# Nikita

# Nikita

AJAY JAIN

HARPER
FICTION

*An Imprint of* HarperCollins *Publishers*

First published in India by Harper Fiction 2026
An imprint of HarperCollins *Publishers*
HarperCollins *Publishers* India, Cyber City,
Building 10-A, Gurugram, Haryana – 122002, India
www.harpercollins.co.in

2 4 6 8 10 9 7 5 3 1



P-ISBN: 978-93-6569-226-6
E-ISBN: 978-93-6569-582-3



Typeset in 11 pt/14 Minion Pro
by HarperCollins *Publishers* India Pvt. Ltd

Printed and bound at
Nutech Print Services Pvt. Ltd.

FSC
www.fsc.org
MIX
Paper | Supporting responsible forestry
FSC® C195953

This book is printed on FSC® certified paper
which ensures responsible forest management.

HarperCollins *Publishers*, Macken House, 39/40 Mayor Street Upper, Dublin 1, D01 C9W8, Ireland

# One Mistake

I made one mistake in my life. At nineteen. An age when you cannot distinguish between right and wrong, correct and incorrect, the good and the bad.

It's an age when there are no precedents, no events to base judgement on. You just do things. You are in the kindergarten of adulthood. When you still have to learn the alphabet, the vocabulary, the grammar to write a story for your life.

When you enter school, you start with pencils. And an eraser to wipe and correct mistakes. Unfortunately, you are only given pens with indelible ink in life. The slate cannot be wiped clean. What's on it determines the course of your future.

When I made the cardinal mistake at nineteen, I had no teachers to guide me. If there were any, I did not pay heed. Had I done so, or even listened to my own heart and soul, I would not have made the mistake at nineteen—and then another at twenty-nine. Just when the marks of the first were fading into oblivion, I splattered ink all over my destiny.

And thus, I need to narrate my story to myself. So I can reflect upon my life. And make another go of it.

# Run Nikita, Run

Run Nikita, run.

I have been running. Ever since Radha didi, my elder sister, told me to. She had been to a hell one would not send their enemies to. And she did not want me to be forced to enter one too. She loved me, she cared for me. She had been my mother ever since we lost ours when I was not even one.

Someone had cast a spell on our family. We were condemned without a trial for sins we were not even aware of. The punishment was serving term in hell. My sister urged me to run before the flames consumed me, before someone locked the gates and lost the keys.

I would sprint on the road to heaven only to stumble into another hell. The curse would endure. I would be hurt, I would be in pain, I would cry. But I stayed defiant. And continue to be.

I will enter the gates of the heaven I seek, I will build the utopia I dream of. Hell be damned.

# Nikita is Coming

Martyrdom is never a good idea. Not on a battlefield. Not at home. Every soldier lost means one man or woman less to fight another day. And every personal life ruined means continued distress for those you are trying to protect.

I allowed myself to get married at nineteen to gift a measure of peace to my father. His sufferings were not easy to bear for a child who loved him. My decision was only a placebo, not lasting longer than a flash in the pan. He could not have been blind to the misery I got trapped in—the resulting grief consumed him till his last days.

Of course, the new decade had started on a more cheerful note. The dreaded high school leaving exams, called the boards, were finally over. Symbolically, history had been the last paper—and I was already doodling the personal history I was going to write in my future. I chose to walk back—rather than hop and dance—from school to home. It was late March and the afternoons were already very warm. The sun was harsh, but it was only brightening up the flower-laden streetscapes. The flaming oranges of palash, the lilacs of rosy trumpets, the reds of silk cotton and the deep pinks of kachnar—these are a few of my favourite things at that time of the year. Just as are raindrops on roses and whiskers on kittens for the characters in *The Sound of Music*—perhaps my favourite movie of all time.

The protagonists sought a life that was rightfully theirs; I believed myself to be the eighth of the von Trapp children, deserving of any life I could envision for myself. I did not need to escape to Switzerland like them, but I would catch a train to Delhi. To study further. To model. To party. And to get a man for myself; I was done with boys.

Hello world, Nikita is coming!

# NIKITA

I exist because my mom wanted another child. Out of remorse. She might still have been around had she not wanted to see me in the family portrait. I am, and thus my mom is not. The cross of guilt became mine to bear. Even though I had no say in a past I was not even conceived in.

We lived in an extended joint family, and my parents were hosts to their parasitic ways. The extended family sucked them financially, and then they messed with their psyche. They took away my parents' jewels, their house, their health, their peace and their second son. My parents took it all in their stride, but the burden of parting with her child weighed too heavy on my mother. I was needed as the counterbalance.

It was a blunder, a fatal one. My mother carried me despite her frail state, and could not nurse or even hold the three kilos of the newly born me. My first meal was formula milk. From what I have been told, my mother's feet rarely touched the ground for a year before she passed on. I was not destined to have a mother who I could have one conversation, one that could have been the touchstone of my life. To keep me from making mistakes, or knowing how to tackle them when I did.

Our family was one notch below the royals of Jaipur in social status. We had served them for generations, and my father continued the tradition. Even though his masters no longer held any political sway except those who got elected democratically to the state and national assemblies.

We were the confidants of the rulers. With extremely strict rules and protocols. At any given time, only one member of our family was allowed to work at the palace. The baton was handed over to my father from a granduncle who lived and served them for a long time. No one from my grandparents' generation got the chance to hold the position.

My father worked closely with the rajmata, the queen of the state without a crown. He had access beyond doors closed to most of the royal family members, and was privy to information he could be killed—or handsomely rewarded—for. But he was not entrusted with this role because someone pulled his name out of a hat. He was groomed and tested by his granduncle for years. He had to prove not just his aptitude for the job, but his trustworthiness to exercise utmost discretion in whatever he did. Everything had to be kept a secret, even from his own family. Despite his proximity to the palace, we saw no more of it than tourists to the city.

My father never, ever spoke of his work. We knew broadly what he did from what our uncles and aunts told us, but much of their accounts were guesswork too. He was the royal family's go-to man, having his fingers in all their pies. He oversaw their finances, ensured the security of their massive collection of jewels and valuables, kept track of their vast real estate holdings, lobbied with the government to protect the family's interests and assets lest they be nationalized, and managed election campaigns when any of the family ran for office. He was the event manager of their opulent weddings, birthdays and anniversaries. Every festival had to be a grandiose celebration. He was the gatekeeper who let guests in at these occasions. The stables were his responsibility—the well-being of the horses and elephants vital for polo matches.

He sat at the table—and often dictated terms—for business collaborations, including those with hospitality brands who took over palaces and forts to run them as hotels and museums. Every will, every family settlement, every legal agreement was vetted by him in consultation with lawyers and would bear his signature as a witness.

He was the perfect employee, not even sharing trivia about the royals lest he let slip any confidential information. The employers were not necessarily ideal though, as paymasters at least. They paid my father well, but he should have been rewarded better. He was steeped in idealism and the tradition of the position he held, and could never get himself to demand more than what he was given. He could have but did not make anything for himself on the side. He had enough insider information to create wealth for himself—and for us—by investing in land, gold and stocks before their values escalated. It would have done his employers no harm, but he still regarded it a crime on his conscience.

In earlier times, his ancestors would benefit from the occasional largesse of the king or the queen of the day; the massive bungalow or haveli we lived in was granted to us in the nineteenth century. As were vast tracts of agricultural land spread across the state of Rajasthan. Such bonuses became scarce after India gained independence, the new republic stripping the former royals of much of their assets and sources of income.

There has been another distasteful tradition in our family. Most lived off the one serving the royals. But as income fell, some made themselves useful by being gainfully employed elsewhere. Others started selling off land and jewellery to pay for their ever-diminishing lifestyle and even renting out a part of our haveli. But that was never enough. My father had the most modest income amongst all his predecessors, and that too was largely mooched off him by his brothers.

I came in late into the story, but by the time I did, my father's spirit was already being squeezed of its juice. I only heard from others of how he was the charmer amongst the city's youth, a man so good-looking to have attracted my mother, herself a head-turner at Jaipur's parties. But someone cast an evil eye on their union; their marital bliss was short-lived as domestic politics, financial stresses and resulting poor health dominated the time they were together.

And yet, they stood firm with their feet on the ground, as pillars of strength for each other. They weathered the gale around them for as long as they could, till my mother could not take it any longer. Leaving my father—and us—forlorn.

I don't know what his siblings—and their respective families—had against my father, but it seemed they were out to bleed him dry and destroy him in every way possible, including the lives of his children.

My father had five brothers and two sisters. The position he held with the royal family should have gone to the eldest brother, Brajesh tauji. But he was too busy managing his wives and mistresses to be entrusted with any responsibility. Next was a sister, Sarla bua, who was not entitled to work. The third, Chand tauji, had some sense and studied medicine in Russia and settled there. The baton was my father's to drop, but he held on to it for dear life. He had grown up dreaming of this job but expected that one of those in line before him would get it. But when destiny offered this gift, he gleefully accepted it.

My father's parents lost their lives tragically about two years after the youngest of their children was born. They were on their way to Badrinath for a pilgrimage when their bus fell down the steep Himalayan slopes. All thirty-four on board perished. The eldest of the siblings was expected to take charge of the family at the young age of twenty, but he was too caught up in his romantic liaisons to bother. The aunt had been married just a few months prior to the tragedy to a lawyer about twelve years older to her. He was struggling in his practice, and he found the perfect pretext to move into our house as the new father figure. My aunt was very docile, and took the task of managing the household upon herself. The husband, Mahesh uncle, went about unchallenged as he sold off properties to not just pay for household expenses but to also siphon off an undue share for himself. The jewels were saved because my great-grandmother was still around, and kept those close to her chest.

We also got by in those trying times because of the special status our family enjoyed in Jaipur as the confidants of the palace. We could raise unsecured loans with no questions asked, seek favours of any kind with the authorities, be assured of admissions to the best of schools and colleges, and get preference for jobs in the private and the government sector. But all of this benefits those who can make good use of it. Doors may have been open to us, but they still required one to study and work hard. The royals themselves were generous enough with gifts and grants to our family, and became even more charitable after the death of my grandparents. But any good fortune squandered off provides little solace to its intended beneficiaries.

The four born after my father were all studies in contrast. Birju chacha, the uncle born after my father was a waster, a bully, a drunkard, a leech and a predator—yes, it's possible for one to be all these and more. Harish chacha, the sixth child, got good guidance from a friend's father, pursued law and moved to Delhi—he built a successful practice helping politicians legitimize their ill-gotten moneys and became fabulously wealthy himself. Rupa bua was born after him—no one bothered looking for a groom for her, and she became a bitter, abusive spinster. All of us kids would call her a witch behind her back and stayed clear of her; she would wallop us on a whim anytime, with or without reason. The youngest, Jagdeep chacha, caught the fancy of a rich Marwari family, the rich business community from the state, and married one of their daughters. The bargain required him to move to Mumbai, live with his in-laws, be employed in their garments factory, and not move anywhere from under the thumb of his dominating wife.

In this family was born Nikita.

Our house was like a hammam of sorts. Everyone's lives were bared for all to see; there were only feeble attempts to be discreet about one's pleasures and displeasures. Illicit liaisons and abuse were rife, as were resultant outbursts and tears. Everyone knew what was happening, and yet no one talked about it. We hurt each other and let wounds fester.

I was the youngest in the family, and was invisible to everyone. I was literally a fly on the wall, and on the floor, and behind doors, and even under the bed; even if others knew

I was around, I would be disregarded as the kid who would not even comprehend what was going on. They were right. I did not, at that tender age. But the images stayed. For me to interpret later in life. We may have been a family of stature for the city, but we would have been condemned socially and legally had our admirers got to peek within.

The eldest, Brajesh tauji, turned out to be an inverted role model. He got married to Lata tai when he was 15 and she was all of seven. Of course, she did not move in with her husband until puberty, but she always remained a child in his eyes even after she did. Brajesh tauji did not desist from bringing his 'girlfriends' home. This was the normal that tai got conditioned to since she was still at an impressionable age. No one read out her rights as a wife to her. She was made to wash and iron his clothes, serve him food, make his bed and even wait outside the bedroom when he was busy with a woman. The audacity of it all was laid bare when she was made to serve drinks to the visitor, and even clean up after she left. She did not know what sex was, and her husband couldn't bear the thought of 'educating' her. Birju chacha took it upon himself to make her wise about worldly matters. For his own motives though.

One day, Brajesh tauji brought home a fair-skinned woman; she was clearly a foreigner. A coolie followed, lugging oversized suitcases and boxes. Tauji was beaming; he had the look of someone who had just won a world cup in polo—his favourite pastime and hunting ground for women. Without a word to any of us, he took the lady straight to his bedroom on the first floor. Curiosity took us all to the central courtyard, to look up and see what that was all about. Servants were continually going up and down, with the luggage first, then water, and then chai. After about an hour, we saw Lata tai coming downstairs, with a servant carrying her personal effects behind her. She did not look towards any of us, save a couple of fleeting glances. Even in those briefest of moments, we could see the humiliation writ large on her face. But her eyes were not wet. They were seething. Rupa bua, the 'witch' muttered: Everything will be finished now. You wait and see. Never forget this moment when the downfall of our family started.

The child in tai was going to throw a tantrum. But she was no juvenile, not anymore. It was time to lay out the chess board. We would discover a crafty grandmaster in her, whose game would be played out over the coming generation. She would show us an art of war that would make Sun Tzu proud.

There were no fixed norms around meals in our house. Everyone had their own schedules, their own menus and their own eating places. Sometimes there was sharing and caring, but people stayed to themselves mostly. There were exceptional days though, like one when Brajesh tauji sent word out for all to have dinner together. He made it sound important and mandatory.

After all, his marriage to Gloria Sternberger deserved a toast, even if it was just over a family meal. She was Jewish, from Israel, in town to write a history of the sports the royals played. The charmer of a man played the perfect game in winning her over. Besotted by him totally, she agreed to marry him despite being fully aware of his personal situation. She could not be bothered about his modest financial condition; her father was an arms trader, a key player in keeping the Middle East well-supplied with weapons and ammunition to be able to keep fighting. He traded with all sides, and they protected him as their own. Gloria was the sole heiress to his wealth. If Tauji's heart fluttered more for those riches than for the woman, then disappointment lay in store. His new wife would not let him have a whiff of her money even if they had vowed to be one for as long as they lived.

Dinner was served on a massive dining table built about a hundred years ago; it was an heirloom, a priceless one. Money cannot buy such wood and workmanship today. Everyone was there—only Lata tai was missing. Not surprising though. There was small talk over starters of chicken tikka and lamb soup, but the corners of all adult eyes were firmly on the white lady. The kids stared at her directly for the entirety of the evening. And then tauji spoke up.

Let me introduce you to Gloria. We got married this morning in Birla Mandir. She is from Israel but will now be staying with us. She speaks English and Hindi very well, so you can all talk to her. I hope you will give her the respect due to the eldest bhabhi in the family. We would have liked a bigger ceremony as the occasion deserves, but we decided to keep it simple. Her majesty, the rajmata, is very close to bhabhi and has blessed our union. Gloria is a historian and a scholar, and has studied at Cambridge in England. She needs her peace and quiet, and I hope no one will disturb her when she is working.

The uncles and aunts exchanged pleasantries with Gloria, but fell short of making meaningful conversation. The children milled around her out of curiosity, pulling at her silken flowing dress, and giggling while testing her Hindi. She was not exuberant in her expressions, but would smile easily.

An unusual chapter had been added to our family biography. It would not make for very pleasant reading.

Lata tai was at war with everyone in the house. But she could not ride into battle alone. Birju chacha, the useless one with all the time on his hands, was recruited to be her ally. He readily accepted a role where he could indulge in the pleasures of fornication, had someone to attend to his daily needs, and was handed over keys to a money chest to fund his wasteful life.

In a house of open secrets, their proximity was not missed by anyone. They became inseparable, sharing meals, going out shopping, socializing, and just hanging out together at home. In the verandah, on the terrace, in the kitchen, in the bar, in each other's bedrooms. They bolted the doors from the inside at times, giving a hoot to wagging tongues. She was out to spite the family; he was being the parasite he was born to be.

Tai discovered the joys of illicit sex with chacha; all was fair in a war where her own husband was lost to other women. She came from a rich family in Bikaner, and chacha would help himself to much of the pocket money her parents sent every month. When this was not enough to fund his wanton ways, he gifted himself his paramour's jewellery to be pawned or sold. The tai was too focused on the bigger battles at hand to be bothered with material losses. She dismissed the embezzlement as fee for the services her brother-in-law rendered.

And then tai struck the first blow. She came pleading to my parents to save her marriage. What could they do? They had no say, certainly not on conjugal matters. It was between the couple, more so when the bull-headed tauji was not one to pay heed to anyone.

I want a child, the tai said.

But how? You don't even share the room, said my mother. She feigned ignorance of her relationship with chacha.

But the white whore has already given him two children. A boy and a girl. How can I bear to see that?

You are our elders, how can we interfere?

I just want one child. I know I will not get one from him. Can I adopt one of your sons?

My mother went pale at the prospect. She had a daughter and two sons, but each were as dear to her as the other. Even the thought of parting with one—even if living in the same house—would be too much to bear. Why would bhabhi put them in such a predicament? Why couldn't she just seek a divorce and go back to her parents? My mother knew that option was worse than death for tai; she would rather continue living in humiliation in her marital house.

My father, who had been quiet throughout, finally spoke up. Addressing my mother, he asked if she would be agreeable to letting Aman, the elder son, be brought up by tai. It really will not change anything. We would be living in the same house. He will have two mothers instead of one. He will be well looked after. No one would be going anywhere.

Tai knew my father would support her. He could not say no to anyone in the family even if it called for emotional and financial sacrifices by his own wife and children. Aman was adopted by my tai and her husband in a religious ceremony followed by legal formalities.

The guilt of giving up one of her children began bothering my mother. It was her turn to talk to my father, and thus the idea of me took shape. I was born two years after my brother was adopted by his tai.

Disturbed, disjointed and dysfunctional—that was the state of the House of Mathurs, as our family was commonly known. It's subset, my immediate family—the one I was born into—was disintegrating even before my birth and the pieces just kept falling off through my growing years.

I lost my mother before my first birthday. An unidentified complication during my delivery had left her extremely weak; despite running all possible tests by the best of doctors, she could not get better. My elder brother, Aman, had been adopted by my eldest tai; it was supposed to be more of a placebo for her hurting soul. He would be living just a few rooms down the corridor. But my tai was playing a grander game with the Mathurs; she took him away much further without consulting his biological father. Aman would eventually come back home, but only after a failed suicide attempt upon being betrayed those he trusted within the family.

My father and sister had their own share of hurt and heartbreaks, their stories running parallel despite the generational gap. My younger brother almost died of burns when his bid to scare Birju chacha went awry. The residual scars—on his body and on his soul—would leave him lesser able to lead a life with any semblance of normalcy.

Radha didi had been a witness—and victim—to all that was wrong around us. I should have run the first time she told me to.

You may be its guardian, but you may not pluck the forbidden fruit for yourself from the garden. Even if the royal family holds you in high esteem for your performance and loyalty.

There are some rules set in stone—rules to remind you of your position in their society. It would be a sin for my father to be in love with a princess, lest an eventual marriage leads to him being counted as one of the royals himself.

For a long time after losing his wife, my father was a dispirited man. He went about his responsibilities at work and at home almost robotically, with dedication but little emotion. And then he got acquainted with Sara.

Sara was a princess but only of a notional kingdom. The royal family had titles only because their 'subjects' continued to address them with such; they had none officially. They did not rule over a single square foot of land anymore. They had their status, their jewels, their real estate, which included a few palaces, their parties, their media coverage and their polo, but no political power. They were one family to the world, but were out for each other's blood within. All of them were embroiled in complex legal battles over assets and inheritance. As the cases dragged on for decades, the number of claimants increased as more children bloomed on the family tree. Deference to the rajmata was holding up the facade from cracking. But only for as long as the aging matriarch was around.

Sara may have been a part of the family, but was far removed. If heirs still counted for anything, she would probably have been two hundredth in line for the throne. She was not even entitled to any dividends or shares of the royal assets. Her father made a living as a building contractor. The only privilege accorded to her were invitations to events at the palaces; but it was more to flaunt her stunning beauty than as a relation. Much of the family was undistinguished in their appearance, and they were conscious of it.

But Sara was all humility and only had love for dad despite being wooed by the finest of suitors from not just within the state, or the country, but even by the rich and the royal of Europe. But she did not want to be a part of their 'shallow world' as she put it, where all she would be expected to do was dress her part and play the wonderful hostess, a doting wife and an indulgent mother to a brood of children. All Sara wanted was to travel to discover the real world for herself and capture it in her camera.

What did she see in my father? A fine gentleman, and a good soul. They never opened up about their relationship to others, coming across as just acquaintances. Whoever saw them together could not miss the love they had for each other, no matter how hard they tried to hide it. Of course, Sara would be affectionate toward my father in private. She would even drop by at his home, spend time with his children, bring them gifts, tell them stories and shoot photos of them. I still hold onto some in my albums with fond memories.

The extended family did not think too kindly of my father's new-found happiness but would not let their displeasure be known; they wrongly assumed that Sara would bring the riches of the palace with her after marriage. One day, Sara told us she would be travelling for four months on a cruise around the world. Even as a child, I could see her eyes were sad despite embarking on a journey she had spoken of excitedly in the past. I could not understand the heaviness in her voice when she spoke; it's the last memory I have of the most beautiful face I have ever seen.

She never returned. My father chose not to carry on the relationship despite Sara being readily agreeable. He feared for his children; how would Sara treat them when she had any of her own? I do not want any, she would clarify. I want to travel, and not be bound by any of my own, and yet ensure your children never feel neglected, she would tell him. Being an empathetic man, my father did not want to burden the young and sprightly Sara with the baggage he carried. My father was also not sure how the rest of his family would treat her.

Of course, there was another reason why the match might not have been possible. The rajmata had summoned my dad and expressed her displeasure explicitly when she heard the rumours. She would not even recognize Sara as her relation for all practical purposes, but rules were rules. If my father did not end the relationship, it would be regarded as treason—he could have been jailed for life or even executed in the past. But in the current scenario, my father would lose his job—the only one he was trained for and loved. He would not know how to support his family. The 'queen' could well have been bluffing with her threats of firing him; he knew he was indispensable and could not be let loose with all the insider knowledge he had. But loyalty toward the royal family was too ingrained in his blood to rebel.

He acceded to the queen. And from that day on, my father was sick for most of his life.

He may have taken it upon himself to be the head of our family when my grandparents died, but Mahesh uncle was like a politician who uses his position to enrich himself and to inflict abuse with impunity.

He had been married once earlier but his wife never returned from a visit to her sister in Canada. His male pride severely bruised at the abandonment, and saddled with the additional responsibility of a six-year-old son, he desperately sought another wife. A common acquaintance set up a rendezvous with Sarla bua who took to him at first sight; he shouldn't have felt flattered though. She would have gone for the first half-decent man who proposed to her.

She was told about the son Vikram only after she reached her new home. A worse shock followed soon after—she lost her parents within a month of her marriage. It set off a chain of events leading to her moving back into her parental home with Mahesh uncle and Vikram. There was too much happening for her to grudge the stepchild; she just took him in as her own, to care for along with her orphaned siblings.

With no one to question him, Mahesh uncle went about consolidating his financial position, skimming whatever he could of the family assets. For the first time, portions of the haveli were leased out; he pocketed all the rent coming in. It did not take long for the gossip mills of Jaipur to go into overdrive, the town wondering what ailed the Mathurs. Why else would they let out their traditional home to the petty traders of Johri Bazaar, the market of jewellers? Our haveli was a landmark in the area, one of the most prestigious of addresses in the city.

If that was not enough, he became a sexual predator within the house itself. The easiest target was Rupa bua, his wife's younger sister. She had just been a child when she lost her parents. Mahesh uncle became the man she looked up to in the absence of any other credible candidates. He showered extra care upon her to win her confidence; soon after she attained puberty, he took advantage of the trust she had in him to rape her. There was no struggle, no resistance from a girl who took such a physical act to be a normal human activity; she had been living in a cocoon and knew no different. It pained the fourteen-year-old the first few times, but she gradually got used to it. As trauma turned to pleasure, she even started looking forward to the encounters.

Mahesh uncle swore her to secrecy, but a child cannot keep things to herself for long. She narrated what was happening to her elder sister after about a year; she sounded as if this was something to be pleased about. Of course, it was a horror story to the older sibling, who went hysterical. She sought her husband out, and screamed and cried herself hoarse with the entire household including servants standing witness. My aunt made the mistake of making it public; this was a matter where discretion and sensitivity was of utmost importance. But the damage was done.

Tongues wagged within the haveli and beyond. Very soon, all those who mattered to us knew. The talk was not so much about what uncle had done; people were more interested in what to do with Rupa bua. The victim suffered even more.

Her schooling was the first to get affected. The principal suggested she go for home tutoring or be sent off to a boarding school since other students and teachers could not stop talking about her. Both these options would have increased the cost of her education, and Mahesh uncle did not want to invest in it. No one else in the family had the money to. She became an introvert, staying confined to her room, mostly in the dark. Tragically, Mahesh uncle continued to visit her; this time he threatened go public if she squealed. She complied out of fear of further ostracization. No suitors came forward when she reached marriageable age. She was the keep, the mistress of Mahesh *babu*; he was addressed with a respectable suffix to his name as he moved up the social ladder in town. His unsavoury—and illegal—actions were glossed over.

Rupa bua turned bitter; she was a reject of society for no fault of her own. The child in her grew up to be a 'witch', venting her anger, frustration and despair at all those who crossed her path. She aged in a hurry. She became scrawny, her hair turned frizzy and grey. Her temper was feared by all, especially the children. She would calm down only when Mahesh uncle visited her, which he did for most of his life. He would still take her despite her appearance. He was the trainer who could tame a caged wild animal.

If he wasn't enough of a scourge in the family, Vikram aspired to emulate his father.

What do you do when you walk into a room and see your sister with her step-cousin, Vikram? With her sitting on the edge of a bed, her dress dropped to her waist, the bra lying on the floor? And he standing over her, his shirt unbuttoned, and his member protruding hard and big?

I was looking for the stray kitten who ventured into our house sometimes and followed its trail into the room. All the curtains were drawn, but there was enough light to see what they were doing. I watched them, transfixed and fascinated, while they carried on, oblivious to my presence. He was moving his hands all over her, cupping her breasts when she bent down to take him in her mouth. They moved and made muffled sounds till he withdrew with a jerk—and squirted something whitish-grey over her chest.

I was too young to understand what was going on. I did not know what sex was. I did not know what a blowjob was. I did not know a man does not 'pee' after a blowjob; he comes and goes limp.

Vikram was all smiles when he was done but my sister was expressionless. As she had been all through. They noticed me standing in the shadows by the door only when they turned in my direction. Vikram smirked, and I still remember him giving me a flying kiss while he fastened his belt. My sister had a look of panic on her face.

What are you doing here? she asked while clumsily fastening her bra and pulling her dress back up.

I was looking for Lora.

Who is Lora?

My kitty.

When did you get a kitty?

She comes to visit me sometimes.

Go out.

Ok.

No wait. Don't go.

She looked at Vikram and asked him to leave. He left, grinning. Radha didi came up to me, went down on her knees, looked into my eyes and asked when I had come into the room.

A little while back, I said.

What did you see? Or forget it, it's ok. Don't talk about this to anyone.

Ok.

Please don't tell anyone.

Ok.

Promise?

Yes.

It's our secret.

Ok.

Want a chocolate?

No.

What do you want?

Ice cream.

Ok, let's go get one.

I also want Lora.

Sure, where is she?

I don't know.

Ok, let's look for her.

So we went looking for the kitten and then the ice cream cart. We found only the latter, and picked up my favourite mango duet bar.

What were you playing with Vikram bhaiya? I asked referring to the big brother.

Nothing.

But you were.

It is not for children.

I am not a child.

No, you are.

I will ask papa.

No, it's our secret.

So why won't you tell me?

I will. When you are my age.

Promise?

Yes.

I went back to licking my lolly. I had seen other people in the house together without any clothes, so there was nothing novel or surprising seeing my sister in that state. I assumed it was something everyone did. Even I wanted to. But in that moment, my priority was not to let any of my precious ice cream drip on my frock.

There were no secrets in our house. Even if there were, I was privy to most of them. I just happened to walk in on events. I moved about silently, barely noticeable; I would describe it as creepy. Even when the protagonists in the middle of an action scene spotted me, they carried on. I was not a witness to be a cause for any alarm or embarrassment.

Maybe. But my photographic memory captured everything. To play back later in life. When the child would be an adult, and would then interpret the meaning of those images. Many events would no longer matter by then, and it might be too late to do anything about some. I would be tormented by mixed emotions; there would be anger, there would be regret, there would be a sense of helplessness. I would want to scream when hindsight showed how things could have been different, how much of the hurt and abuse could have been prevented. It would not be possible to turn the clock back, nor could the dead be woken to demand an apology for their misdeeds.

But back then, I did not understand why Vikram bhaiya was 'peeing' over Radha didi. Or why Birju chacha was moving fervently on top on Lata tai without any clothes on. When Gloria tai had a relation from Israel staying with us, why were they taking a bath together when Brajesh tauji was travelling to Bombay? Why would Rupa bua be crying when Mahesh uncle had his hand between her legs and moving a finger in and out?

I would also see Vikram bhaiya lock up his room at times when he had his male friends visiting. Why would they take their clothes off and feel each other and 'pee' again and again? Who were the women who would come into the house from the door in the back at night with Mahesh uncle, follow him to a room on the terrace and let out loud moans from behind closed doors? Why were those women painted with heavy make-up and deep red lipstick, smelling of revolting perfume, and be wearing flashy clothes over their buxom bodies? Why did they come in a group sometimes led by an old woman, wrinkled with age but equally flashy, and argue over payments due to them? Why would Mahesh uncle need to pay those women?

It was all happening in our house. I was the roving camera, secretly recording the goings-on. I wish I had stayed innocent to the ways of the House of Mathurs.

If I could erase one memory, one image, it would be of the night when my sister's life changed forever. If I wasn't habituated to sneaking around the house, I would not have witnessed her being ravaged. There would thus be no flashbacks to torment me, to haunt me till the end of my days.

My father was in Udaipur for an extended period of time to settle a knotty property matter. Birju chacha was hosting four men over drinks in the living room. The guests included a police officer in a khaki uniform and a politician dressed in white trousers and shirt. They were guzzling down liquor as if it were water and getting boisterous by the minute. Who was the bartender? Radha didi. They were not only ordering her to make drinks, but to also keep the supply of ice and snacks going. I was being her tail, one step behind her throughout. My sister would ask the servants to carry the food but Lata tai, who was supervising the cooking, would order her back. Whenever she crossed the men to pick or serve anything, I could not help noticing them patting her bottom or running their hands wherever they could on her body. She was being molested in plain sight of the elders.

With their decibels at its peak under the influence of excessive alcohol, chacha ordered me out of the room and closed the door with my sister still inside. I promptly climbed onto the windowsill to see what was happening inside. The men put on raunchy Bollywood numbers on a tape recorder to dance to—around my sister. They were trying to get her to match her steps with theirs, but she would not move on her own; they had to hold her by the hands and force her to. She was being pulled and pushed. My chacha, who was already unsteady on his feet, passed out on the carpet. The other four men got bolder with my sister, taking turns to press their bodies against hers, gripping her tight with their arms, and trying to kiss her as she shook her face vigorously to avoid theirs.

It got ugly after that. The police officer took out his belt and tied her arms behind her back. While he held her, the politician gagged her with his white scarf. The two gripped her arms and legs and lay her writhing body on the carpet next to the unconscious chacha. The cop unbuttoned and lowered his trousers and went down on his knees. He lifted her skirt, yanked out her panties, and thrust himself inside of her between the legs. He moved hard and fast, even as the politician held her down by the shoulders. After a few minutes, the officer stopped heaving, and moved off, walking on the carpet on his fours like a dog to pass out next to the couch, his trousers still crumpled at his ankles.

My sister, crying like a baby, drained of all energy, watched in horror as the politician did exactly what the officer had. When he was done, he stood up, fastened his trousers, and walked out to the toilet leaving the door ajar. Before I could go in, Lata tai walked in, surveyed the scene, looked at the two men with lust in their eyes waiting to have a go at my sister and said, Not today. It's enough. Next time. Go home.

By then the police officer was coming to his senses and the politician was back. She told them to leave too. All four men tried to behave as if it were just another party breaking up, and casually filed out of the main door.

My sister was lying unconscious next to my chacha, her skirt still lifted, her crotch on full display. Tai looked at them both, turned around, saw me at the door and walked up to me. Taking my arm, she took me away from the scene of the crime and deposited me back in my room. She bolted the door from the outside. I looked out of the window to see her walking back into her room, closing the door behind her, and switching off the light.

I don't know how long my sister lay next to her father's brother in the state I last saw her. I don't know who woke up first. I don't know if they were both conscious at the same time and looked each other in the eye. I don't know what my sister made of her chacha lying next to her.

I just know my chacha would not have suffered from any remorse at what happened to his niece. He had orchestrated it after all.

Something changed in the house. A hush set in. It seemed no one was talking to anyone even as they went about their chores. All eyes would be on didi—when she would be seen. She barely stepped out of her room for days and weeks.

We shared a room, and I knew something bad had happened to her. That's why she was sobbing all the time, even in her sleep. No one came to our room to talk to her, to console her. My father called a month after the incident to say he would be home in two days—he asked for Radha didi but Sarla bua said she was not home.

My sister finally snapped out of her stupor when she heard papa was coming back. She stopped crying but could not get herself to even fake a smile. She tidied her room and our father's too. She did all the laundry, went out for a haircut and bought a new saree to greet our father.

Seeing her go about the house, there seemed to be a collective sigh of relief. Time had been standing still, the household frozen while she was cooped up. The thaw set in, and the clock could be heard ticking; the corridors were chattering again. The woks were back on the fire to cook rich delicacies and desserts. The mourning period was over for the world. It would never be for my sister though.

My father did not get to grieve. He would never know what happened to his elder—and favourite—daughter. Despite his meek persona, I am sure blood would have flowed in our haveli had he been told.

My sister could have been saved had my father married Sara.

My sister could have made herself sick with anguish. She could have harmed someone—or herself—out of loathing for her perpetrators. She could have dug a hole for herself to go into hiding in. But she chose to go out. To become the toast of town.

Trained as a fashion designer, she cut herself the most provocative of dresses by Jaipur's standards. She camouflaged her grief under heavy make-up. And then went partying. She needed people around her so she would be forced to keep her tears from flowing out. She could be anyone she wanted to be with strangers. She sought attention. And she got it. The rich, the famous, the royal could not take their eyes off her.

Everyone wanted to be seen with her, everyone wanted to see her. If an event was covered by the press, photos of her were sure to be published. Men wooed her, and she teased them back. She would dance with them, let them seduce her, and then leave them heartbroken when they swore their love for her. She hated men, hated all of them. She could not bear to be with anyone for long. She wanted to avenge what had been done to her. She did not know how to. The company of men—bastards most of them as she called them—might teach her to.

And then she met Ranjit. He was technically a royal—the grandson of the rajmata's sister. He had no entitlements but the 'rulers' were fond of him. He was a trader based in Jodhpur, exporting the art and handicrafts of the state. They met on New Year's Eve—at the biggest party in town in Rambagh Palace, a heritage property owned by the royal family and converted into one of the most luxurious hotels in the world.

They may have been introduced to each other by a common acquaintance, but their meeting was no happenstance. He was famous—or infamous depending how one looked at such things—for being a playboy and yet a highly sought-after bachelor in all of Rajasthan. She set up the 'chance' meeting and charmed him right away. He did not let go of her all evening; flirting with her, wooing her, bringing her drinks and offering to drop her home. She accepted the ride in his Rolls Royce where he tried to make out with her. She let him up to a point; just when he was set to go all the way, she zipped her dress back up, leaving him high and dry.

He was besotted with her. He wanted her. He loved her. He wanted her all for himself. He had finally met a woman who could rein in his wanton ways. He proposed to her.

She held back. Told him the family would never agree. Neither hers, nor the royal. She narrated what happened with Sara and her father. Ranjit was determined. He would do anything to marry her.

She agreed to marry him if he could figure how. And then, just like that, she was missing from the house. There was a note to say that she was going away and promised to be safe. No one should worry, she would be happy wherever she was and was sorry for leaving in that manner.

I did not know what my elder sister had done. I was too much of a child to comprehend what was happening. But I still knew Radha didi had done the right thing by running away to wherever she had.

Birju chacha was beside himself with rage. He was mumbling away like a madman, flailing his arms, moving about the courtyard like a headless chicken holding the morning newspaper. The whole state was abuzz with the news of the year.

A leading politician, tipped to be the next chief minister of the state, was dead. As was his son. Chacha was banking on the deceased leader for government contracts to finally make some money of his own. I saw the photo in the newspaper. It was the same man who had done bad things to my sister.

There was more to the story. The son had been in London the past few years to develop the market for their export business. He had returned recently with his wife and son. There was a welcome party for them at their home in Jodhpur, attended by close family and friends. Around 2 a.m., the politician's wife woke to see her husband frothing at the mouth. She raised an alarm. Her son was displaying similar symptoms. Both were dead by the time the doctors arrived. Post-mortem revealed poisoning by a chemical not known to the forensic department of the city. Samples had been sent to New Delhi for further investigation. The bodies were released for cremation.

A week after the news broke, we had two visitors. My sister, and an infant boy in her arms. She was back. My father started crying with joy and relief. I ran to hug her. My brother Raghav just stood and watched, as did others in the house. My father tried asking questions, but my sister evaded answers, feigning fatigue. She asked to retire to the room we had shared. I felt privileged to have exclusive access to her.

Where have you been? I asked.

I got married, she said.

Why didn't you tell us?

No one would have agreed from either side of the family.

So what did you do?

We ran away.

Where were you staying?

London.

When did you come back?

Last month.

Who did you marry? Where is he?

He's no more.

What? How? When? What happened.

Someone poisoned him. And his father too.

Oh my God! Why would someone do that?

Probably to avenge something bad they must have done.

I was still very young when we had that conversation. But I understood what she meant about what can happen when one does bad things to someone. My sister would be my hero for the rest of my life.

Radha didi felt I was mature enough to be taken into confidence. She told me what she had been through. Not in one go, but in bits and pieces. Not everything, but most of it. I figured the rest out for myself; there was no need for her to say it.

Why was she involved with Vikram bhaiya? The two of them would see what the adults were doing through windows and ventilators and wanted to try it for themselves. She was too young and naïve—but had reached an age to be curious about and be attracted to the male body. Vikram seemed an accessible candidate to try stuff with. He was her age, and they were not related by blood; he was Mahesh uncle's son from his first marriage.

Not much happened initially; they would hold and feel each other with their clothes still on. They would kiss a little, awkwardly. It was not long before she realized it was wrong of them to be indulging in such acts, and wanted to put a stop to it. He resorted to blackmailing her, threatening to expose her to our grieving father. Radha gave in under duress, not wanting to risk calling his bluff. She allowed him to have his way up to a point, but stayed a virgin.

Until she was raped.

She had sought out Ranjit knowing he was the son of the politician who had raped her. She wanted to get back to at least one of her rapists, but had only a fuzzy game plan for it. It was important to stay close to the family while she figured out what to do. She seduced the son to rebel against his family and to go away to London.

Why did they come back? Did his family agree to accept her? The politician never realized who his daughter-in-law was; he was too drunk to remember, and he had too many victims to bother remembering each. Looks like the son may truly have been in love with Radha didi, but he had his father's genes. He was known to be a playboy, but he gave girls no choice. They either played along, or he would force himself upon them.

Villainous habits die hard, if they do at all. Ranjit made the fatal mistake of raping his son's young nanny, a Scottish woman, while in London. Didi did not realize anything had happened till the cops came knocking the following day. The nanny had filed a complaint.

Somehow Ranjit knew he was going to be in trouble. He had left home early morning and caught the first flight to India before the police could apprehend him. He called when he was safely home and tried to pacify a distraught Radha. He pleaded innocence, saying there had been a misunderstanding, the nanny was lying, it would be her word against his, and the cops would trust the white woman more. He had no choice but to leave the country in a hurry.

He sent tickets for Radha and their son, assuring them his family had accepted his wife, and were eagerly waiting to receive them. Radha's mind could not stop replaying images of her own rape in a loop. You will get justice, she made a silent promise to the nanny. And to herself too.

Her father-in-law and husband died under tragic circumstances soon after the family was reunited. She did not even try to fake sorrow. She went into a Zen-like state, not communicating with anyone. One early morning, without informing anyone, she left for Jaipur, never to return. No one from her late husband's family ever contacted her. The cops would never find the murderer.

Run Nikita, run.

Radha didi uttered these words for the first time when I was in high school and would repeat them time and again so I would never forget the warning, and take it seriously. You should go away, she would say. As soon as possible. This place will destroy you. Like it has destroyed me.

Go where? I would ask.

Anywhere. Any place will be better than this one.

What about you?

Don't worry about me. I will be fine.

What about papa? He is not keeping good health.

I will take care of him. I will do what I can. But you cannot stay here. At least you can go make a better life for yourself.

Our father was chronically ill. There was no identifiable disease afflicting him, but his body seemed to be in a state of permanent decline. Every healthy moment would be spent at work to make up for lost time. He would strain himself by putting in long hours, exacerbating his health further. We were always worried for him, and administered whatever care we could. I could not think of abandoning him but Radha didi insisted I look at my life ahead. She would hold the fort now that she was back for good.

I had to run before someone broke my spirit.

The infatuation between Brajesh tau and Gloria did not last long. Even a child could see they were an outright mismatch. What were they smoking when they pledged everlasting love to one another? Actually, the question to ask was: what was she smoking? What did she see in my tau?

They did manage to have two kids together, a wonder in itself. They were in a competition to out-humiliate each other with their respective harem of lovers even before the first of the two were born. Her genes seemed to have been the dominant ones; the eye could not discern any Indianness in either of the children. Tongues wagged away, having a field day trying to answer the big question: was tau really the father of those kids?

Not that he seemed to have cared if he was or not. He was as blatant as he always had been with his affairs. He would go missing for days at a time, and tai would always announce the name of the woman whose house he could be found in. On a couple of occasions, when he was needed urgently for legal work, he would be found precisely where his first wife said he would be. Uncanny.

Gloria carried out her charades with greater discretion, or so she thought. She would host guests, mostly from Israel, whenever tau was away. The men were introduced as cousins or even uncles and the ladies as friends. While others had their suspicions, I was probably the sole witness to what transpired between Gloria and the visitors. She was sexually involved with most of them—male and female. There were times when there were three together, and once even four. Her quarters were on the terrace floor, and no one dared go up to satisfy their curiosity. Her temper was to be feared, and she would be particularly vile when anyone invaded her privacy. I had my vantage points from where I could see everything without any risk of being spotted.

And then, just like that, Gloria packed her bags and left; tau was not home, missing as usual without intimation. Do you want the address of the house he is at so you can say your goodbye? Tai hissed at her. Gloria looked at her with all the derision she could muster, held each of her sons by their hands, and said it no longer mattered.

I was standing in the corridor too, and she came up to me. And hugged me. I will write to you; your father's family are the only decent people in this house, she said.

And then she walked out of the main door to head straight to the airport to catch a flight to Delhi and then a connecting one to Tel Aviv. She never returned to India. But she stayed good to her word. She wrote to me, and continues to. At least once a year. Each letter ends with an invitation to visit her beautiful country and spend time with my cousins.

I still don't know if they are my cousins.

Brajesh tau was thunder and lightning for weeks after Gloria left. We all scurried for cover, staying away from him lest he strike. This storm turned into a highest category hurricane when Lata tai also left—for her parent's house in Bikaner. His screaming and raving turned violent. He beat servants without reason—with his hands, with his legs, with a stick, even a chair. The family were spared bodily harm, but he hurled a full lexicon of expletives at them. Even if the provocations were all of his own making.

Tai had been stripped of all dignity while in our house. Her husband never consummated his marriage with her, never gave her the status of a wife. But he availed of all entitlements as her husband. She may have allowed herself to be in a relationship with her brother-in-law, but it only added to a sense of humiliation for her. Theirs was a secret known to all. It became public knowledge because tai wanted it to be—to spite her husband. Her lover could not care what anyone knew, and what they made of it.

Birju chacha was a gigolo to her in many ways. He extracted the price of his services by relieving his lover of all her money and jewellery over time. She had come from a rich family, and had brought a sizeable dowry with her. They would send her money on a regular basis even after that. They knew how she was being treated by her husband, but they preferred to bribe her to stay where she was than return to her parental home. Despite all that she was going through, she stayed put. She focused on running the house and bringing up her adopted son, my brother, Aman.

Things came to a head after Gloria left. Tau would openly abuse her and accuse her of driving Gloria away with her cursed presence in the house. Her self-respect could not take it any longer. With both her soul and pockets empty, she packed whatever material belongings she cared about and left with Aman. She said a goodbye only to my father, and promised him unhindered access to his son whenever he so desired.

My father, my sister, my younger brother Raghav and I were heartbroken. We felt cheated at the breach of contract, in spirit if not in letter. Aman was given up for adoption to tai with the understanding and consolation that he would live in our haveli. With him gone, it felt like we had lost one more member of our family.

❧

We now had two mad men in the house—Brajesh tau and Birju chacha. Tau's pride had taken a beating after being abandoned by not one but two wives in quick succession. Chacha was in dire financial straits since tai's money was no longer his to spend. He was sexually frustrated too. The two brothers lost all sense of balance and were constantly in a foul mood. They made the house a living hell, as if it wasn't one already.

Tau sought sanctuary in his mistresses and prostitutes, and was increasingly away from all of us. Chacha was losing it though. He was too broke to even step out of the house. All the money he had extracted from his lover had been squandered off in partying and foolish business ventures. For some reason, he made my brother Raghav a target of his bitterness.

He would taunt Raghav about anything that came to mind, without any logic or justification. It could be about the way he looked, the clothes he wore, the grades he got or the way he performed in sports. He would imitate Raghav when he stammered, and that only made him stutter more. He would give him money to buy cigarettes, and then openly accuse him of pocketing the change when there would be none. He would tell him he should never marry because impotent men can never please their wives. Raghav may have been in his teens, but he was still a child and would get psychologically distraught easily. Whenever my father saw him upset, he would go and have a word with his brother. The teasing would pause for a while, only to resume with greater venom a few days later.

In a moment of weakness, my father told us about the money he had been paying chacha to not trouble Raghav. It turned out to be a business opportunity for chacha—he realized the money would keep coming as long as he caused distress to Raghav. The pay-offs turned out to be counter-productive though.

When Raghav learnt about the money, already in scarcity for us, being given away for his 'protection', he decided to teach chacha a lesson. He poured kerosene over himself and threatened to burn himself in the presence of all those present in the house. My father was at work. The intent was just to create a scare, but it went awry. A spark from the lit match in his hand flew onto him and his clothes caught fire in an instant. He suffered 80 per cent burns; the only consolation was that his face and genitals were completely saved.

Run Nikita, run. These words resonated louder and louder in my head as I saw my brother burn and scream in the house, and moan in pain for months on end in the hospital and then back at home. The lives of all my siblings had been cursed in one way or the other. I would not let the curse touch me. I was determined to run as fast as I could, as far away as I could, and would not let the curse catch up with me. I needed a plan to give myself the life I wanted.

❧

I was tall. I was slim. I was beautiful. I was in love with the girl I would see in the mirror. And this girl would be the mistress of her own destiny. But I needed to prepare myself for it.

It had to start with styling. I enrolled for fashion design weekend courses while still in high school. I had a good sense of grooming, but the training helped me create scintillating outfits with my meagre savings. I learnt the art of make-up. I made myself knowledgeable about wines, cigars, exotic holiday locations, parties, music, cuisines and all things important to small talk in high society. I observed how to hold a wine glass and a cigarette as a lady should. I used my sister's and father's social connections to make friends amongst the who's who of town; like my sister before me, I caught the attention of men.

I looked for maturity in my dates; I hung around with those at least five years older to me. No one could guess I was still in school going by the way I carried myself. My first boyfriend, Armaan, was preparing to be a professional golfer;

he would train during the day while I studied. We would be an item at night, hanging around at the golf club or party hopping. The last hour together would always be on the back seat of his car before he dropped me home.

He was the first man to touch me. I regarded him less a love interest and more a teacher. I needed to learn how to be with a man and how to please him—and what it was like to be pleased. I let him do whatever he wanted to. He would kiss me on my lips and on my neck. He would cup my breasts in his hands, and suck on my nipples. He would feel me top to bottom, and shag me with his fingers inside my vagina. Strangely, I never came no matter what he did to me; I did not even feel the pleasure I assumed I would. So I would pretend to feel aroused and would moan as I had seen in movies lest he regard me inadequate for him.

It was more terrifying initially to do things to him. I had no idea what I should be doing the first time. I kissed him awkwardly on his lips despite the taste of alcohol and tobacco in his mouth. I unbuttoned his shirt, and kissed his nipples camouflaged in his highly off-putting chest hair. It got more daunting when he guided my hand to the hardness between his legs. I felt him with his trousers on, but he lowered them double quick. He wrapped my hand around his thingy standing stiff in a shrub of pubic hair, made me rub it and move the skin up and down. He put a hand behind my head and lowered it. Something told me what he was expecting and I took him in my mouth and moved up and down despite feeling choked. He came. In my mouth, and on himself too. It was nauseating, and I wanted to get out of the car and throw up. But I managed to control the urge to. Maybe this is what sex is all about, I told myself. And feeling this way is the pleasure of it all even though I was not feeling any yet. Anyway, I was with Armaan to learn, not to marry him.

As an instructor, he threw me into the deep end from the word go. He tried everything the first few times itself. It was not slow and steady with him, there was no stepping up the act gradually. We stayed together for just under two years, but he never got around to penetrating me with anything but his fingers. I was not ready for it. He did not need me to satiate his sexual desires anyway. I was at the club late in the evening once and spotted his car in the parking. There was no reason to, but I walked toward it intuitively for a peek. He was in the car with a girl. They were making love. He was getting his release with other girls.

I was not angry, nor did I feel any pangs of jealousy. Armaan had played his part in my life. It was the cue for me to move on.

❧

I wanted to do something big in life. To make me rich and famous. And powerful too. I wanted to savour the high of achievement. Naysayers warn the youth to keep their optimism in check, for disappointments and heartbreaks would challenge the spirit. The path would be riddled with potholes, and the skies would unleash storms. These are not warnings to be disregarded, but I was being fuelled by a strong belief in myself. I knew I would pull myself out of the potholes, and rebuild what storms blew away, and would keep my date with the destiny I chose.

So what did I want? A career in fashion design and modelling. The economy and media were being liberalized, people were being exposed to money and lifestyles like never before. I had to move to Delhi where the action was. Glamour, a closeted vice, was being embraced as a virtue by society. I would mark my place under the spotlights.

And date men I deserved and desired—but only if they coveted me. I would not let any belittle me, humiliate me. I needed to be treated well, I did not want to suffer at their hands like my sister had. I would flit between men like I would taste my wines. I would assess them for complexity and character, for their suitability for maturing and consumption, and for their faults. Till I find the one balanced right for my palate. He's the one I would settle down with, and raise a family. A happy one. I had not known such a home thus far, but I will know when I make it.

I needed to get on with my life. My career aspirations placed a premium on my youth, and I could not afford to deplete even a day of it on unrelated activities. I somehow managed to clear my school leaving exams and enrol myself in a university. I would devote only as much attention to academics as was necessary to earn a degree.

I enroled in a digital design institute to be useful to the fast-growing creative and fashion industries. I was a quick learner, and got a job with the agency side of the institute. I developed a lifelong relationship with my first client—as my mentor, my shoulder in times of distress, the first man I really loved and continued to long after he passed away.

Alok was exactly ten years older than me; we shared birthdays. He was separated, had a four-year-old daughter and was doing well for himself financially. I would not call him good-looking but he charmed me with his ability to make conversation and by being genuinely interested in what I wanted to talk about. He listened, he reacted, he acted. He would do things I would ask him to, and would also do stuff proactively without waiting for me to ask.

At that stage of my life, I had little to offer him back except my companionship. And love, albeit platonic mostly. He would treasure even that, never demanding more than what I offered.

❧

There is no definition for my relationship with Alok. We had everything going on between us—but he was also my guardian. Maybe that's why I could not get myself to have sex with him, even if we were physically intimate in most other ways.

I picked up valuable professional skills from him. How to sell, how to write impressive business letters and proposals, how to deal with people, how to be a team member, how to be a leader. Money was just currency in hand for me till he showed me how to value it and draw up budgets.

He went out of his way because he loved me dearly. He was exceedingly fond of me. He was a doe-eyed adolescent around me, melting in my arms when I would hold him. His kisses would send shivers down my spine, his arms would wrap around me in the warmest embrace I had ever felt, and the caress of his hands on my body relaxed me both physically and mentally. I would forget all troubles at homes, and all worries about the future, when in bed—or on the rug, or on the couch, or on the office table, or in the car—with him.

I want to marry you, he said one day. It was a surprise to hear those words. I wasn't even thinking about marriage at that stage of life. I was only planning a starry future for myself.

But you are married, I replied.

We are separated. I will file for a divorce.

No, I cannot let you do that on my account.

It would happen, with you or without you in my life.

Anyway, I am not even thinking about marriage. There is so much to do. I want to go to Delhi and be a model. And make a career in fashion design. You know that.

I know. You can still do that. While we wait for my divorce to come through, and even after we are married. I will not have a problem.

It is easy for you to say that now, but things will change. You will have your compulsions, and that would come in the way of my ambitions.

Trust me, it will not be so.

I trust you. I don't trust myself yet. I have not seen enough of life to take such a big step at this point.

Please.

Dad won't agree either. He would not want me marrying someone so much older, divorced and with a child. Don't get me wrong here. These are not issues with me, but my father would be concerned. He is yet to come to terms with what Radha didi went through. He would want a more ideal situation for me. I know you, I value you, I love you. But don't ask me to marry you. Please.

Alok did not push further. He never asked me to marry him again. He did not divorce his wife. They would get back together eventually, and have a second child too. I was not ready to commit myself to marriage for many years to come. But fate dealt the wrong card, waylaying my best laid plans.

❧

Dad collapsed. We were having late-afternoon tea, and he was in fine fettle when he suddenly slumped over himself. He would not regain consciousness no matter what we did; an ambulance was called to rush him to hospital.

It took a few days for the doctors to diagnose a problem in the lungs; he collapsed due to a shortage of oxygen in his system. He was required to stay in the hospital for as long as it would take for the doctors to fix him. He had been sick earlier, and hospitalized too. But I had never seen him in that state on a ventilator before. I was scared, very scared.

I was trying to spend as much time by his side as possible. He had been admitted for five days now, and I was walking the corridors of the hospital well past midnight. I could not sleep, and I could not stop worrying. Just then, I bumped into Krishna, carrying a wad of papers in his hand.

Krishna was Armaan's second cousin, and we had met a few times at the golf club. What are you doing here at this hour? he asked. Everything all right?

Dad's not well. He's in intensive care, I replied. I did not know Krishna very well, but I was glad there was someone I could talk to.

What happened to him?

Something in the lungs. The doctors told us but I can't remember the medical jargon. Only my sister can explain.

Can I help in any way?

Thanks, but it's ok.

Can I get you a coffee?

I looked at him. I wanted to say no, but I didn't want him to leave. Sure, that would be refreshing, I said.

Take a seat, I will be back soon.

He was back with two cups a few minutes later and joined me on a bench in the corridor. We made small talk about news in town, gossip at the club, and about my father's earlier bouts of illnesses. It was three in the morning when I realized how long we had been talking. I thanked him for being with me, and excused myself to take a nap in the rooms reserved for attendants of patients. He offered to check on my father the following evening and left.

I had not asked what he was doing in the hospital at that hour. He did not do anything while he was there except chat with me. I should have asked him. Maybe, just maybe, I would have been alerted to what lay ahead.

❧

The word cocksure was invented keeping the youth in mind—because that's what they feel about their decisions. It leads to mistakes or poor judgment calls. If small, they amuse or leave you scarlet in the face. If big, they can leave lives in ruin in their wake.

What big mistake did I make? Make that plural. I made two in one go. I put my dreams on hold. Dreams to go to Delhi, and make a career in fashion. There would be ample opportunity for it in the future, I assured myself. Let me make the other big mistake in the meantime, I must have told myself. Of marrying Krishna.

How did that happen? Well, he dropped by at the hospital again the following day. And then every day after that. He would offer to drive me around, bring home-cooked food to save me from the unpalatable hospital fare, and take me out for coffees to cheer me up. He would spend time with the doctors, follow the progress, arrange the medications, do the paperwork. He was just the help we needed when we were lost. He uplifted our deflated souls.

His presence, care and proximity to me was not lost on my father. He was curious about Krishna's place in my life, and would quiz me about him when he was in better spirits.

Nothing, he's just turned out to be a good friend, I would say repeatedly.

Would you like to marry him? asked my father.

Where did that come from?

Krishna spoke to me and expressed a desire to marry you. He assured me there was nothing on between the two of you, so I should not get any wrong impressions. He sought my permission and blessings the old-fashioned way.

I have not even given it a thought.

Why don't you? But there is no compulsion or pressure from my side. I don't know how long I will live, and I would like both my daughters to be settled and secure. It will be a big load off my chest. But it is your decision to make.

My father did not say I have to do anything if I didn't want to, but he also underscored a heartfelt wish in the twilight of his life. We could see he had given up, and was just going through the motions of existence. If the grim reaper knocked the same evening, he would open the door without hesitation and give up his earthly existence. He had had enough.

But I was not ready to give up on him yet. I wanted to see him happy. I was not being morbid, but I wanted him to have a few sips from the cup of happiness before he died. He wanted me married, he was ok with Krishna. Even if he was ten years older, and I was still in my teens.

I put my plans of going to Delhi on hold. I said yes. To buy some cheer for my father, and to extend his life. My dreams would be delayed, but they will come true. I was cocksure about my decisions.

❧

Charity begins at home, and happiness starts with the self. It may sound selfish, but one can be a source of happiness for others only if they themselves are happy first. When I agreed to marry Krishna, I knew I was making sacrifices for my father's sake. I wish someone had told me things don't pan out the way I thought they would. By going off-track in the pursuit of my dreams, I would have regrets. Despondency would set in when the life I desired turns into a mirage. My plight would torment my father till the end of his days. I should have rejected the idea of marriage in my teens.

Ours was an important match in town. Krishna also lived in one of the palatial havelis in old town, not too far from ours. Their family business went back centuries when they traded with caravans passing through Rajasthan; at one time, they had significant stakes in the manufacture of salt, a valuable and uncommon commodity. They were still a big deal. Or so it was believed by everyone. The reputation built by their ancestors endured till the present day.

Once word got out, congratulations poured in from even long-forgotten acquaintances; everyone was fishing for invites to the wedding. Even at the club, friends walked up and wished me. How come none of these people knew the inside story about Krishna's life? And his character? And if they did, why didn't they alert me? When I reflected on the events of that time, I promised to cut myself off from all those who were privy to his state of affairs but did not care to warn me.

Alarm bells could be heard well before the big day, and the damage would have been limited had I bailed out when there was still a window to. We learnt his parents were separated—ok, these things happen. But the father was leading a life of penury, confined to a shanty, isolated by the family. His sister was in Calcutta, married to a distributor and producer of Bengali films. They were both in the thick of sex scandals in the region, even pimping wannabe actresses as prostitutes to the rich and the powerful—in exchange for money or favours. His brother-in-law also ran a chit fund company, where investors save and seek credit on the fringes of the regulated financial and banking system. Apparently, he was a much sought-after person—by those he had swindled. What did Krishna do himself? He was in the process of setting up a company to export handicrafts from Rajasthan but was yet to build a steady source of income for himself.

None of the above could be confirmed. The truth was drowned under the cacophony of hearsay. We did not dive deep to dig out facts to be sure. Who would have done it? My father was not in a state to go probing. The brothers could not—one had been given away, another was still recovering physically and psychologically from the burns. My sister was in a shell, but she would mumble run Nikita, run, even as the wedding date got closer. I wanted to, but would look at my dad. My father had recovered enough and was out of the hospital. Busy with the preparations, he now had a spring in his step, and a spark in his eyes. He had discovered something to be enthused about. I did not want him to sink again.

How would I know that this decision would take all of us down? A decision none of us could be held responsible for. Fate was in a grumpy mood when I crossed its path.

Thank you for saying yes. You don't know how happy you have made me. I have really liked you from the time we got acquainted, but could never express what I felt.

Krishna opened his heart to me over our first dinner date but I could not get myself to reciprocate with any words of affection. My head was still in a swirl. What was I doing? Who was the man across the table from me? He was a stranger until recently; how did he become my fiancé? Wasn't I supposed to be heading to Delhi as soon as my dad had recovered? When did those plans get derailed? Was all this for real, or just a dream? Or worse, a nightmare? Who was scripting those chapters of my life?

Why didn't you say so earlier? I asked. I could not think of any other response.

Well, you have been a popular girl with the guys and I did not think you would pay any attention to me.

Don't be funny. You are making it sound like I am some Miss Universe.

You are to me.

Aawww, that's sweet, I said. I was genuinely flattered.

I have never been able to take my eyes off you whenever we met. And there were times when I would see you but you probably didn't know I was around. I would just admire you from a distance.

You are making me blush.

It's a fact. I have been your fan for a long time now.

You should have just walked up to me.

I did. Finally.

When?

At the hospital.

You mean when you spoke to my dad?

No, when I met you the first time in the hospital at night.

You didn't walk up to me. We bumped into each other, and we just spoke about my father and some random stuff in the middle of the night. I am surprised we spoke for hours. But wait … I am so sorry. I never asked why you were in the hospital. It's so insensitive of me. I hope all was fine?

No, no, it's ok. You were so distressed, it was perfectly natural for you not to ask. So please don't chide yourself.

So why were you in the hospital?

May I make a confession?

Yes.

I came to meet you.

Meet me? I don't get it.

I got to know your father was unwell, and that you were spending time in the hospital. On a whim, I decided to drive over and try to see you.

How did you know I would be there?

I didn't. I just took a chance. Got lucky the third time.

Third time?

Yes, I went twice earlier and looked all over but could not spot you.

Who told you about my father's hospitalization?

Aman.

Aman who? My brother?

Yes.

How do you know him?

We got introduced a few months back to explore business opportunities together. Nothing has come of it yet, but we have become good friends.

But Aman is in Bikaner with his adopted mother, my tai.

He visits Jaipur from time to time. He mentioned a possibility of moving back.

He did? No one knows about such plans.

I don't know. I am telling you what he told me.

Why is Aman coming back? My mind was racing but kept hitting a wall. He is supposed to handle his grandfather's business in Bikaner, or that's what we all assumed. If he comes back, will it by himself or with tai? If both, where would they stay? Does Brajesh tau know? Will they move back to the haveli?

Run Nikita, run. I could hear this echo in my head, but it was too feeble. I wish it had been louder. I might have realized something creepy was afoot; there was something amiss about the whole thing. Why would Krishna corner me in the middle of the night in a hospital, when circumstances had left me highly vulnerable? Why did he just hover around before finally 'running' into me? How long had he been eyeing and stalking me? Why did he zero in on Aman of all the people to do business with?

My senses failed me when I needed them most. I could not see the red flags shrouded in fog. I was asking the right questions but could not hear myself speak. I did not see through the man who was manipulating things to marry me. I would have realized the situation was red hot and would have retreated instantly had I touched it. I wish I had smelt the coffee.

You sound like such a romantic, is all I could get myself to say to him. I should have put on my running shoes instead.

And then I got married.

My father sold his farmhouse—his sanctuary—to fund an impressive reception. The wedding must have been an important event for the city. The rajmata herself came to bless the couple. It was a rare occasion when the royals allowed themselves to cross into my father's personal life. We even got coverage in the city's leading newspapers. I did not know our families were such a big deal.

All the guests had a merry time; I would recall it later as a wake before the death itself. I was then taken away to my husband's house in a car decorated with flowers—and reeking of alcohol inside. I ignored it. We reached his grand haveli, brightly decked with fairy lights. The mother-in-law had reached in advance to greet the new member of the family at the door, performing a brief auspicious ceremony with oil lamps and flowers. And then I stepped in, for the first time—I had never visited the house during my courtship. Why didn't I?

If I had, I would have called off the engagement no matter how far we had gone into the preparations. Count Dracula's castle would have looked like a children's amusement park in comparison. The haveli was dilapidated. That's it—one word should say it all. The residents looked morose and unsmiling—just a few hours back, they had been dressed in their finest attire and were all cheer and gaiety at the wedding. How could they have undergone such a transformation? Were they the same people? Did they die on the way and was it their ghosts I was seeing?

Narrow, winding steps, in near darkness, took us to a two-room set at the far corner of the terrace. One was ours, one the mother-in-law's. There was a small, dirty kitchen and a dirtier shared bathroom. The walls had not been painted for years, the lighting was dull, the furniture old but the sheets smelt freshly laundered. I stood in a stupor. Is this the future I signed up for, gave everything up for? I felt like throwing up my dinner.

I collected myself, and steeled myself to bear up with that one night. If I live to see the morning sun, I will figure out what to do. I took off my jewellery, secured it in a steel wardrobe in the room, and went to the bathroom to change from my heavy saree into a comfortable salwar suit. I was not ready to undress in front of my husband yet.

I returned to the bedroom to find Krishna sitting on the bed, stripped to his boxers, with a tumbler of whisky in his hand. This was getting worse, but I kept counting till ten over and over again. This too shall pass, I prayed. It would not. Not in a hurry at least.

Evading eye contact, I went to the other side of the bed to lie down. So, we are officially married, I said, trying to make small talk to take my mind off my surroundings.

Yes, we are, he said. He was smiling.

I hope your family and guests liked the arrangements.

Ask my mother. I was too busy getting married, he said and laughed.

I will. But it was quite tiring. I think I should get some sleep.

There was no energy left in me and I lay down sideways with my back to him, but he seemed full of beans. He did a bottoms-up on his drink and slid towards me, feeling my legs with his hand. I could feel his hardness against my hips.

What's the rush, he said. We need to make our first night memorable.

Tomorrow please, I am really tired, I mumbled. I was not tired. I was disgusted. I was trying to hypnotize myself into believing this was a bad dream; I wanted to sleep quickly and wake up in my father's house. God knows how difficult it was to fight back my tears.

But he was very focused in his mission. Feeling my breasts and kissing my neck, he asked if I liked it with the lights on or off.

I don't know. I have never done it, I replied.

Really? I did not know you had a sense of humour.

You don't believe me?

No one would.

Why?

You were quite an item in the club.

What makes you say so?

Everyone knew.

What did they say?

Want some fun? Pick up Nikita.

That's nonsense.

You can't change facts.

Why are you talking like this about me?

Because it's the truth.

Then why did you marry such a girl?

Because she ignored me. I promised myself to win your heart.

Can we sleep for now? I am in no mood right now. I was almost pleading, and getting turned off further with his words and touch.

He responded by sliding his hand under my bra, squeezing me, hurting me. He started kissing me even more profusely, and had his body weight almost completely on me.

I am getting crushed, I whimpered.

It's ok, he replied. He pulled my salwar pyjamas down, unhooked my bra, and pushed my shirt up in almost quick succession. He was pressing against me, increasing my discomfort. The smell of liquor on him was making me sicker.

He was a strong man, and turned me over with one flick of his arm. Holding me in place with one arm, he used his free hand to take the last of my clothing off. He tried to enter me, but I was as dry as a woman could be. How was he expecting to have sex with me?

Painfully.

Without even trying to arouse me, and without warning, he thrust himself inside me. My head could have exploded with the pain. He could not have cared. He moved despite the friction, and continued to for what seemed an excruciatingly long time. He came, finally. Inside me. I was sore and itchy by then and did not know what to do about it. I felt a trickle down my thighs, and I could see no tissues around me. I just had the sheet to dab the icky liquid with.

Don't do this again, he said after a few minutes.

Don't do what?

Dislike me in bed.

What do you mean?

You were not aroused. Clearly, you did not find me desirable.

It's not that. I was tired, I told you.

How come you are tired only for me?

It's not about you. I have just been having long and tiring days lately.

Anyway, I am warning you. Don't ever humiliate me again.

I was not humiliating you.

I have said what I wanted to. Don't ever say no to me for sex. Ever. Good night.

And with that, he shut his eyes and passed out. What happened to the gentle Krishna I had liked? Where was that side of him? I lay on my back, naked, covered with a cotton sheet, staring at the ceiling. I stayed like that for hours. Till no more tears would flow out. I had never cried so much.

I woke up with the first light of the day, my stomach feeling tight, my spirits low. I looked sideways—Krishna was sleeping without any clothes on, not covered with any sheets. I saw not so much of his nude body as his bared soul, and both made for an ugly sight. I did not wake up in my father's house. I was not in a nightmare the previous night. It was reality, the new reality I would have to live with.

I closed my eyes and visualized myself sashaying on a ramp in the best of designer wear, all attention on me with flashlights popping and spotlights following me. I flicked them shut.

All my jewellery had been stolen. From the steel wardrobe—despite being secured by two locks. The house itself was not easy to break into. And yet, it was gone! Within thirty-six hours of arriving in my new home.

I was trying to reconcile to my situation. Even if I wanted to, I could not just walk away. I decided to face one day at a time to see where the road would lead to. It might not be such a bleak journey, I thought optimistically. Things change, as do people. What if our fortunes turn for the better, and we are out of this gloomy place? Krishna's disposition could improve too. I tried to settle into my new home, helping my mother-in-law with the cleaning and the cooking.

The second day after the wedding is a big one. As per custom, my brother would be coming around noon to take me back to my parents' house. And I would return in time to get ready for the reception dinner in the evening—it is the party hosted by the groom for their guests. Krishna had left for work, and I was getting ready for Raghav to come pick me. He was being brave for me despite his scars. I unlocked the wardrobe, and the locker inside, and put my hand in for the jewellery. It was full of air.

Hold it, I told myself. This is a mistake. I felt the dark space inside and found nothing. Panic started setting in. I threw all my clothes out, opened the cabinets and bags, lifted the mattresses, bent to look under the bed, shoved my hand into the sides of the sofas—it was all in vain. I went to my mother-in-law's room, and asked if she had seen my jewellery. Maybe, just maybe, she had taken it elsewhere for safekeeping. But she had no idea where it could be. Some of the collection were heirlooms going back generations, some my parents had been investing in when they could over the years, and some had been purchased recently for my wedding. I feared I was going to get a heart attack.

I called Krishna. My jewellery, it's not there, I blubbered. It's been stolen. Call the police. It's urgent.

Calm down, he said. No need to call the police.

But why? The thieves can't be too far.

First, don't sound so hysterical.

Why? Do you know it's worth?

I know.

Then what are you waiting for? Let me call papa and ask him. He knows people.

Wait. Don't do that.

Why?

After what seemed like an extended period of silence, he said he took it. His tone was sheepish. But the thought of it being with him had an immediate calming effect on me. Must be to keep in the bank locker, I told myself.

So where is it? I need it. Raghav is about to come and I don't have much time to get ready.

I don't have it.

Then who has it?

I had to give it to someone.

Who?

I owed money to some people and could not pay on time. They were putting a lot of pressure on me. They left me with no choice but to give the jewellery. They will return it when I give them the money. Don't worry, I will get it back.

I had a sinking feeling like never before. My system was feeling choked. What mess had I landed myself into? I kept holding the phone to my ear, not speaking a word. Krishna was evidently bankrupt, and in debt too. He did not have a shard of decency about him. How could he have taken his wife's jewellery without her permission? Without even bothering to inform her. That too within two days of being married. What kind of a man was he?

The signs, the whispers, the conversations of the past few months flashed before my eyes. Was I being set up for this?

He had gone to the hospital looking for me. Was it for me or for my money? On our first night, he insinuated nasty things about my character. If that were true, how could he bear to love me? Does he even love me?

I snapped out at the sound of a hello from the other end of the line. Are you there? he asked.

Yes, I mumbled.

It's ok, I will sort it out.

What will I wear when I go to my parents'? What will I wear in the evening? What will I tell my family? What will my father think? He will be shocked.

You don't have to think so much. Just wear anything.

I don't have anything, you took all of it. My tone was developing a sharp edge.

Don't talk to me like that. We are one now, and all problems are for both to bear.

Why didn't you tell me all this before we got married?

I had expected to sort it out.

I am feeling like such a fool, I said. I was crying.

Can you shut the fuck up? he retorted. Stop crying for God's sake.

Why did you do this?

It's done, I can't do anything about it for now.

But what do I wear?

It's not my problem. I have work to do. You go figure.

He put the phone down, but I kept holding the receiver, feeling incapacitated. Raghav would be over soon. I needed to get ready. I did, sans any jewellery. Our houses were a seven minute walk apart, but he picked me up in a car.

A cheerful lot was waiting for me—comprising mostly my mother's side of the family. They were the white sheep of my life. I was conscious of my appearance—it was unnatural to appear for an occasion like that without any jewellery on. I could feel eyes on me, but no one said anything. But they would. My mother's elder sister took me aside eventually and asked how I was.

I am fine, I replied.

Then why aren't you wearing any jewellery?

Oh, that! I was so tired, having to wear heavy clothes and jewellery continuously and meeting people. It was weighing me down, so I decided to give myself a break.

But this is an important ceremony.

I know, but I am with my family. I can be casual with them.

The aunt did not look convinced with my explanation but decided not to press further. I was glad for it. I wanted to enjoy myself for the time I was there.

Evening came and I got ready quietly for the reception. Even Krishna did not make an effort to make conversation. I still didn't know what to wear. I had some costume jewellery—there was no option but to put that on. Jaipur is a city where it matters what you flaunt, and I had nothing to. Not even a husband. He was barely beside me. He spent the evening surrounded by his male friends, downing one whiskey after another.

My family was there too; they knew something was amiss. They may have bought my story of no jewellery earlier in the day, but there was no plausible excuse for the evening. I could see the pain on my father's face, although he didn't speak a word on the matter.

Eventually the last of the festivities associated with the wedding were over. It was time to figure out the marriage.

What do you do when you open the door to two strangers, one sporting a rifle and the other a revolver? More so when you are in a dingy mansion, it's night, and it's raining?

You quiver.

It had been two days since the reception and I was just sitting in my room, staring into blank space. That had been my state past few days. My mother-in-law was in the adjacent room when I heard fervent knocking on the back door. This one led straight to our part of the house. Realizing no one else was opening the door, I went out myself to find two men standing there. They had clearly not come in peace.

Where is Krishna? asked the man with the rifle. The other did not speak anything but his gaze was fixed on me; he was clearly the boss.

I don't know.

You are his wife, you will know.

He does not tell me.

When will he be back?

I don't know. He hasn't called.

Tell him we had come. He has two more days to pay up.

Who are you?

He knows.

And they left. I kept looking in their direction long after they were gone. I was motionless; I was the lull before the storm.

And then I screamed. With as much power as my lungs could crank up. I was livid. I was angry. I was scared. I was helpless.

Why didn't you tell me about all the problems? I ranted at my mother-in-law when I could get myself to close the main door and march into her room.

Everyone has problems, so does Krishna. They will get sorted, just give him time, she replied in as composed a manner as she could.

But you should have told me.

How could I have? Krishna really loves you. I didn't want to take away his happiness. He has been stressed for so long, you were his hope.

But you have ruined my life for the sake of your son. Who gave you that right? I was shaking, stammering with nervousness.

He told me not to say anything, she said.

Did you ever think about me? How could you be so heartless and cruel?

That's enough, boomed a male voice from behind me. I didn't need to turn around to know it was Krishna's but I still did. Don't you dare speak to my mother like this. She has nothing to do with this. It is between you and me.

Apparently, he had been there for a while, listening to us. Then who should I speak to? What do I do? I wailed in exasperation.

I told you this will pass. Can't I expect any understanding from my wife?

You should have come clean before I married you, I said.

Women don't need to be told everything. They don't understand.

What I understand is that my jewellery is missing. Where is it?

I told you I had to give it in lieu of my debts.

How much are your debts?

You don't need to know.

I do. Because you have used my jewellery to pay for them. Do you even know the worth of my jewellery?

I am not discussing this further.

And what do I tell those people?

Which people?

The two people who had come asking for you. With guns.

In a flash, Krishna mellowed down. I could see fear on his face. When did they come? he asked.

Just before you returned.

What did they say?

They want the money in two days.

What else did they say?

Nothing. They just left.

Mother and son were clearly scared. Krishna turned around and dragged his feet to our bedroom. The mother-in-law went off too, leaving me alone. I had never felt so alone. I so wanted to be with my sister. And with my father. And with the mother I recognize only from her photographs.

Run Nikita, run. But where to?

Standing face-to-face with gun-toting debt collectors alone at night is terrifying. The sight of them drinking with your husband in your bedroom is downright macabre.

I had stepped out of the house for the first since I got married—I needed a bit of shopping therapy. Not that I had much money to spend. I had walked straight into the bedroom when I returned—only to freeze at the door seeing the men.

I just stared, holding my bags, not knowing what to make of the sight before me. My marital life was playing out as a never-ending tragic saga. The rifleman just looked at me, not saying a word. His boss smiled at me, raised his glass, and said

'Namaste, bhabhiji,' a respectful term used to address the wife of an elder brother.

Where were you? asked Krishna.

I had work in the market.

You didn't tell me.

You weren't home.

You could have called me at the office.

You are hardly there.

Did you try?

No.

Don't do this again. I should know where you are. I get worried, he said. The fake concern was just a way of keeping track of me, to control me. He was showing the visitors he was the man of the house, the dominant one.

Can we get some snacks? We were waiting for you, we are all hungry, Krishna continued.

Where's your mother? I asked and turned around to go out.

Krishna's face turned red, and he followed me out. What was the meaning of that question? he asked.

I just asked where your mother was. She could have prepared something if I was not there.

I will not tolerate such impertinence again, and certainly not in the presence of outsiders.

Outsiders? I thought they were younger brothers to you.

Enough of this nonsense. Can we get some chicken tikkas? And ice too. And fast. They are getting restless.

I decided to back off and went to the kitchen quietly. I put together what I could and took it to the room. I wanted to leave the tray on the table and come out immediately, but the boss invited me to join them.

It's ok, I will be outside, I replied.

No, join us. We would like it.

I think my mother-in-law is calling.

She's not at home. So you are free to join us.

I looked at Krishna for help, but his expression was ordering me to stay. I could not find a suitable spot to sit on. Krishna and the rifleman were on the bed, my bed, the bed I slept in with my husband. The only vacant space was on the couch where the boss was sitting. He patted the empty seat and beckoned me to join him. I did after a brief hesitation, avoiding any contact with his body.

Would you like a drink? he offered raising his tumbler of whisky toward me.

No thank you, I don't drink.

You can, with us.

No, it's ok.

Try a sip.

I don't drink.

He edged closer, and held the tumbler under my nose. Have a sip, he said in an increasingly insistent tone. I was not drinking, and certainly not from his tumbler. I shook my head, looking down, not making eye contact with anyone.

A sip won't kill you, piped up Krishna. Especially when Ranjan bhai is offering it so nicely. I heard the name of the boss for the first time, bhai referring to brother.

When I stayed still, Krishna got up, took my arm and dragged me out of the room. You do not insult Ranjan bhai like this, he hissed.

I am not insulting him. I cannot share his drink. It's disgusting.

You have to do these things in business sometimes.

What business? Don't you have any shame, asking this of your wife?

What am I asking? I am just asking you to be a good host to him.

Right, and then you will ask me to sleep with him, I snapped.

He replied with a tight slap across my face. It was the first time someone had hit me. Even my father had not. I was stunned. I must have looked so pitiful, so pathetic. He stared at me for a few seconds and then, without even a hint of remorse, asked me to go back in. He literally shoved me back inside.

I am sorry Ranjan bhai, she met you the first time so is a bit shy, said Krishna.

That's ok, these things happen between husband and wife. Nothing that a drink cannot fix. The tumbler was back under my nose. I slowly raised my hands, held the tumbler, and took a sip. The boss had not let go of the tumbler; his touch was sickening.

See, it was not a big deal at all, said the boss. Can we have some music?

The rifleman got up, went to the cassette player, browsed through the collection of tapes and inserted one with Bollywood dance numbers. He knew what his boss liked.

Let's dance, said Ranjan bhai looking at me. He got up, and started moving gently to the tunes filling the room. He bent toward me, and extended his arm for me to take. I sat, not moving, looking down, noticing his shiny green leather shoes for the first time. Come on bhabhiji, one dance, he said. I still did not move.

Krishna got up, and literally pulled me into a standing position. The boss put his arms around my waist, and moved around me, but I stayed a statue. Krishna bhai, why is your wife in a bad mood? Don't you let her dance with your friends? he asked.

No one said anything. Ok, continued the bhai, for every dance bhabhiji does with me, I will waive off ten thousand rupees of the interest you owe me. That's a good business deal, isn't it?

One dance is all that bhai is asking for, don't be shy, Krishna said softly. Anyway, it's not about the money bhai, he said to the boss.

Of course it is Krishna bhai, said Ranjan. Why else did you marry bhabhiji? You promised all debts will be cleared after you are married. But she did not bring enough. The jewellery did not even pay for a tenth of what you owe the market.

I was aghast at what I was hearing. Krishna had married me for the money. He had set me up. Ranjan still had his arms around me, and I was being prostituted now.

What happened to the dowry you got, he continued. Oh yes, I forgot. You got none. You were an idiot not to have asked. Didn't you say her father was dying and would give in to any demands you make? Why didn't you use the opportunity? What will you do with a beautiful wife with no money? Ask her to dance with me at least to reduce your interest burden.

Run Nikita, run. My sister was again urging me. What do I do? God, help me.

I was going weak in the legs. I felt dizzy. I don't know what happened but I found myself lying in darkness when I came around. I was in my bed. I could not see him but I could hear Krishna snoring. I prayed it was Krishna only next to me.

What had happened to me after I fainted? Was I raped in an unconscious state? The way those goons treated me felt like I had been anyway. My husband was a willing party and witness to whatever those characters wanted. What can be worse for a woman?

There could not have been a bigger trigger for me to escape from the marriage. I had every grounds to—moral and legal. I was with a sick man from a sick family in a sick house. If I stayed on, I would become sick too.

But where do I go? I asked myself. I did not have the means to be on my own. How do I go back to my father? How do I tell him about how I was robbed? Of my jewellery, and of my life. How will I bear to see him in torment? It could kill him.

My sister was still pounding away in my head, urging me to run. I will find a way to navigate through a new life, but only after I was out of the current one. I continued with the make-believe conversations I often had with my sister. I wish I had called her for a real one.

She would have only repeated what she had been telling me: to run, no matter what. I was not moving out of my marriage for dad's sake. She would have told me to move out for dad's sake. He would rather see you cut your losses and rebuild your life than continue to suffer.

I wish I had reached out to my sister then.

I was stuck. I had nowhere to go. Divorce was not on my mind yet. I told myself to bear with my situation for a while. It was a storm I had to sail through; I would figure my options if I make it to land.

And so I went about doing what I had to. I resumed my classes to learn fashion design. I had dropped out of university, and could thus spend more time practising what I was learning. The head of my institute was impressed with my work, and referred me to a designer looking for an apprentice. I was hired for a stipend of five thousand rupees a month, a princely sum for me at that time.

It paid for my fee, as also for milk, bread, vegetables and other groceries at home. I was the breadwinner at home, and I had to feed myself. Others dug into what I brought home. I likened myself to a cheetah, the hunter, while the others were hyenas scavenging off my kill.

I still had a few trinkets left, but those too kept disappearing one at a time. I questioned him once, and he responded by downing his whisky in a swig, and slapping me. Not once, not twice, but three to four times in succession. What do you think I am, a thief? he slurred. How dare you interrogate me?

I did not question him again. Why bother about pennies when the main valuables were gone?

And so it went on. For a few years surprisingly. Life was never short on events—all dark ones, save the silver lining in the form of my daughter. But hers was not a smooth entry into my world either.

God seemed to have prepared an arsenal for a world war, but decided to direct all firepower at me. What was He smoking when drawing up my destiny? God has to be a He, a She cannot do this to a woman.

Two months into my marriage, I missed my period. I was scheduled to visit the gynaecologist anyway, to be examined for a likely infection in my urinary tract. I made a casual mention of the cycle being delayed, and he offered a quick test just to be sure. I was pregnant!

I was not even twenty. The quicksand was pulling me in deeper, and no one was throwing me a rope yet. This is not happening, I told myself. I went home, and we had another fight.

How could this have happened? I asked in a shrieky tone.

These things happen, he said without making eye contact. He was engrossed in his newspaper.

Why didn't you take precautions?

You could have asked me to.

I didn't know any better. You are much older. You should have known.

We are both adults, he said without looking up from his newspaper.

I am talking to you.

Even I am.

No, you are not. Are you listening to what I am saying? I am pregnant.

That's good news, no?

Really? Who is going to pay for the baby? We don't have money to feed ourselves. You have sold everything.

That got the attention of his male ego. He threw the newspaper aside and stared hard at me, trying to control his anger.

What do you mean? Just because I am going through a lean patch does not mean things will stay this way. What is this sarcasm for? he said, his voice getting louder with each syllable.

It's the reality.

Don't you dare humiliate me.

Humiliate you? Look who's talking! Do you know what I have been going through ever since I married you?

What have you been going through? You only want to make mountains out of molehills.

If that is so, then why don't you get your sister to share a drink with Ranjan bhai?

In an instant, I was on the floor. With the impact of his slap; it had never felt so hard before. I could not feel any sensation on my left cheek. My head hurt upon hitting the wall on the way down.

He was towering over me, eyes glowing. And then he kicked me—with the leather boots he had on. The first landed on my stomach; I was sure it would have killed the baby. The next few struck my thighs, calf and shin, as I squirmed on the floor avoiding blows on the more sensitive parts of my body. He gripped me by the hair, and brought my face close to his.

Don't you put my sister and yourself in the same category, he said.

I was choked. I was crying, and was not able to make any sound.

You ever talk like this again, I swear I will kill you and feed you to the dogs, he continued. Do you hear me? Do you understand me?

I nodded. I just wanted to be released from his grip. He was hurting me. He let go with a jerk, my head hitting the floor. He got up, and walked out of the room. Through my moist eyes I saw my mother-in-law standing at the door, watching everything silently. I tried to ask for help—but I could neither gesture nor speak. Maybe I was dying, I thought. She stood rooted to her spot for a few more minutes, and then turned around and left.

I just lay there, and slipped into unconsciousness. I don't know how long it was before I stirred awake. I could see the night sky through the windows. I had come home a little after lunch. I had lain in that state on the floor for hours, but no one had bothered to come to my aid.

My first instinct was to feel my stomach. I hoped nothing had happened to the baby. But I also wished the baby had aborted. Both emotions were playing up simultaneously in my head. Nothing felt amiss. I managed to get up, found water to drink in the room, and went to the bathroom. And stood under the cold shower with all my clothes on. I stayed that way till I could feel the shivers. I went back to the bedroom, dripping. I changed, and lay down on the bed. The prospect of dinner crossed my mind, but I found the thought of food revolting.

I slept off again, to wake up the next morning only. I looked at the other side of the bed; it was still made. He had either not come home all night, or he was sleeping in his mother's room. Had something happened to him? I shocked myself by being concerned for his well-being. What is wrong with us women? I thought. Shouldn't I be wishing some debt collector shoots him? I could not get myself to, even though my body was bruised and paining from his blows.

I just sat on the bed, pensive, broken. No one cared to enquire about me. I got up eventually and went to the kitchen to eat something. My mother-in-law and Krishna were both there, eating rice and dal on a small dining table fitted in the space available. Neither made eye contact. I helped myself to some rice and took the plate to the bedroom.

He came in after a while but didn't say anything. He pretended to be looking for something, he opened the wardrobe absent-mindedly to take out some clothes, and then sat down on the couch with his newspaper.

I want an abortion, I blurted out.

He looked up; he was relieved the silent tension was getting dissipated.

Are you sure? he asked.

Yes.

Ok.

I will ask Dr. Manchanda.

Ok.

The conversation ended there. He got up, changed and left. I picked up the phone to call my gynaecologist.

Make sure you are fasting tomorrow. It's Karva Chauth. Since this is your first time, I want you to know it's a very important festival in our family.

These were the first words I heard from my mother-in-law in two days since the thrashing. All she could think of was her son. Hindu married women are expected to fast all day and pray for the health and prosperity of their husbands. The fast is broken only when the moon is sighted at night. Men could suffer if their wives failed to follow the rituals, or so dictated deep-rooted beliefs going back centuries. There is no equivalent festival for men to observe for the well-being of their women.

The special day came, and Krishna and I had to go out early in the morning itself. For an appointment in the clinic. I was aborting the child. Long live the husband—wives and children be damned.

The procedure happened. I fasted despite being physically and psychologically messed up. The moon shone, I prayed to it for my husband's health and prosperity and then bent to touch his feet for his blessings. I was thinking of the abortion when I did. I was wishing for something to happen to the man whose long life I had fasted for. I was praying not for my husband but for myself. I wondered how my mother-in-law would react if she could read my mind. For just a moment I derived sadistic satisfaction imagining how terrified she might be for her dear son if she could.

Life settled back into a routine. As if nothing had happened.

❧

I got pregnant again. And again.

For someone poised to take flight at the first possible opportunity to, what was so endearing about my husband for me to be sexually active with him? There was no love lost between us; fear and insecurity was forcing me to be the submissive wife. I was biding my time till I could bail out. Escape is never an easy option. I had to try maintain some semblance of peace in the house. A routine is important to that end: wake up, clean the house, cook, socialize with your husband when required to, and have sex with him. Without contraception. Krishna did not use condoms; he said latex came in the way of the pleasure.

I got pregnant the first time because I had not even given a thought to taking precautions. The second time was foolishness—I was not careful enough despite what had already happened. The third was an accident, call it bad luck. It seemed I was also suffering from—or was blessed with—high fertility in my genes if I looked at how easily and rapidly my mother produced the four of us siblings.

I got my second abortion but Dr Manchanda was not pleased with me. He prescribed oral contraceptive pills but I could not take them for long. They caused nausea and headaches, affecting my work; I could not risk being jobless and stopped taking them. I tried other methods but I still became pregnant again.

Despite monitoring my menstrual cycles and forcing him to use condoms on fertile days. Despite him drinking more. Despite his volatile behaviour. Despite being physically abused more regularly. Despite the sex being painful. Despite feeling like I was being raped every time we had intercourse. Despite hating him increasingly with every passing day. None of these caused a decline in either his or my fertility.

I decided to keep the baby. I did not know how I would bring him or her up. I did not want to think about it. Anyway, the gynaecologist was strongly against the third abortion. God was not.

It was Karva Chauth again. I was returning from the market in a cycle rickshaw when a mini truck struck us from behind. I fell on the road, my abdomen taking the brunt of the impact. Miraculously, it happened right across the street from Dr Manchanda's clinic. And he was around to clean up the damage.

I fasted the rest of the day. I prayed for my husband's longevity. I touched his feet for his blessing when the moon was shining upon us. He would live. The baby would not.

The doctor had given me a stern warning earlier in the day. Another mishap, another abortion and I may not be able to bear children when I wanted to. My body might not even survive another trauma.

Another abortion might be the way to go if I felt suicidal, not an entirely outlandish proposition. But not before I had given life a few more chances.

❧

If he didn't use condoms, I would get pregnant. If I insisted he does, I would get a slap.

When he wanted to have sex with me, he was like a wild animal on heat—not that he was very docile otherwise. And because he was in a drunken state more often than not, he would get violent if I interrupted him to put on a condom.

For my own safety and dignity, or whatever was left of it, I allowed him to have his way. And, not unexpectedly, I was pregnant again. I was already into the second trimester when I shared the news. I just had not felt like bringing it up sooner. But the baby bump was just about beginning to take shape and it could no longer be a secret. I also needed him to go easy on me from then on. I tried to stay calm when I was telling him but I could not help sounding caustic.

Why the fuck do you talk in such an accusatory tone? he said. As if I am solely responsible.

You are. You refuse to use contraception, I said.

Says who? Of course I do.

No, you don't on most occasions. You don't even remember, you are so drunk when you come close to me.

What do you mean I am drunk? I drink, but I know what I am doing.

Then you would know why you wake up to unused condoms on the bedside.

Keep your tone down. Why are you making such a ruckus?

Ruckus? It's my life at stake here. I have a job to go to. I am the only one earning money in this house. How do you get food on your table? Who pays for it? You still steal my few remaining trinkets to pay for your booze and God knows what else.

He punched me hard on my stomach the next instant. I fell over and hit my head on the corner of the bed. I was bleeding. He had lost it again, and I would be branded the villain who provoked him.

Who are you calling a thief? And what is this thing you keep saying about providing for us? You are not doing anyone a favour, he said in a raised voice.

I am bleeding, I said in a broken voice.

That is also my fault. Why did you accuse me?

Oh my God, the baby is not moving. Help! I cannot feel the baby. Krishna, do something. I was getting hysterical. I was running my hands over my abdomen to try and feel any life within.

Just as well, he said, without a care about what I was saying. You are out of the house all day. And now some evenings too. I don't even know who you are with. It's not even my child. I took all precautions.

I was in a state of shock, but I could still hear him. And could not believe my ears. He was capable of such low talk. How can you say such things? I wailed. After all that I have done and given up.

What have you done? What have you given up? I married you even though Armaan warned me about you. Told me you are frigid.

You are lying. He would not say such a thing.

Really? Then why didn't you let him fuck you? He left you because he knew you were cheating on him. That's why you would not let him go all the way with you.

You and your cousin Armaan are scums. How can you discuss me like this? And just so you know, he was the one multi-timing on me.

I felt a twinge in my abdomen, and remembered the lifelessness within. Help me, please, I pleaded. My baby will die. Take me to the clinic. Please. I am sorry, we can talk later. I need to go now. I cannot feel anything. Please. I beg you.

I knew why I was being tortured. My earlier abortions were over in a day, but the guilt lingered. I had terminated human life, and not just any life. They were my own babies. There would be punishment for it, and God was meting it out.

Thankfully, Krishna calmed down. He helped me to the door and down the stairs. The blood on my forehead had clotted; it was not a deep wound. He hailed an autorickshaw to take us; he would let me suffer the gyrations of this three-wheeled transport but was too broke to hire a taxi.

Dr Manchanda excused himself from a patient who had come for a routine check-up to give priority to me. After a preliminary examination, he ran an ultrasound test on me. I felt something, and looked at the doctor's face. He half smiled at me. Looks like you have a gutsy kid inside you, he said. Will be able to handle more than a few knocks in life.

I could not hold back my tears even as I laughed in relief. He held my hand in his, and asked me to be strong. He called the nurse to administer first aid to my wound. Please be very careful from now on, he advised. Do not strain yourself mentally or physically. You cannot go to work. Watch every step you take—don't lose your balance at any time. You have had a close call. You might not be lucky again. Don't provoke that husband of yours. Save your battles till after the baby is born.

If I had left for New Delhi as planned, I would have certainly secured a foothold in the fashion industry in two years. I boarded the wrong train though. In the same time period, I ended up being battered, bruised, broken, broke and a mother of a daughter. Her father named her Vani.

Things had quietened down at home and I could feel myself breathe without effort for a change. Krishna was actually trying to be nice; him being so meant he was not loud after drinking, did not hit me, and kept his hands off the last remaining pieces of jewellery. In fact, some trinkets came back.

Jagdeep chacha had been inviting me to stay with him in Bombay for a while, and I finally decided to make the trip with two-month old Vani. He was one of the grey sheep of the family; he stood out considering most were black and my father was the only white one. We stayed there for nearly three months, uneventfully. We stepped out of the house for shopping or entertainment only when our hosts were paying. I would have been on welfare had I been the citizen of a developed country.

Krishna called a few times to update me. Business was looking up, and he had found investors to take a stake in his company. He bought a car finally. The break in Bombay and the news from Jaipur had a healing effect on me. His conduct gave me reasons for hope—there might be a future yet with my husband. I attributed his past behaviour to the stresses he was facing in life. He may actually be the good person I was acquainted with initially, I thought charitably.

I was looking forward to going home for a change.

In a surprising act of extravagance—and a show of wealth he did not possess—Krishna paid for us to fly back from Bombay, saving us a tortuous train journey. I landed in Jaipur, but there was no sign of him at the airport. I called home from a phone booth, but the line would not connect. After waiting for over an hour, I took a cab.

We reached home and picked the phone to call his office—there was no dial tone in it. I asked the mother-in-law about his whereabouts but she had no idea. The phone had been disconnected due to non-payment of dues, she said. Do you have any money? I could not believe her audacity to ask me. But I had seen worse.

He tumbled in eventually, well after dinner, reeking of alcohol. Hi baby, he slurred, trying to hold me and kiss me at the same time. I withdrew.

We kept waiting at the airport for you, I said calmly.

I am so sorry baby, I had to meet Aman and our discussion went on too long. I could not ignore him—he is your elder brother after all.

Aman? What are you doing with him?

Nothing. He just wanted some advice on investments.

From you?

Yes.

Why from you? What do you know about money?

Now, now, come on. Give your husband some credit. A bit of bad luck does not mean he's not smart, he said. He was not steady on his legs, in his speech and in his gaze. I was not even sure he knew what he was talking about.

Vani and I were looking forward to being driven home in our first car, I said, changing the topic.

Oh that! Of course, soon soon.

Tomorrow morning.

That's a problem.

Why?

You see, ummm, someone stole it.

Stolen? From where?

At night from outside. I mean, from outside the office.

What was it doing at the office?

I had to leave it there.

Why?

Some friends picked me up, and it got too late. So I came straight home.

When was that?

Day before yesterday.

I thought for a moment and realized something. But that's the day you called me from home around ten in the night, I said. That's not late at all by your standards.

Actually, it was last night.

Have you filed a police complaint?

Yes.

Where is it? I will ask Harish chacha to pursue the case. As a lawyer, he knows everyone.

I lost it.

Lost what?

A copy of the complaint.

Did you ever buy a car?

Are you accusing me of lying about the car?

Did you buy a car?

Yes, I did.

Where are the registration papers?

In the car.

There was no car. There never was. If he had no money to pay the telephone bill, how could he buy and maintain a car?

For that matter, he had no money to pay the milkman, the grocer and the newspaper vendor. I got to know within twenty-four hours of my return. All of them came calling, asking to be paid for months of overdue bills. Why didn't you ask sahib, I enquired.

Whenever we did, he said you would pay upon your return. They took turns to speak, but they were three heads saying the same thing.

Why me?

We don't know, that's what we were told.

How did you know that I was back?

Sahib told us. He said to come today to pick up the payment.

He told you when I would be back?

Yes.

That hollow, sinking feeling again. Nothing had changed. Nobody had. Nikita could not even run now. She was further weighed down with Vani's responsibilities.

I encashed a fixed deposit my mother's elder sister had presented on my wedding. I restored the telephone line—it was my lifeline if I needed to make a call in an emergency. I bought time—and fresh supplies—by settling a part of the dues of the vendors.

What do I do? What do I do? I had to do something, but my brain was short of ideas. The fuses were all blown.

Alok called. For the first time since I got engaged. I was surprised—and pleased—to hear his voice. He wanted to know if he should do it. All I had to say was a yes or a no. He would do it, no questions asked, if I gave my consent. When he figured out that I did not know what he was talking about, he asked if we could meet. I readily agreed, and went across to his office the same afternoon. Something was amiss, and I did not want to hear it over the phone.

I had not seen Alok in over three years. His smile, his warmth, his hug, his pecks on the cheeks brought memories flooding back. I wanted to continue holding him. I did not want to be anywhere else. I wanted to be with Alok. I wanted a home with him. Even if he had a wife living there. I wanted Alok in whatever packaging he came in.

But I had to snap back to reality. We exchanged pleasantries and made small talk about our respective personal lives. But I was itching to get to the point. And I did.

What was the cryptic question all about? I asked him.

It was about the money.

What money?

If I should lend it to him.

Lend what money to whom?

The twenty-five lakhs you and Krishna need.

Twenty-five lakhs? Rupees?

Yes.

We need?

Yes.

Says who?

Krishna.

Why would he say this to you?

Because he only speaks on your behalf every time.

Every time? What every time?

Every time he borrows money. I figured you would be embarrassed to ask me directly so you had been asking Krishna to. I give it without asking you since I did not want to make it awkward for you. But this was a very big sum and I just wanted a quick yes or no from you. There is no need to justify or explain anything.

I don't even know what twenty-five lakhs looks like. That's two and a half million. I was earning ten thousand rupees in my last job, including bonuses. I never asked for any money from you.

You didn't? Then why would Krishna say so?

Because he is Krishna, the crook, the smooth-talking con man. If he had reached out to Alok, he would not have spared others either. I made calls. My husband had been borrowing money not only from Alok but from other friends and acquaintances too. All in my name. No one checked with me thinking I would be embarrassed to talk to them directly. They just assumed I was in the know. Which husband would use his wife's name like this? they said. He swindled good people, trusting people, the ones who cared for me even if we had not been in touch lately.

How will I ever repay those people? I will never be able to, even if I sold myself.

Radha didi called. To enquire if I knew where Aman might be. He had not been home in four days and had not informed anyone about his whereabouts. She sounded worried. I could not prove it yet, but I knew Krishna had something to do with it. My nightmare with him was playing out like one of those never-ending television soaps where the characters would never live happily ever after.

We should call the police, I said.

Are you sure? Maybe he's gone somewhere and not informed us?

Does tai know? He would tell his mother.

Even she has no idea actually. And she's particularly worried since there has never been a day of his adult life when he has not called her, no matter where he is, didi said.

Did she have anything to say about his behaviour or state in the recent past?

Yes, I spoke to her. She mentioned that he had been stressed about financial matters lately but would not open up to her with details. He would laugh it off when she insisted on knowing more.

Do you know anything?

Not really. But Krishna might.

Why Krishna?

They were in business together.

Who was in business together?

Aman and Krishna.

Since when?

For over a year. Why, didn't you know?

No. Krishna mentioned he had met Aman the day I returned from Bombay to give him some advice. Nothing more.

Oh, I thought you knew. They had floated a company together to trade in real estate.

Where did they get the money?

Aman put up the money.

Aman? What kind of money?

He had inherited about fifty lakh rupees when his grandfather died. He was figuring his investment options when he and Krishna got talking. He really liked Krishna; he would speak highly of him as a professional. He found him to be the truly caring man in the family.

My knees felt weak. I was fearing the worst, and I knew who was behind it.

Listen, you talk to Harish chacha and ask him to call the police chief. They are friends. File a complaint. Don't delay. And don't ask questions. I will call you soon, I said and hung up.

I was about to call Krishna to ask where he was when he walked in anyway. He was in a happy mood.

Where is Aman? I asked.

How would I know? he replied.

You should, he is your business partner.

Says who?

Says I. Why didn't you tell me you were not just advising him, but were actually working with him?

There was nothing to tell. It's business talk. Women don't like it.

This woman needed to know if her husband and her brother were in business together.

Well, she knows now.

And she wants to know why you were borrowing money from her friends in her name behind her back?

Why are you getting so touchy? I will repay them. They are just loans.

You had no right to approach them for money.

They did not have a problem. What is your problem?

They had no problem because they thought I had sent you. They trusted and cared for me.

Bullshit! They gave it because I am the man who can earn that money back and repay them. No one would give you a rupee as a loan without me standing collateral.

You are worse than I thought.

Whoa! I am in a good mood today, but don't push it.

Where is Aman?

I just told you I don't know.

He is missing.

He is an adult. He will come back. Must have gone off with a girl somewhere. Let him have fun. It's his age to.

No, something is amiss. And I know you have a hand in it.

One more word, and I will thrash you like you never have been.

You touch me once more, and I will kill you. I am going to find my brother. God save you if anything has happened to him.

I went to the police headquarters to meet the investigating officer. He greeted me politely, offered me a seat and chai. He was working the phones to find my brother, and issuing instructions to officers moving in and out of his office. I was impressed. I knew they would find him soon.

They did. In a run-down hotel in Ajmer. The news came on the wireless. The officer got up to leave in his jeep to confirm for himself. Ajmer was a two-hour drive away. I requested to be taken along and he agreed.

I was greeted by a sight that would make anyone wail in anguish. Aman was in a dirty room, looking no cleaner himself. He had locked himself in four days ago according to the hotel manager. No one had come to see him, and he had not stepped out. The staff had not checked on him either. This was a hotel where most guests preferred to be left alone, and did not appreciate anyone snooping in on their affairs. What was Aman doing here?

He had gone there to die. Krishna had swindled him of all his money. He was broke. He could not tell tai; she would be so ashamed of him. He could not tell me; Krishna was my husband after all. He had gone into a depression when he learnt that all his money was gone. He had not eaten in four days; he was trying to muster up the courage to hang himself with a rope he had purchased on the way to the hotel. When the police notices went out, an alert bellboy decided to check on Aman's room. The local police came immediately since this was a case involving the top brass. They had the presence of mind to call a doctor who put Aman on a drip right away. If the rope had not killed him, dehydration would have.

Aman stayed in a hospital in Ajmer for a day before being transported to one in Jaipur. I was by his side till he was back home.

It was Vani's first birthday. No celebrations had been planned. Instead, I took her to an orphanage run under the patronage of the royal family. I requested to meet the administrator but she was on the rounds of the dormitories. I was asked to wait; it would be at least an hour before she would be free.

I took the time to play out a story in my mind. Vani had lost both her parents in a road accident; the mother was my sister. There was no one to take care of her. The surviving grandparents were too old, and my husband refused to accept her. There were no other uncles or aunts who wanted to bring her up either. There was no choice but to have an orphanage take care of her till a suitable family adopted her.

The story had to sound authentic and plausible enough for the institution to accept the baby. The more I played the narrative in my mind, the more confident I got. And the sicker I felt. I was going to give up my baby when she had two perfectly healthy parents, even if they were estranged. What was I doing? Would this be the gift I give my daughter on her first birthday?

The secretary finally said that the administrator was available to meet. It's ok, I mumbled. I will see her another day. I need to be somewhere else. Thank you.

I got onto a rickshaw with Vani still safe in my arms. How could she have been such a quiet angel all through even as a gale blew in her mother's head? I had sacrificed three unborn children already, I could not get myself to give up the living one now.

I headed to my husband's house—for the last time.

❧

I reached home to find that my sister-in-law had come over. She was screaming at me even before I came into full view. What have you done to my brother, you bitch!

But isn't it your brother who does things to people, I thought. What happened? I asked her from the landing of the steps, holding Vani close to me.

You don't know? You should join the film industry, actresses like you will do very well. Come to Calcutta with me, I will set you up, she said.

Can you tell me what's the matter?

Where have you been all these days? Do you even care about your husband? You have pushed his life to the brink; he wants nothing of it anymore and took a bunch of sleeping pills to end it. Mom spotted his state timely to call the doctors, he would have been gone otherwise. All because of you.

Me? What did I do?

He wrote to me to say that you have destroyed him, and that he's ending his life. I took the first flight out to find you missing. What Krishna said was true then.

I could not be bothered how Krishna was. I was done with him. He could be sick, he could be in pain, he could be bleeding, he could be dying but I would not feel anything for him. It was time for me to go far away from him.

I brushed his sister aside, asked my mother-in-law to handle Vani for a while and went into my bedroom. Krishna was lying in bed, reading *MAD* comics and chuckling to himself. He had not realized I was back; he turned cheerless the instant he spotted me.

Why did you do this? I asked him.

I have no desire to live any more, he said.

I don't give a fuck whether you live or die. I am asking why you did what you did to my brother.

What did I do?

You swindled him. He tried to commit suicide. We saved him in the nick of time.

I did not cheat anyone. Losses happen in business. He was too weak to handle it.

Losses happen in business. Cheating happens in crime. You are a criminal.

Go fuck yourself, and your brother can fuck himself too.

I am going.

Where?

Away.

Away where? For how long?

Away from you. Forever.

You dare not.

I dare yes.

He got up and tried to hold me. Come on, forget what happened, he said. Don't overreact. I am sure we can sort things out.

Fuck you.

I will not let you leave.

Who are you to stop me?

I will not divorce you.

We will see.

I will not let you take Vani.

Keep her. I will come back for her. And take her. She will be mine.

That was it. I pulled out a suitcase, threw in whatever clothes and shoes I thought might be handy, and closed it. I put other personal effects and the remaining trinkets in a handbag. I stooped to pick something when I noticed an empty strip of paracetamol tablets under the bed. I remember it being full before I left. And I realized he never took any sleeping pills. It was paracetamol. He just wanted to raise a storm but didn't intend to die.

Anyway, he was dead to me. I picked my bags and walked out of the room. My mother-in-law was standing outside, eavesdropping. Vani was in her arms. I took her in mine, held her close and kissed her. Mumma will be back soon to take you, I whispered in her ear. I handed her back to her grandmother and turned to leave. My resolute expression and body language kept Krishna, his mother and his sister from coming in the way. They knew I was going for now. They let me.

I was finally out. Why had I not walked out on the night of my wedding itself?

I had been married for nearly three and a half years, and I rarely showed my face to my father. I could not. He would have known that his daughter was troubled. And that would have pained him. Didn't I marry so he could have had the satisfaction of knowing I was well settled, and he could be happy and healthy for the remaining years of his life?

Any visits to him were brief. I had not spent a single night in his house since I got married. And here I was now, with a bag, and without my daughter, keeping to myself mostly in my old room. For days. And then weeks. I slept. As if to make up for years of sleeplessness. I would get up for a bite once or twice only every twenty-four hours. I just lay listlessly even if awake. It was obvious that something was wrong, but he let me be. Till I was ready to talk. I would be ever grateful for the space and the respect.

My father finally came to my room one morning. I was reading a book in bed. How are you feeling? he asked in his usual gentle tone. He sat down beside me.

I am ok, I said. I tried to sit up as a mark of respect but he patted me back.

Keep lying, he said. You must be tired.

I have only been resting for the past three weeks since I came.

You know the fatigue I am talking about. It must not have been easy for you.

What must not have been easy?

I am your father. You don't think I know what you have been going through? I was not born yesterday. And I have people who are my true friends. Some belong to Krishna's family. They tell me what I need to know.

I have been trying to make it work.

I am sorry for what I made you go through.

What did you do papa?

I made you marry him.

No, you did not. It was my choice. You told me to be sure before I said yes. I remember you giving me the option to reconsider even after I said yes; you assured me that there would be no shame as my life was more important than what society and family thought. But I still went ahead.

I should have investigated more about him. It would have been so easy for me given my network.

You were not well. I would not have liked for you to take on any additional burdens.

If I had not survived my illness, you would not have married Krishna.

Please, don't ever talk like this. You are the only parent I have ever known. You don't have to feel guilty about anything. Promise me you will not take it upon yourself. It was destiny.

I wish I could make it up to you.

You can.

How?

By never engaging in morbid talk again. Can I have your word for it?

Yes.

Thank you.

What do you plan to do now? he asked.

I don't know. I am trying to figure out if we can still make the marriage work.

No, you will not.

I will not what?

You will not try to make your marriage work.

What are you saying?

It is not easy for a father to say this, but I will. Krishna is not the man for you. He does not deserve you. A better life awaits than what he can give you. If he was just inept professionally, but was a good man otherwise, one could still have figured something out. Everyone has their strengths and weaknesses. I have seen all kinds of people in my life, and he's not one you will be able to find your happiness with.

What about Vani?

Let her be with him for now. Go and build a new future for yourself, Niki. Both my daughters are fighters. They can be down, but never out. I know you will do well for yourself. Don't dwell on a past you cannot change. Focus on the future you can build. And once you are on a strong wicket, come back and claim your daughter. Legally and morally, no one can deny you your right to her custody.

Are you sure?

Yes, I am. You also need to leave Jaipur.

How can I do that? I have to be around Vani and you.

No, you need to be far from Krishna for a while. It could be months, it could be years. Vani will be fine. And don't think about me for even a moment. I have three other children to take care of me. You have to think about yourself now. Be selfish. Take your destiny back in your own hands.

Where will I go? I have never been away from Jaipur.

You will figure out a way. I hope you do. For your sake. And I will make you another promise. I will not die till you are reunited with your daughter.

He leaned forward and kissed me on my forehead. He smiled at me, got up and left the room.

I sat upright. I could not lie around any longer. I had a life waiting to be lived.

My biological age was twenty-three. You could add a decade or two to it if you considered my biographical age. So much had happened in my life already. Some of my friends from school were still studying. I knew of at least two who were still virgins. What must they be thinking of me when I came up in their gossip sessions?

By corollary, there was still so much waiting to happen. I had the juice to tick for a long time. Very long indeed. I had to make it count. Starting with a job. Outside of Jaipur. I agreed with my dad. I had to be away. Only then would my soul, and body, rejuvenate.

I opened my little telephone book, tucked away in the corner of my bag; it was coming apart and needed tender handling. Just like I did. It was bound in cheap plastic and had tabs cut out for each letter of the alphabet. I browsed through it for contacts who could help me. Easiest to call would have been Alok, but I was still too ashamed. Even though it was no fault of mine, I was in debt to him. He kept insisting I owed him nothing; he was too graceful to even tell me the amounts Krishna had swindled off him.

I zeroed in on Anurag Prasad. He and his sister trained people to work in the hotel industry. We had got acquainted at the institute I was pursuing my design courses at. He was always keen for me to join him—to teach his students the art of grooming and to improve their diction. I could not accept as it would have required me to relocate outside of Jaipur.

He had two offices. His sister managed the one in Delhi while he handled the Bangalore branch. He had kept me updated as their venture expanded, and had always ended each conversation with an invitation to join him. I decided to take him up on his offer.

I could sense his excitement at the prospect of having me on board. I would have to move to Bangalore though—that's where opportunity lay. The city's hotel and eateries sector was growing exponentially due to the rise of its software export and back office industries; they all needed quality manpower and could not get enough of them. I asked him if I could work in Delhi, but all positions were filled there at that time.

I would have to travel to Bangalore and set up home there on my own dime; my net worth was down to a few thousand rupees. I was considering selling some of my last remaining trinkets when my father handed me an envelope.

What is this? I asked.

It's some money you could use until things stabilize, he said.

How much is it?

Twenty thousand. If you need more, let me know.

I knew this was a sizeable fortune for him to spare, considering the precarious state of his finances. Aman had lost everything to Krishna, and Raghav had still not fully recovered from his burns; he was supporting his sons for the time being. No, you need this more than I do. You keep it, I will sell some jewellery, I said.

No, it's ok. I will be fine.

I insist.

So do I. Your jewellery is your insurance should there ever be a financial emergency.

He patted my hands and ended the conversation. I did not argue further. I knew I had to hold on to every rupee to get by in the uncertain future waiting.

I booked my train tickets to leave for Bangalore in a week. You are my Lakshmi, the goddess of wealth; you will spread prosperity wherever you go, my father said as his parting words.

From the grand haveli of my forefathers, to a shack of a corner in a grand haveli of my husband's forefathers, I had to move into a shared room in a small apartment in Bangalore. I did not complain though. My husband had housed me in dingy quarters, where the environment was nothing short of being psychologically demeaning. The modest space did not irk me one bit; I toasted my new-found freedom.

I was a paying guest in the home of an old couple; they let out four beds in two rooms and stayed in the third themselves. Anurag was kind enough to not only find the accommodation for me in advance but to also pick me up from the railway station and help me settle into my new home in a new city. Despite the constraints, I would be living a life I had aspired to for the first time.

Actually, Anurag was too kind. He would pick me up and drop me to and from work. At times, he would bring me fruits, teas and snacks knowing these were indulgences I could not afford. Whenever we would take a coffee or a meal break, he would insist on paying. I could not have paid anyway; I was barely making ends meet. Not that he had to shell out much. We would usually go to client restaurants, and they would not charge us.

Anurag's care restored my belief in the goodness of people. I did not make much of the attention he was paying me since he was married. Anyway, my mind was too preoccupied with thoughts of my daughter, of my current situation, and of a future I had no inkling of. I missed my daughter, and could not stop feeling guilty for abandoning her. I would feel miserable about myself. I would cry for her, but consoled myself with reminders of why I needed to be where I was. If I did not become financially independent, we would never be together. The prospect of reuniting with her kept me motivated to give Bangalore my best shot.

But I was still happy. I was away from Jaipur. I was working. I was getting results. I was meeting new people, and interesting ones. Murli stood out from amongst those I did.

Have you run away from home?

That's the first thing Murli asked me after introductions. I had never met him before. He was still a stranger to me. There wasn't even the remotest possibility of him having any links to my life. How would he know? Was my personal history etched on my forehead? Why would he ask me this question anyway? Wasn't it a little crude?

What makes you say that? I asked.

Something told me you had so I asked, he said.

Did I say or do something for the world to think so?

No, but I felt so intuitively and blurted out the question on reflex. I am sorry, it was totally uncalled for. And not right of me.

Yes.

What yes?

I have run away from home. Not literally, because my family knows where I am, but I have deliberately created a distance.

I am sorry to hear this. And I will not make any more intrusions into your personal life. Even though I will admit I am curious.

You can ask me, and I might tell you. But I need to get going with the agenda of our meeting. I have another appointment to keep, and I have a boss waiting expectedly for news of a sale by me.

It's a yes, he said.

What's a yes?

We will be happy to offer internships to your students, and also consider them for permanent positions if they clear our tests. You will be paid your standard fee for every hire.

Wow, that was easy, I thought. Murli was the head of training at a leading luxury hotel chain. I had sent him our proposal in advance; he neither played hardball nor did he haggle on our terms. If only we had more such clients.

Thank you so much. This means a lot to me. I have achieved my target for the month with ten days still to go, I said.

Great. If it's not inappropriate, we can have a coffee or a drink sometime and you can tell me why you ran away from home. We have excellent baristas who can brew the perfect cuppa. In all immodesty, I can claim credit for training them. I am a coffee afficionado and developed the art of coffee appreciation in Italy.

Sure, I will take you up on your invite. Will see you soon, I said.

I turned to leave, trying hard to suppress a grin. I was feeling joyful for the first time since the day I got married. What did Murli say to please me so much? I don't know. I hoped we would become friends. He seemed a nice guy to know.

Was the tide turning for me? I wish it were, even if one wave at a time.

Murli recognized those who had 'run' away from home because he had too. Married for five years, he could no longer take what he called marital mental abuse. With his wife not willing to give in to his pleas for a divorce, he mustered up the courage to walk out from their home in Cochin.

It truly was courageous of him because her family were the owners of the biggest spice plantations in all of Kerala; they claimed their ancestors were the first to trade with the Portuguese. With a legacy and wealth like theirs, the police and politicians ate out of their hands. If they chose to, they could hound him till he pleaded for mercy and forgiveness. It was his good fortune that they let him be, for now at least.

Murli and I got acquainted when we both needed a friend. He called me two days after our first meeting, and invited me for a coffee over the weekend. Don't judge me, but I could do with a beer instead, I said.

Of course, that would be swell, he said.

So we met. In the bar of one of the hotels he worked for. I would have had to save for a year to have been able to afford an outing at such a plush place, but he was entitled to special employee rates. In reality, he did not pay even the discounted price. All employees depended on him for their recruitment and training; they would figure ways to serve his table without raising a bill. Not ethical if one went by the book, but every job has its perks.

It did not take much time for us to become the best of pals, hanging around with each other whenever we could. He had a car, making it convenient to move around. We watched movies together, walked in the famed gardens of Bangalore, attended live theatre and music events, and tried all kinds of food—especially on the streets and hole-in-the-wall outlets. We did not make much use of privileges at his hotels—he did not want to be the centre of his staff's attention all the time.

He lived in a small, cute apartment but it needed a woman's touch to set it right. Once I was convinced he did not entice women to come to his place where he could rape and murder them, it became a second home for me; it was cheaper than going out too. We would cook, watch television, clean the house, do the laundry, read books—we were both in a comfort zone with each other. Physically and emotionally.

All our interactions happened when Anurag was not in town.

I was a caged bird with Anurag. But I accepted my situation for the time being; I had no choice. Not that I was letting him have his way when he started making advances.

Anurag would only talk about work and my living arrangements initially. But the conversations started getting more personal—and suggestive—one snail step at a time. He would motivate me by saying I should be strong and stay the course; I had everything going for me and success and riches would be mine for the taking. He would also tell me not to worry; he would take care of everything. Including my daughter when I am able to bring her over.

I could have viewed his conduct through the prism of naïvety or tried to read between the lines. I was not sure. I did not want to judge him wrongly; he was married and had a son. He may just have been trying to be helpful and caring. But the signals he emitted indicated otherwise. He would try to keep me at work till late and then suggest we go out for dinner and drinks. I would go along, but my discomfort increased with every outing. He took me to dimly lit places and tried to sit on my side of the table. As close to me as possible, brushing his body against mine, and allowing his arms and hands to take a few liberties. He would pick a table closest to the speakers, so he could bring his face close to mine to make himself heard over the music. He was being creepy.

He left me with no choice but to come up with excuses to minimize interactions outside of work. But he was of the persistent kind, always countering my reasons. He would even call my landlords to request them to let me stay out late when I would remind him of their curfew. He started sending me cards and letters—he would write about how good it was to have a friend like me, how he enjoyed my company, how he would always be there for me, and so on. He would not say anything romantic directly, but I knew what was coming.

And it came. He invited me to accompany him to the launch of a new hotel in town. He even described a dress he had in mind for me for the evening. He was talking as if we were a couple and would walk in as one. Even as I dithered, I could see his face twitch with impatience. And then he burst out.

I know why you don't want to go with me, he said.

Do you? I asked.

Yes. I know who you spend your spare time with. He even picks you up and drops you off when I don't or can't. You have the time and inclination for him, but not for me.

Whoa! Aren't we crossing some lines here?

Are we? Why didn't you see those lines when you were making me do all the things I did for you?

Do what? I asked for a job, you gave me one when I needed it. And I will always be grateful for it. But I have also repaid the favour, if you want to call it that, by bringing in much more business than targeted. Yes, I acknowledge you went out of your way to help me settle in, but you did not need to beyond a point.

You know what I mean. I did not do what I did because I had any ulterior motives. I like you, and care for you.

Anurag, you know everything about my situation. Do you really think I am in any state of mind to even think about a man in my life?

How come you don't have the same thing to say for Murli?

Are you crazy? Murli is a very good friend. There is nothing on between us.

I am ready to divorce my wife.

What? Now you have lost it. Please understand what I am saying. You are making me uneasy.

You cannot do this to me.

Listen Anurag, let me make one thing clear. If I wanted to be dictated to, be beholden to someone, be made to do things I didn't want to, allow someone to steer the course of my life, then all this was being done very well by my husband. I left him, and I left my infant daughter, for a life I want. If you try to control it, it will backfire. For both you and me. I have no interest in you. For that matter, I have no interest in anyone. I just want to work and make a living. Can you grant me that?

Ok. But you know what I feel for you. I hope this conversation does not change anything between us at work, he said and left.

Things change when such incidents happen. It may not show up right then, but they do.

You can do what you want with me, but make sure you kill me after that. Because if you do what you intend to, and I walk out of this room alive, I will come after you. I will make your life hell. You will regret what you did to me, or you will regret letting me live, or both. Go ahead, I will not resist. Do what you want to.

The words had the desired effect on Anurag. Just a few moments ago, we had been taking a tour of the new hotel he had been invited to. I had acceded to his request to accompany him for the launch in the interest of maintaining harmony at the workplace. He suggested we check out the property while the party was on. The hosts had given him a key card to see the rooms from inside, and we went into one. Just when we were done inspecting it, he grabbed me and pushed me onto the bed.

Before I could get up, his body was asserting itself over mine. I could not move under his weight even as his lips and tongue tried to get a taste of my face, neck and shoulders. At the same time, he unbuckled his belt and lowered his trousers. He used one hand to grope my breasts and to try open my shirt buttons, while the other found its way up my skirt. I gasped and surfaced for oxygen when he put his hand inside my panties, and delivered my ultimatum in that one opening I got. Would he be willing to kill me after he had done the deed?

He froze in the position he was in—his body over mine, his left hand cupping my right breast, his right hand caught in the elastic of my underwear. His stiffness, piercing my right thigh, went limp. His loosened his hold over me as his body strength gave way. We both lay silent for God knows how long; fortunately, his male ego did not come in the way of good sense prevailing.

He withdrew. He shifted his body away from mine, and pulled his trousers back on. I had turned my face away from him. He got up, croaked a let's go, and walked out of the room. I found my own strength, got up from the bed, went to the washroom to look presentable, and stepped out of the room. I took the elevator to the lobby and went straight out to the porch. The valet was just pulling his car in. Without asking, I sat on the passenger seat. We did not speak a word all the way till he dropped the bitch home.

Men are such fools. Why did Anurag have to do what he did? I was indebted to him, he had proven himself to be dependable in my hour of need, and I liked him as a friend. He had expressed his feelings for me; he should have left it at that and been more patient. We might have got into a relationship at some stage. But he adopted the wrong approach. He forced himself upon me; he felt he owned me.

He should have known better. When men have tried to own me, they have lost me.

Anurag had been pursuing me to work with him ever since we got acquainted in Jaipur. I had no qualifications or experience for the role he wanted me for, and I used to be surprised at his offer. If he thinks I am the right person for the job, then I must be the right person for the job, I would tell myself.

Upon reflection, I figured he was not recruiting me for my professional credentials; he was just lusting after me. He had gauged that I was in a financial pickle and he could take advantage of that by being charitable towards me. Everything in life is an exchange, and he had expectations from me. He did not expect to be rejected though.

He could have easily asked me to join the Delhi office. Not only was it much closer to Jaipur, but I would have been more useful there. But he wanted me close to him so he could find his way into my pants.

He also had a poor sense of judgement as a manager. I got him results he had not imagined. The business expanded multifold; hotels and restaurants were queuing up to hire our students. As our rate of placements rose, so did classroom enrolments since we were assuring jobs to almost everyone. I would take credit for a large part of the success. I was a highly effective trainer. And I figured I was a natural at networking within the hospitality industry. I was trusted by human resources departments to deliver what I promised and they gave top preference to our candidates.

Anurag should have seen me as his goose who laid golden eggs. And rewarded me financially too as I deserved. Despite rising profits, he gave me only miniscule bonuses to try controlling me. He could cage me for a while, but I was meant to fly. And I did.

His loss was a gain for my future employers. And for Murli too.

He moved his fingers slowly along the back of my neck; he had never touched me like that before. I liked it and did not stop him. He moved closer to me. He took my fingers with his free hand to play with. I was enjoying whatever he was doing. He stretched forward, buried his nose into the side of my neck, and let his lips kiss me.

What are you doing? I asked only because modesty demanded I should.

He mumbled something and let go of my fingers so his hand could caress my left breast. Keep going, I was thinking. What are you doing? I kept asking.

And then, just like that, he turned my face in his direction and planted his lips on mine. I was loving him for it. It had been so long since a man had touched me—a man I wanted to be touched by—until Murli made the move. And what a man to break the jinx!

He kissed me generously with his lips and licked me with his tongue on my neck, my ears, my face, my lips, my breasts, my thighs, my hands, my feet—the sensation made my body squirm and twist. But this was just the warm-up. My head exploded when he went down on me and literally smooched my vagina; he pushed his tongue in to taste my wetness. It was lava, he told me later.

I was too overwhelmed by the sensations to reciprocate with oral sex but he did not mind. My eyes closed and head swimming, ecstasy ran up and down my spine when he penetrated me. He was big and hard as a rock inside me; his member seemed to have a life of its own. He moved, gently at first, and faster later. I came. And then I came again. And yet again before I felt him come, the warm fluid filling me up. I lay exhausted.

But there was more. He was up again within fifteen minutes. Already satisfied once, he did not need to rush things. We settled for gentle, lolling sex till sleep took over.

❧

Murli just happened. I had not been planning on having a man in my life. Yet. After the showdown with Anurag, I had been spending more time with Murli. He was my security blanket. Maybe I was his too.

It was not easy to work with Anurag anymore. The air between us was always charged, and it just needed a spark to get inflamed. That scared me. I would have nowhere to go if he fired me at short notice. I could not go back to Jaipur. I had to find another job lest I be stuck without one. I let the word out.

Murli introduced me to Zarina who headed public relations for a national chain of upscale restaurants. She was looking for an assistant, and I went in for the meeting wondering where I would fit in. I had no idea how communication worked. Zarina and I hit it off from the word go. A half-hour interview over an Italian lunch lasted till wine at sunset. We spoke about the job, and everything else in our respective lives. I had been hired in the first five minutes of the conversation, even though Zarina kept a formal confirmation on hold till her boss signed the appointment letter.

I had the job by the following afternoon; my salary doubled overnight. The position also came with health benefits. Zarina advised me to befriend the chefs; they always had leftovers for the staff to gorge on. The much-needed salads and vegetables were in abundance. I was malnourished, living on one miserly meal a day. I had to save every rupee I could to send for Vani. To pay for her clothes, her toys and her playschool. Her father claimed to have no money for the daughter he wanted to cling on to badly when I was walking out of his house. Since he never gave me an account of the spends, I was sure I was funding his alcohol too.

As expected, Anurag lost it when I quit. He threatened to make my life hell for being the ungrateful wretch that I was, leaving his operations in dire straits. He recognized, but never acknowledged, my true worth to his business. The choice had been in his hands: to retain me as an invaluable employee, or to pursue me to be his lover. He could not have both. He got neither.

Of course, he did not back off. He called me at my new office persistently, threatening to take legal action for breach of some imaginary contract in his mind. I had warned Zarina that he might be a nuisance. She finally called him and threatened to file a police report and to also call his wife if he did not disappear from my life from that moment onwards. Zarina's tone could have made any man pee in his pants. I never heard from Anurag after that.

I wanted to move out of my current accommodation; the landlords were quite close to Anurag. I did not want to take any chances, nor have news from my life reaching him. I advertised for girls willing to share an apartment. Sabina was one of the respondents I really wanted to live with. We did not agree on co-living, but we did become besties.

❧

Sabina was the first woman I kissed. Actually, she kissed me first. I allowed her and then kissed her back.

We met at a coffee shop after office, but Sabina proposed we go for a drink instead at the Black Cadillac pub. It was a Thursday evening, and most pubs had specials for ladies on the day. My remuneration had gone up; I deserved to splurge on a few shots of vodka to celebrate.

What do you do? I asked. We had to quiz each other if we were considering being flatmates.

I work for an escort agency, and I am their star performer, she said.

Seriously? Is that even legal in India?

No to both questions. But I would have liked to work for one if Indian men were not so repulsive.

Not all are.

They are not. But I am assuming those paying for an escort would be the lecherous, stinking, misogynistic, violent, flashy, repugnant kinds.

Hahaha! Are any men listening? I hope they are. Could not agree more, I said.

Even if there are some desirable specimens, one would have to work through a lot of muck to get to them. Not worth getting your shoes, and your body and soul, dirty for it.

So what are you doing till men change enough for you to become an escort?

I am a chartered accountant. At First Pacific Partners.

Accounts? And you go dressed like this?

Sabina was dressed in a short sleeveless cotton dress reaching just above her knees. She wore heels, had adorned herself with costume jewellery, and cut her hair short to look spunky. She was tall and lean, her frame very similar to mine. I could not help admiring the shape of her breasts. She would have been a star performer had she chosen to be an escort.

I belong to the high-flying universe of investments and fundraising. It helps to show off glamorous women to banks and investors. In a way, I am an escort. The company prostitutes my looks and style to increase valuations of their clients. I am very good at my work though—I even topped my class—so you cannot say I am the doll in the team. But it still helps to be the way I am.

I liked the way she described her place in a world dominated by men. We could not be roommates because she earned much more than I did and was looking for better quarters than what I could afford. We continued chatting and were already on our fifth vodkas when she asked if I wanted to dance.

Oh yes, I haven't danced in years, I said.

The DJ was playing slow, dreamy music; I swayed to it, eyes closed, happy to be lost. Sabina put her arms around my neck. I let her be close. She smelt good. Her breasts, ones I was staring at all evening like a man would, gently pressed against mine, feeling warm. We moved in sync, not like soul sisters, but as sex sisters.

And then she kissed me. On my lips, nowhere else. I had imagined being kissed by a woman in the past, and the idea held little appeal to me. Until then. Her lips felt better than any man's I had been close to. I moved my hands to her backside, and up her dress in the dark. She had lace silk panties on. I was turned on. I felt wet between my legs. I could sense her getting excited too; she came closer and kissed harder. Bangalore was the only place in the country where you could do this openly.

As if on cue, we both withdrew. We looked at each other for a second or two and then burst out laughing. We were happy.

I have to go, she said.

Home?

No, to a friend's.

Boyfriend?

Friend. With benefits. I cannot be committed. But I need this friend tonight. Vodka and kissing a sexy woman like you has me all turned on. I need the release.

I felt flattered at being called sexy. I was glowing. I was already loving Sabina. I would have liked sex too but Murli was travelling.

I will see you again soon baby, said Sabina. She winked, waved as she turned away from me and left.

I could not sleep that night till I had masturbated. And I could not masturbate till I was sure my roommate was fast asleep.

Sabina and I became an item, inseparable socially. Not that we were sleeping with each other; we didn't even kiss again. But we were two cats on the prowl, hunting as a pair.

We went out at least two to three nights a week. My workday started closer to noon—that's when restaurants and media wake up—so I could sleep till late in the morning. Sabina had the energy of ten women—she could get by with minimal sleep. She would be in office sharp at nine daily no matter what the previous night had been like; she was never drowsy, never sluggish, never hungover.

How did I afford that lifestyle? Our group usually gathered at someone's home for a few rounds of drinks before heading out to a pub where we would order just one or two drinks. I stuck to the cheapest drinks—Old Monk black rum, beer or a shot of vodka. I would also identify places staffed by those who had been trained or placed by me while working with Anurag. I was in touch with many of the owners and managers from that time. Not only did I get special rates, but someone would usually give me a refill or two without charging for it. In any case, I drank in moderation; I did not want to wake up with a stranger in my bed. I wouldn't have actually; Sabina always had an eye on me and would ensure I was home safe and untouched when high. She never got sozzled no matter how much alcohol was in her system.

She and I had got together for a beer on a warm Sunday afternoon at the NASA pub, one you enter through a porthole of a door but packed with its loyal following at all times of the day and night. We noticed a guy at the adjoining table wearing a noticeable pair of maroon leather shoes, embellished with studs and coloured glass pieces, with leafy patterns embroidered using golden thread. We had not seen such footwear, nor a guy like him. He was tall, slim, taut, very fair and with long wavy black hair. Would you like to buy us a drink? Sabina asked him. It was so sudden, and so unexpected. What was she doing? I wanted to hide under the table.

The man looked in our direction, smiled, picked up his drink, and came over. I would love to, but I can do better than that, he said.

What is that? asked Sabina.

I can invite you to come along to a party I am going to.

In the middle of the afternoon?

This is Bangalore. Anything goes here.

You are not a serial killer, are you?

I am, but my victims are men competing for the attention of lovely ladies like you. You have nothing to fear.

That makes us feel safe. Ok, we are on. I am Sabina, and this is Nikita. And you are?

I am Zulfiqar. Let's go then. I am on a bike. You could follow me in an autorickshaw if that's fine with you. We don't have to go far.

Sure. You lead the way.

I kicked Sabina under the table to keep her from embarking on the risky adventure, but she had already settled the bill and was getting up to leave. If I am raped and murdered today, I will never forgive Sabina for it, I promised myself.

Two women go off with a stranger to a house party on a Sunday afternoon. When they reach the destination, they see three men lounging on couches and rugs, smoking, drinking, and dressed in nothing more than their underpants and vests. The women didn't run when they could. They just gawked at the sight till one finally spoke up.

Where's the party? I asked.

Now we are a party, said Zulfiqar. It will not take long to set one up.

He clapped his hands to rouse the three men. They smiled, sheepishly, and went off to an inside room. They came back wearing clothes befitting respectable men and introductions followed. The alpha amongst them introduced himself as

Mahesh. We were at his and Zulfiqar's place. He set up the bar and ordered sandwiches for the famished guests. He put on jazz on what seemed a very fancy music system. Although a doctor by education, he did not see himself exploring people's insides all his life. He got into representing and producing gigs for both upcoming and established bands.

The party happened. The guys made a few phone calls and more people joined, carrying alcohol or food; we apologized for not contributing anything but Mahesh just dismissed it. We will be left with excess, you wait and see, he said. He was right.

Come midnight we found ourselves in the company of Mahesh and Zulfiqar only. All the others had left. Even in my inebriated state my brain was telling me to watch out; this is when the hosts will do stuff to us. No one would even find our remains. I started crying. I must have looked like such a fool. Did I see others laughing at me? Everything was so fuzzy. I passed out but don't remember when; I woke up on the same couches where men in their underwear had greeted us the previous afternoon. I looked at the time; it was seven in the morning. Sabina was stirring on the adjacent couch.

Mahesh served us much-needed coffee in our beds and then graciously drove us home. We survived with our honour and lives intact.

❧

I did not ever have as many people caring for me as I had in Bangalore. Zarina, Sabina and Murli took it upon themselves to help me get by in the new life I was trying to create. Each exceeded themselves in their role as my guardians; they did become possessive and a bit overbearing at times though. The three were not particularly fond of each other, but they all loved me dearly.

I was spending most of my time with Zarina in office. She knew enough about my life to write a book on it. She would want to have a say in everything I was doing and would actually sulk if I followed my own mind. But I took her behaviour in my stride. I knew she cared and was always willing to help when she could. I had my lows—thinking of Jaipur and Vani—and Zarina would cover for me if I needed to be with myself, away from office. She was a brilliant mentor too, playing a big role in shaping me into the professional I was to become.

I was a trophy friend for Sabina, flattering since she was the hottest and the smartest chick I had ever met. She wanted me to be with her everywhere outside of work—not just for drinking and partying but for shopping, for running errands, at salons and as a buddy to hang out with. She was always trying to pair me with guys, even though she knew I had a thing going with Murli.

There are no promises, no commitments, no future with Murli, so why are you being so loyal to him? she would say. It was true. Things were easy with Murli because there was no pressure on either of us even though we were a couple of sorts. He was very nice and considerate towards me and was always there for me. But there was a tacit understanding between the two of us: both were free to take any path for our respective lives whenever we wanted, with whoever we wanted.

And yet, Murli tried to violate a few boundaries. He did not approve much of my new friends. Was he being protective or just jealous? He could never fit into the groups I went pubbing and partying with. I was still young. I was having a good time, seeing a new world, flirting with men but not sleeping around recklessly. Actually, I was having sex only with Murli, but the frequency of our encounters was gradually dipping. We were moving apart, and it was not lost on either of us. Neither made an attempt to bridge the gap. We both understood that it would be time for our paths to diverge soon.

I was meeting a lot of men, and they all seemed to be smitten with me at first sight. Each—without exception—wanted to marry me even if they had not yet kissed me. But I did not have the luxury of getting deeply involved with anyone; it would have been too complicated.

I could not allow anything or anyone to derail my agenda of divorcing Krishna and reuniting with Vani.

❧

Hello auntie.

I burst out crying when I heard those words. Why would a daughter address her mother like that? Because she had not seen her for over a year. It was the pivotal year, when the infant learnt to say her first words. And to recognize—or not recognize—people. I was just an auntie to Vani.

Krishna was making sure that I would suffer for leaving him. I had been in Bangalore for over two years but managed to go to Jaipur only twice. On each occasion, he made it hard for me to meet Vani. When I could, it was only for short periods under the watchful eyes of his mother. If I would call from Bangalore—it was not cheap making long-distance calls at that time—he would always come up with excuses to keep me from talking to her. I knew he would be lying.

I might have tried to go to Jaipur more often during that period, but his behaviour deflated my will to. It seemed less tortuous to stay far from Vani than to be in Jaipur and not have free access to her. But when she said thank you auntie for buying her an ice-cream, I was forced to question my decision to separate. What if I was wrong? What if relationships always have problems? What if it's about making peace with your circumstances and learning to live with them? Why was I causing so much upheaval?

I created a test to see if I should go back to Krishna. I would spend a night with him. If I felt ok about it the following morning, I would stay; else go away, never to return. I got him to agree to meet me for lunch to talk things over. He arrived and we placed our orders. And then I froze. I could not get myself to speak a single word, I could not get myself to eat a single morsel of food, I could not get myself to even take a sip of water for my dry throat.

I did not need to spend a night with him to figure out if there was a future together. I could not sit across a table from him for even an hour. I whispered an apology in Vani's ear and promised to take her away very soon. And then I returned to Bangalore.

❧

I know this may sound absolutely wrong, but could I request you to leave the company of your friends for a bit? And join me for a drink? I had no choice but to reach out to you this way—because if I had not, I would never have got another opportunity to meet you, let alone have a drink together.

This is how I met Ravi. Our group was in the poshest bar in town—at the Sheraton—it was an indulgence, but we allowed ourselves to splurge once every few months. Two drinks down and this tall, well-built, totally bald, clean-shaven, good-looking man walked up to our table and requested me to join him for a drink.

All eyes at the table were on me. Will I or will I not? I was pondering this myself; what can possibly go wrong if I agreed? Nothing, we would be sitting openly in a seven-star bar. Ok, I said, but there is a condition.

You have my attention, he said.

You will have to buy my friends a round of drinks, of their choice, whatever the price, if you want to have one with me.

That's not a problem at all. In fact, it would be my pleasure, he said without hesitation. He waved to the server, and instructed him to add the next round for the table to his tab.

He led me to his table in a corner, secluded from much of the bar. Thank you for accepting my invitation, he said. I am Ravi.

A drink can't hurt, I said. I am Nikita.

What can I get you?

Surprise me. Order anything.

He did. I don't know what it was, but it was quite a treat. You have good taste, I complimented his choice of drink.

I know I do. That's why you caught my attention.

Beware the flatterer, Aunt Agatha warned.

Who is Aunt Agatha?

Agatha Christie.

The writer?

Yes.

When did she say this? I have read most of her books.

She told me privately.

She did? When? She would have been long gone when you were born.

We have a karmic connection. She talks to me.

Aha. What else does she warn you about?

Don't drink too much with strangers.

I am Ravi, no longer a stranger. Can I get you another drink?

Sure, I am happy to repeat what you ordered.

He promptly did. Do you live in Bangalore? he asked.

Yes, currently.

Where are you from?

Jaipur. Where do you live?

I am a nomad. Always on the go. But Mumbai comes closest to being called home.

What do you do?

I facilitate businesses and individuals set up base in India.

Interesting. Married?

No.

Girlfriend?

Not currently.

Hmmm.

Ok, I am really going to push my luck now, he said. I am leaving for Muscat tonight. I am staying in this hotel itself. I check out in three hours for my flight. Would you like to join me for another drink in my suite?

Whoa! You mean just a drink in the suite?

Yes.

Naah! That's a waste. Let's stay here only then, I said in a merry tone. I was on my fifth drink of the evening. Friends tell me I lose memory of whatever happened after the second.

Ok, then let's go for a drink and more.

You look like a decent guy.

I am.

Then I have a condition.

It's a yes.

Hear me out at least.

Tell me, but it's a yes anyway.

You pick the tab for everything my friends order for as long as I am with you.

It's a deal.

We were playing a game, and I asked Ravi to pay for my friends in the spirit of the moment. But in a way I was returning a few favours to my friends; not that they ever made me feel in any debt to them. I was the newbie in their town, bogged down with my struggles and barely earning enough to make ends meet. They went out of their way to make me feel wanted and loved; they enjoyed my company. Without making me feel small about it, they often picked my tab—partly or fully. If they didn't, I would be mostly cooped up in my room. I could never repay what they did for me.

Ravi again beckoned the server, gave him some instructions, handed over his credit card and got up. He took my hand and whisked me to his suite on the top floor.

Wow, I said. What a grand room and view. How do you pay for it?

I don't. My clients do. A drink?

Another drink, and you will have a sleeping beauty in your bed. Or worse, a sick one. You got anything else to offer?

Yes, he said taking me in his arms, planting his lips firmly on mine. I was ready for him as much as he was for me. I made it easier for him by unzipping my own dress and letting it fall at my feet. He took me to the most comfortable and luxurious bed I have lain my naked self on, and that too in the company of a gorgeous hunk.

We made love once, and then once more. My friends could be sponges when offered free drinks, and Ravi's tab was mounting. But he couldn't care less. He was having a good time, and I was having the best casual sex of my life. Actually, I had never jumped into bed after knowing anyone for such a short while as I did with Ravi. I didn't even really know him—it might just turn out to be a one-night stand. It was not me—I did not conduct myself that way. But then again, things were changing. And so was I. What kind of an avatar would emerge from the churn my life was going through?

He held me close even after he had come twice, a rare quality in men; they are usually jumpy when the deed is done. But he made me feel warm and desirable, and I liked that. As much as I hate to, I have to get dressed for my flight, he said eventually.

You can't do this to a lady, I teased.

Trust me, my loss is greater than yours. But this is a flight I have to catch.

Where is Muscat by the way?

Oman, in the Middle East.

Aah, of course. Sure, I understand. Have a good flight, and a fruitful trip.

Thank you. I will. Will you see me again?

Will ask my friends, I laughed.

Where do I find you? Do you have a number to call?

Try me at my boarding house.

He smiled. I scribbled my number on a piece of paper, and he gave me his card. We both dressed and took the elevator down to the lobby. We hugged, he kissed me on the cheeks, went to the bar, signed the bill without even looking at it, waved to my friends and left.

All eyes at the table were on me again. Whenever you want free drinks, sell me to the richest guy in the bar, I winked at the group. If they were expecting any spicy accounts from me, they were disappointed. They had to settle for whatever their imagination could project.

Ravi was in town every alternate weekend, with an occasional visit on other days too. He would call to meet me, and I would—to have sex. It had to be preceded with a bout of drinking, no matter the time of the day. I had to lose a bit of control over my senses to sleep with him. I would not be able to otherwise. I felt nothing for him emotionally. But I liked his company and did not want to miss any opportunities of being with him.

He called me at least twice or thrice a week, from whichever part of the world he was in. Disappointment usually awaited at my end of the line. I was rarely home when it was ok to call on my landlord's line. Office was unavoidable as Zarina and I shared a small cubicle. I could not afford a mobile yet; they were new to the country, devices were prohibitively priced and calls expensive. One had to pay for both incoming and outgoing. Ravi offered to gift me a mobile, but I would not accept it. So you want to pay for my services now, I quipped. He didn't get, or appreciate, the joke.

Sabina did not know what was happening between Ravi and me. She tried to probe further, especially when he called on her mobile in desperation to get through to me. I dismissed him as a long-distance admirer, one who would not leave me alone just because we made out once. I didn't tell her about our subsequent meetings. In fact, I told no one. I did not want my mother hens to lecture me on the futility of such a dalliance.

I needed a mobile of my own. I convinced my employers to buy me one so journalists could contact me at all hours since their routines were different from ours. Ravi was more relieved than anyone else. I was thrilled for a different reason; I could now call Vani anytime.

What was the status of our relationship? Neither Ravi nor I brought it up. We just continued being with each other whenever he was in town. We did not even enquire too much about each other's personal lives. He knew about my separation from my husband and daughter. I did not ask who he was with when not with me. The knowledge—and the lack of it—suited us both.

If I was emotionally attached to anyone, it was to Murli. He was family, he was my comfort zone. Even if I was involved with another man, I would not feel guilty if I slept with Murli. Not that I would; this just described how I would always feel as one with him. And yet we drifted apart.

I seemed to attract men. It would not go unnoticed by others. Including Sabina. I found her more vivacious than me, but men always seemed to gravitate towards me. But to her credit, she did not allow any competitive jealousy to cloud our sisterhood. In fact, we would feel sexually charged up in each other's company, just like when we first met. We never got physical with each other again, but we loved the sensation when we were in proximity of the other.

I may have been sexually active with Murli and Ravi in Bangalore but did not see myself committed to either. I would continue to seek a partner who I could build deeper connections with. I would enjoy myself when I had a male companion but would not pine for one when I didn't. I never lost sight of the key purpose to be in Bangalore: secure myself financially so I could rescue my daughter from the clutches of a man who was unworthy of anyone's affection. I wish I had ventured outside my marriage and got impregnated by someone else just to spite Krishna; it would have laid to rest any claims he would have on Vani. The smear on my character might have been worth it.

Everyone took it upon themselves to find me a steady boyfriend or even a husband-in-waiting. It was flattering but would get too much at times. But I enjoyed the tease part of it anyway. Zulfiqar and Mahesh both had the hots for me, and I could sense it. Not that I was interested in either but if I was, then Zulfiqar would have got my vote. The attraction between us was mutual but neither made a move. He was a true friend, always watching out for me, ever willing to lend a hand. I did not want to risk our bond by getting involved romantically with him unless I was sure it was for keeps for both of us.

Mahesh really likes you, he said one day.

Don't we all like each other? That's what makes us such great friends, I said.

You know what I mean.

No, I don't.

Now you are playing me. It's obvious to everyone.

Yes, it is. As are other things.

What other things?

You.

Me? What about me?

Don't you like someone?

Not really.

Come on, say it.

No, there is nobody, he said.

How would you like this nobody dating Mahesh, I asked. Will you be able to bear it?

It's not about me.

I wish you would sometimes make it about you.

That was Zulfiqar for you—always keeping his own emotions under a lid. He never sought anything for himself even though we all knew he could do with some help—and a loving companion—from time to time. Life had not been easy for him. He was from Kashmir, and his family had a healthy business trading in agricultural produce from the Himalayan region. They lost everything with the onset of terrorism; the youth dispersed across the country for education and livelihood. Those who had the means to would send money back to the elders. Zulfiqar's parents and two sisters stayed on in Pahalgam; he remitted all his savings to them. That made him conservative with his expenses. His battles may have been his own, but his struggles were not very different from mine.

Both of us were bearing burdens from our other lives, and neither could make long-term plans for ourselves. He liked me, and I really liked him. Under more benign circumstances, I would have even considered marrying him. But we could neither commit to each other, nor hurt the other. So we never acknowledged our feelings towards each other. We would never know what might have been.

I did not get involved with Mahesh either. I did not feel drawn towards him. In any case, when Zulfiqar suggested I date Mahesh, I was already warming up to Kenneth.

I was not willing to commit to a relationship till my divorce was through, and yet I said yes when Kenneth asked me to marry him.

Kenneth was a part of one of the groups I used to hang out with. He was dating Falak when we first got acquainted, and I had not yet broken up with Murli at that time—but we were gradually drifting apart by then. Kenneth was not one to beat around the bush. He proclaimed his intentions with his actions from very early on. He would pay special attention to me even when his girlfriend was around—I could see her discomfort, and even others would find it an awkward sight. He would sit close to me, chat endlessly with me as if no one else was at our table, carry my drinks and ensure I got safe transportation home. Falak was a very cheerful and friendly girl, but only had daggers for me. I could not blame her.

I was fond of dancing, and was good at it. Kenneth was the only other person in the group who could match up to my skill and enthusiasm for the floor. We would whip up a frenzy as a pair even as his relationship with Falak was icing over. It was no surprise when we began seeing less and less of her. We broke up, confessed Kenneth finally. He did not give any reasons, but it was obvious to all. He advertised his affections for me on his forehead.

I love that apartment block, I told Kenneth. We were at someone's house party together, and smoking on the terrace looking out.

It is very well-built and designed from the inside. I had checked them out a few weeks back.

Are you planning to buy one?

Yes, but only if the right woman agrees to live with me there.

Oooh, looks like Kenneth is ready to move on or already has. Who is she?

I haven't told her yet.

Do I know her?

Yes.

Who? I am curious.

You.

I cannot say I did not see it coming but jumping straight to the idea of living together did come as a surprise. Aren't we supposed to date first and get to know each better before moving to the next level? Normally, I would have been put off at such a suggestion, but I liked where the conversation was going.

You are quite an optimist to even consider buying an apartment for us, I said. You don't even know what I feel about you. My personal situation is an open book—I can't commit to anyone until I sort out my matters.

I am willing to wait. And I can see you have a fondness for me even if it's not love. I know I really like you; I really love you. You are just the woman I would want to make a home with. Maybe in one of the apartments we are looking at right now.

I won't deny my attraction to you. But I do feel guilty for your break-up.

It's not your fault, it may not have lasted long anyway. Falak was prone to extreme jealousy if she spotted any woman around me. It would get a tad suffocating and irritating.

The attention you pay me sends out clear signals about your intent. No woman would have tolerated it, jealous types or otherwise.

I could not help being drawn to you. Once I knew you, I could not be with another woman.

Things moved very fast between us after that. I let everyone know we were dating; I had never been so open about a relationship in the past. I was partying—and dancing—harder than ever before. He had an insatiable appetite for sex, and he whetted mine further. We made use of every opportunity to make out with each other. In his house, in the car, in the bedrooms of those hosting house parties, and in the washroom of a pub once. We did not take a break even during my period.

I was working late at the office once, and he tried to do it on my workstation despite my efforts to push him away. The desk collapsed. Fuck, I said.

Ok, he said. Let's do it on the floor.

Shut up! How will I explain this?

Don't.

What do you mean?

Scoot from here. No one saw this. Feign ignorance tomorrow. Anyone could have been here. You don't lock the office behind you.

I was fretting, but he was absolutely cool and logical about the incident. This is what I liked about him—his ability to be composed no matter the situation. We made haste from the office. Fortunately, Zarina was travelling for a few days and the desk was fixed before her return. She missed the breaking news altogether.

He wanted me to meet his parents. I didn't want to till I had Jaipur sorted out but agreed to since he sounded very keen. I am glad I did. I had never met such a sweet couple, happy and content with their lives, living in a small but pretty house cluttered with potted plants. I saw them filling the parental void in my life.

Kenneth was the first man I wanted as a husband from deep within my heart. And then he blew it.

If his best friend claimed to have slept with me, Kenneth should not have believed him if he truly loved me. Even if he had reasons to be in doubt, he should have had a conversation with me about it. And then taken my word over his. He certainly should not have called our engagement off. Unilaterally. Over the phone. Without meeting me. What a dork of a man!

I had to go to Delhi for a job interview. I had been in Bangalore for over two years and there had been no noticeable progress on my divorce and getting custody of Vani. I needed to be in Jaipur or close to it for things to happen. Kenneth introduced me to his best friend, Atul, should I need assistance while in Delhi.

I flew this time; my prospective employers were paying for the tickets. This was sign enough of their heightened interest in hiring me. Atul picked me up from the airport and dropped me off at Harish chacha*'s* place. I did not want to be with family but could not afford to stay at a hotel. I knew he would have a thing or two to say to me. I had not spoken to him after leaving Krishna; he was surprised to hear my voice when I called to ask if I could stay with him for the week. Of course, he said. He had sounded genuinely pleased.

Atul took time off from whatever he was doing and took me around town, meeting job consultants and a few hiring managers he was acquainted with. I landed the position I had interviewed for; it was for a new brand of pubs owned by my current employers. In a way, it was an internal move within the same group of companies.

Kenneth had been open to my moving to Delhi. He was agreeable to relocating himself after we got married. As an airline pilot, he anyway spent half his life in the air and in hotels. Private airlines had been allowed in the country only recently; they all needed pilots to fly their rapidly expanding fleet. In short supply, pilots could get away with most of their demands. He could easily negotiate terms to be posted in Delhi, the biggest hub for air traffic in the country.

Only when I had expressed my intent to relocate to Delhi did he officially propose to me. I did not want to make promises till I wasn't sure of my own divorce. But he asked, he begged, he cajoled and he pouted to get an answer out of me. I am in, I finally told him. But I have conditions.

You know I will say yes to all, he said.

I have to relocate to Delhi, or even Jaipur. Only then will I be able to sort out my past life.

Of course. If you don't get your divorce, how will I marry you anyway? So it's in my interest to say yes.

Thank you. What about your job?

I will get a transfer to Delhi. Even if I don't, I get offers from other airlines all the time. I could switch to one agreeable to my terms. I am sure they will give me a raise too.

Great. Fingers crossed, I will get the job in Delhi. I will figure other issues out too soon. And then marry you. And fall in love with you after I do, I said.

Kenneth cancelled the booking of the apartment, the one I had admired, and got his deposit back. It would make more sense to invest in the city we finally settled in. I went to Delhi, got the job I sought and managed to stay in the good books of Harish chacha. I told him all that had happened with me and his lawyer brain and family heart approved of the stand I had taken. He assured me that no court could deny me custody of my daughter even if I was the one who 'deserted' her.

I had accomplished my mission in Delhi, and was readying to fly back to Bangalore. I had a house to pack up there, and a Kenneth to make future plans with. I was lost in his thoughts when he called. Telepathy. I noticed his gruff tone right away. He had never sounded so.

I don't think it's a good idea for us to marry each other, he said.

What? Why are you saying this? What's happened suddenly? I asked.

You know.

What do I know?

Atul told me.

Atul told you what?

About going out to night clubs with him.

You know that. We even called each other when he was taking me around town. And you sounded happy for me.

Yes, but not about what followed.

What followed?

I did not expect you to sleep with Atul. How could you?

When did I sleep with him? Who has been filling your ears with such hogwash?

Who else would know other than Atul?

Why would he say such a thing?

He had always warned me about you. He was right.

How can you believe such nonsense if you love me?

Atul and I are not just friends. We are like brothers. We have known each other since I was three. I trust him with my life.

He is lying.

Don't talk like this about him. I will not believe a word against him.

And you will not take my word for it?

I would. But I can not disbelieve Atul.

And it's ok for your brother to sleep with your fiancé?

He did it to prove your true character.

What does it say about his character?

I told you, I will not hear a word against him. He always watches out for me.

And I don't? Have you been drinking? Get a hold of your senses.

I have not been drinking. I have a flight tomorrow morning, so need to be clean. I don't even know if I can fly in this disturbed state of mind. I did not expect this of you.

And I did not expect this of you. I am glad I saw this side of you before it was too late. I don't even know what Atul has against me. Don't ever call me again. Have a nice life.

I disconnected and sat down on the steps leading to the upper floor of the duplex house. I did not cry. I felt relieved. I may have been saved. I had been feeling a heaviness ever since I had consented to marry Kenneth. I was not ready to commit yet. But I really liked him and agreed to the proposal out of fear of losing him.

I lost him anyway. I was free.

Even while I was dating Kenneth, I continued to meet Ravi whenever he visited Bangalore. I enjoyed his company for a movie, a meal, window shopping and the occasional long drive beyond the city limits. And for sex.

I may have been considering marrying Kenneth, but I did not feel any guilt in sleeping with Ravi. But I did not have an iota of emotional attachment to him. Sex with him was just a casual social act for me. It may not justify my actions, but I allowed myself the logic. In any case, my relationship with Kenneth soon imploded and he was relegated to just a footnote in my personal history.

Ravi was taking us more seriously than I was; he would behave as if we were a couple, or would be in due course. He would tell me not to fret over a career and money matters once I was married to a well-off guy. Did he know something about my marital plans that I didn't? I wanted to ask him. He observed and frequently commented on my domestic skills, especially cooking. He persuaded me to accompany him when visiting homes of top businessmen and diplomats. At first I was queasy about the idea; how do I explain what I was doing with him? You don't just take a lady friend along to your business acquaintances, no matter how friendly you were with them, unless there was something on between the two of you. Emotionless sex counted for nothing in my book. He would fuss over my dress, my make-up, my hair and my overall look when socializing with others. I could see where all that was headed, but I played along. Even after I moved to Delhi.

And then the inevitable happened. He called me mid-December and asked what I was doing on New Year's eve. No plans yet, I told him.

Can I suggest one? he asked.

Sure.

Let's go to Kathmandu.

Kathmandu? Where did that come from?

It is a delightful city. You will love it. And you don't need a passport for Nepal.

I will have to think about it.

I am sitting with my travel agent. The place will get sold out soon. Please say yes. Now.

Hmm, ok, I said. For some reason, I could never say no to Ravi. He drew me to himself, but I could not get myself to stick.

Thank you so much for making me happy, he said. I will be in Delhi on the morning of the thirtieth. We will fly out the same afternoon and be back on the first evening, he said.

Cool. Sounds like a plan, I said and hung up.

He was there as scheduled and we were off. The trip almost did not happen. There was a lookout notice for my namesake, and I had no document to prove I was not the same person. Fortunately, we had reached the airport with time to spare and were able to sort the matter out. Ravi gave a personal guarantee in writing, and we also managed to get my office to fax a confirmation about my identity, occupation and address. We might have missed the flight if the airline had not agreed to keep the doors open for an additional five minutes longer than scheduled; business class passengers do get treated differently especially by the tourist-friendly Royal Nepal Airlines.

I made full use of the upper class of travel, downing as many wines as one could in the short flight of just over an hour and a half. We had barely checked into the penthouse suite of the Soaltee Crowne Plaza when the sloshed me was taking her clothes off, and helping him take off his. He did not resist. We made out on the carpet, passed out for what might have been two hours, woke up at dusk, dragged ourselves to the bed and made out all over again. He asked if I wanted to go see the city at night, and I mumbled a no. Please order dinner and champagne, and stay right here, I said.

I was dictating the agenda, and he was happy to be led. I was wasted by the time the bottle had been emptied; I was over him all over again, taking charge and making love all night long. If the poor guy was exhausted, he did not show it. It might have been four in the morning when I finally passed out. I woke up to a bright afternoon, exactly twelve hours later.

Did I make a fool of myself? I asked Ravi. He was sitting on an easy chair, reading the *Time* magazine.

Of course not. And if you did, please make sure you do it more often, he said and winked at me.

When did you wake up?

I have been up since nine.

Nine? Why didn't you wake me up sooner?

You were sleeping like a baby. I didn't want to disturb you.

I don't remember when I last slept like this. It must have been during my school days.

I wish you get to sleep more often like this. I hope I am able to help you sleep like this.

It's strange, but I never sleep soundly nowadays except when I am with you.

Either it's me or it's the sex with me.

I guess we will know some day.

You must be hungry.

I don't mind a chai first. Will figure what I want to eat later.

Sure, he said and called room service to order. I got out of bed to go to the washroom; the tea was already there with freshly baked cookies by the time I came out. It felt heavenly.

Thank you, this is just what I needed. I don't think I would want anything until dinner now, I said.

I have something planned for tonight to ring in the new year.

What's that?

I have booked a private table in the casino to play blackjack; butlers will wait upon us to take any orders for food and drinks.

Casino? I have never been to one. And I don't know how to play this game. I have never gambled.

Never gambled? I have not met anyone who gambles so much with her own life. You will be fine. I know you will pick up the game within minutes and beat both the dealer and me.

Ok, if I lose your money, don't blame me.

I won't. And oh, another thing.

Yes?

I took the liberty of buying you a dress for the evening.

A dress? What kind?

Should I show you?

Of course.

If I had one weakness, it was for good clothes. It stemmed from my desire to be in the fashion industry. I could never say no to an opportunity to try out, or own, any outfits. He brought out a backless, thigh-high slit, sea-green dress designed for feisty ladies who could pull it off without a malfunction.

It's beautiful, I said. I love this colour. What do you want me to be in this dress? The showstopper?

You will be one no matter what you wear. You are a stunner who makes heads turn wherever you go.

Not right now, I said. The mirror reflected the mess I was after the doings of the previous night.

That's what you think. I can prove otherwise.

How?

He came over me, lowered his boxers, lifted my night gown and was inside me before I could count to ten. It had not taken much for him to recharge his batteries. And I was surprised to find myself ready for him. It was the first time I made love to him when sober.

I could not help thinking of Ravi's motives for this trip; he was definitely going to try something. I had wanted to decline the invitation but he did not give me any window to. He played it well when he called with a sense of urgency to book lest we miss out. He could only do things in a classy way, but he was exceeding himself; he was clearly setting the mood for something bold. I hoped I was wrong.

I was not. The evening played out to perfection. I won sacksful of chips; I didn't see the equivalent of cash at the end of the evening though. We had a butler waiting on us, serving us whatever we wished for. I did not consume any alcohol, sticking to lemonades to detox. I also wanted to be in control so I could give a rational reply if Ravi was planning to do what I suspected him of.

The lights went out at a minute before midnight, the countdown started and shouts of happy new year reverberated across the hall after sixty seconds. Strobes came on to light up the space in flashes, and the sight of Ravi kneeling greeted me when my eyes could see clearly again. He was holding a ring with a gleaming solitaire on it. I was not waiting for this to happen.

Nikita, I love you. Will you marry me? he asked.

I don't know what to say, I said. A bottle of Brunello, a premium red wine from Italy, had been placed on our table but I was so glad I had not given in to the temptation of consuming it. I needed all my wits to be at their sharpest best to counter the proposal.

Try yes.

I can't.

Why?

This is too sudden.

Why do you say that? We have been together for long now so it's not something quite out of the blue.

I am not prepared to be married. Yet.

I will wait.

No, I thought. Not again. Kenneth had retarded any progress I had made about the idea of getting remarried. I was not ready to commit, I was not ready to be hurt again. Kenneth had let me down. I was not going to let myself fall into another trap, more so since I was still caught in one.

The party ended for us with this discussion. The mood changed. We returned to the room and slept off. There was no sex. I didn't feel like eating all morning, nor in the afternoon. Neither of us made any attempts at conversation, but he hovered around as if waiting for me to initiate one. We checked out and left for the airport.

I was finally hungry in the flight and ordered black coffee and a sandwich. He spoke first.

I had to say what I did because that is what I feel about you, he said.

That's fine, it is perfectly ok for you to. You don't need to feel you have done anything wrong, I said.

I have been thinking long and hard and realized that I really want you with me for the rest of my life.

Under normal circumstances, I would have been inclined to say yes to you. But I am in no emotional or psychological state to. Things are coming to a head in Jaipur. I have to file my divorce case. If you knew my husband, rather ex-husband, you would realize what a battle I have at hand. He is not a reasonable human being by any standards; he is vicious and cruel. I have never used such words for anyone, and I would not for the father of my daughter, but I cannot restrain myself.

I can be by your side in this struggle.

I know I can count on you, whether I say yes or no.

Yes, you can. I truly care for you.

Thank you. It is very reassuring to have someone like you in my life. I am blessed in a way.

Ok, there is no pressure, but I will ask you once more. If you want to say yes, say so. If you want to say no or are undecided, don't say anything.

Ok.

Nikita, will you marry me?

I did not speak a word after that. Till he dropped me home. Thank you for a wonderful time, and thank you for everything, I said while getting out of the cab. I hugged him—fondly I would say—and pecked him on his lips. It was the last time I would be touching him as a lover.

I like to be in control, but I don't like to be the alpha with a man. That's his job. He has to ensure I keep growing intellectually in his company. I will get bored otherwise. And go away.

That's just some of the rules—or conditions—men need to keep in mind if they hope to have me in their lives. If I can learn something from them, I will be attracted to them. And they will get one foot in the door.

Talk a lot, sense of course, in bed. That's a big turn on for me. The man can then take me as many times as he wants to. Be wild in bed and I will keep up with the frenzy. But be gentle in your words—and actions—with me. I have only seen chaos in my life, and I need to feel calm in the company I keep.

If I ever managed to be with a man for an extended period of time, it was because he had more than a few of these traits. Murli came closest to checking all boxes, but I could not get my head around the thought of settling in with him. It may have been the timing.

He came into my life soon after I left Jaipur. As did some others after him. I may have got into relationships with them, but I could not get myself to fall in love even if my heart wanted to. I did not want to commit to anything long term. I was legally married then, so marriage was not a possibility. But even if the guy was willing to wait for a formal divorce, I was scared to get hurt.

I curbed any strong feelings I may have had. I was in survival mode. The war to win my daughter back was still raging. I was holed up in the trenches and there was nowhere to go till victory was secured.

Ravi did not call me in the new year until Valentine's Day. He did so shortly after a courier delivered a bunch of orchids and a stuffed teddy bear early in the morning.

Hi, happy Valentine's Day, he said.

Thanks, and the same to you, I said.

How have you been?

I have been good. And you?

All good. I am in Singapore currently.

Are you? That's nice. How is it there?

The city is excessively decorated with pink and red hearts, and I was missing you more than usual.

You should get yourself a date there. I am told Chinese women love Indian men for their build and looks.

Good idea, but I love an Indian woman and I would rather date her.

Nothing has changed, Ravi. You are a very loving and caring man, and you really should find yourself someone who can reciprocate likewise.

I was, rather I am, happy with how you reciprocate.

You don't know enough then.

Just one thing, Nikita: why are you saying no? If you are open to being in relationships with men, why can't you get yourself to marry one?

I have told you, Ravi. My situation does not give me the liberty to make long-term plans. Having said that, I have my own ambitions. I eventually want to be the chief executive of my own company. I cannot be with a man who expects me to stay at home, wants me by his side for his social obligations, and treats me as his trophy wife. I can be all this, but my work would take precedence over any other expectations, and that is not acceptable to most men. And I want to settle in with someone who is not jet-setting all over the place. Again, I would not grudge his professional stature, but I would want him home at the end of a day's work, by my side, loving me, letting me love him. I need the emotional stability I have not known so far.

These are all adjustments we can make. I can look for alternate opportunities so I am around more often, and you can pursue what you like.

I know you, Ravi, and I know you will not be able to confine yourself. You like the high life. Even if you were to do what you say, it would be too much effort to make it happen. Yes, couples who care for each other can do all this and more, but I have no energy and time to. And I don't know how the future will pan out. I do not want to make any promises to you, nor do I want myself to be bound by any.

I hear you.

Can we not talk for a while? I cannot have these conversations anymore. We can always be good friends once this phase of my life is over, and you have moved on too.

Sure, Nikita, I can respect your request.

Thank you. I wish you all the happiness you deserve.

And I to you. Happy Valentine's Day.

Thank you. And to you too.

We hung up. I felt heavy in my heart, but light in the head. By the same evening, I was out partying. I did not think of Ravi again.

It's funny but in all the years I had known him, I had never called or messaged Ravi. I only responded when he reached out.

Diplomacy was over. It was time to go into battle since the enemy was not willing to come to a settlement any other way. At stake was my freedom from Krishna and the custody of Vani.

My lawyers fired the first salvo by serving him a notice. He did not even bother talking to the lawyers or to me about it; he rubbished it like a scrap of paper. We then moved the court, seeking divorce. He ignored the court summons and did not appear on the appointed date. I never had any illusions of him being an easy adversary.

After what happened with Kenneth and Ravi, I figured I needed to stay away from men for a while. Whenever someone would enquire, I would talk about a fictitious boyfriend just to keep suitors at bay. There were still a persistent lot, regarding any current love interest of mine as mere piffling to be dropped when someone better came along. Morals were going abegging too; some said they did not mind me having a boyfriend, or a fiancé, or even a husband. They just wanted a piece of me, not all of me. I would of course say a no, thank you.

Not that I had much time for anyone. I was busy as hell at office; the concept of weekends did not exist in a start-up I learnt. If I got any days off, I would head out to Jaipur. My father's health was deteriorating, and I wanted to spend time with him. I did not want to sound morbid, but I knew he would not be with us for long.

Of course, I would try to meet Vani too on every visit but her father would always make it stressful. Even when he gave me a time to pick her, he would cancel plans last minute. A justification for his erratic behaviour was too much to expect. He had a sadistic streak to him; he revelled in torturing me.

I lost it on one of the occasions when I was supposed to pick Vani up but he did not even open the door to me. He called out from the other side, asking me to meet her on my next visit. I dug my heels in. Literally. I told him I would be waiting on the street outside till he let me see her. And I did. For eleven hours. Without food and without water. In the sun. Only at dusk did an uncle of his, who lived in another part of the house, come out to enquire what was happening and why I was not leaving. Not without my daughter, I told him.

The uncle invited me in but I declined. He returned with lemonade and requested me to have it while he sorted the matter. Although they were barely on talking terms, he used his position as a senior in the family to give Krishna a dressing down for his inhuman behaviour. Vani was finally allowed to spend the night with me.

I took her home in my exhausted state but still mustered up the enthusiasm to try and have fun with her. Come bedtime, she started crying for her father and grandmother. She was not used to me, not used to idea of any mother for that matter. She did not know what one was. Despite my best efforts, she could not be pacified. I requested my younger brother to drop her back; I did not have the heart to see her go into that house again.

Krishna eventually became agreeable to attending meetings with lawyers but we would never be sure if he would turn up or not. He did not engage a lawyer; he represented himself. He would poke holes in all terms, acting unreasonable over the simplest of clauses. I was not even asking him to pay any alimony or reimburse me for the stolen jewellery. I knew he had nothing to offer; even if he did, he would not give me anything. All I wanted was shared or sole custody of our daughter.

In retaliation, Krishna went about town maligning me. He filed cases with the police, accusing me of being alcoholic and a drug addict, to be restrained from visiting my daughter. With the help of his golf club friends, he started a whisper campaign questioning my sources of income. For someone with no qualifications, who was paying for the rich lifestyle I was leading in Bangalore and Delhi? No one could check how I was getting by, and people took his word for it. I was supposedly leading an opulent life, paid for by my lovers; he even suggested I was into high-society prostitution. Jaipur being a small city, word got around fast. People believed what they heard, for it fed their appetite for spicy gossip, hard to come by in a conservative city. Fortunately, those closest to me—the ones who mattered—did not believe a word of his insinuations and stood by me, never doubting my character.

My lawyer came recommended from Harish chacha but I had to fire him too. He was ostensibly a gentleman, a courteous one, extremely helpful and ever responsive when I reached out to him. He would comfort me and boost my morale when I had my emotional meltdowns—more a norm than an exception during sessions in his office. He would never tire of reassuring me about us emerging victorious; it just needed patience and a willingness to walk over a bed of thorns. He never told me he was one of those pricks.

He was dropping me back after a late-evening session and put his hand on my thigh. It was purportedly to console me, but his intent was not so. When I didn't move his hand away, he took it as an approval for more. He stopped the car by the side and reached out to kiss me. That's when I jolted and pushed him away.

It's all right, I mean no harm, he said.

Why are you doing this? I asked.

I am not just your lawyer, I am also a friend. I care for you. I know you are going through a lot, a bit of affection is always good for the soul. I know you well now, and I know there is no one else in your life. We all need someone.

That's being very presumptuous of you. And you have someone in your life anyway. She's also the mother of your two children.

You know the fire between a couple dies out after a few years. So it's ok to seek comfort in other arms from time to time.

I suppose you would approve of your wife seeking such comfort too with another man.

How dare you speak like that about her? She's not that kind of a woman. She is the daughter of a Supreme Court justice and a very respectable woman herself.

And what am I? And what are you for that matter?

I don't think you are in a position to show such an attitude towards me. Certainly not after all that I am doing for you.

Then do one more thing for me. Drop the case.

I uttered those words without thinking. I was shivering. I was scared. What will I do if he goes off the case? Who will I turn to? I will have to start all over again. But I have taken enough shit in life already, I reasoned with myself; firing my lawyer was no big deal in comparison. I don't need another sick human being in my life. I need to surround myself with good people, ones who create positive energies for things to happen as I want them to.

Yes, please do, I said.

Please do what? he asked.

Drop the case.

You don't need to react this way. We are adults. It's ok if you want to say no to me. But we don't need it to affect our professional engagement.

No, thank you. I do not need this. I will figure out a way. You can talk to my uncle for your fee so far. I will collect all case files from your office the next time I am in town.

I opened the door of the car and stepped out. I will find my way home. I will find a way to get to the life I seek.

❧

The more I resisted the idea, the more my destiny steered me towards prospective candidates to get married to. Even as memories of Kenneth still tugged at my heart, Simran walked into my life as the designated medium to connect me with Nakul.

I got acquainted with Simran at a press conference we had hosted; she was a freelance lifestyle journalist. We realized we were near neighbours when I was booking her cab. Since I was headed back too, I saved myself a sweaty bus ride and hopped along with her. By the time we reached home, we had both been acquainted with each other's personal lives; a mutual fondness had developed in the one-hour peak traffic drive back. She invited me over for a drink and dinner. I was staying with Harish chacha till I found my own place and I readily accepted the invite—anything to stay away from the ever-hovering, ever-preaching uncle.

I had a sinking feeling when she introduced me to her husband, Anand. I wanted to turn the clock back in that instant, go back to being nineteen, and dismiss my life of the past few years as a bad dream. Why couldn't I have met him when my dreams had hopes? Why couldn't I have met him when I was raring to go, to make a name and career for myself in the world of glamour? Why am I meeting him now? I may still be young by all measures, but the burdens I was carrying made me feel much older.

Anand was a fashion photographer. He was the Anand. He was the prodigy who was more famous than most of his clients. Every model, every Bollywood star wanted to be shot by him. Every fashion designer wanted him to shoot their collections, every movie director wanted him to shoot the stills from the sets to send out to newspapers and glossy magazines. When I would visualize myself as a model, I prayed that Anand would shoot me. Stardom was assured for those Anand chose to shoot.

And here I was, sitting in the icon's living room, talking to him like he was no big deal. I was so tempted to ask him if he thought I still had a chance to be a model, if he thought I was worthy of his camera. But I held myself back. I could not insult a God of mine by asking him to stoop so low. I felt like a dump. Of course, it was not too long ago when I had all the self-confidence to approach the best in the field. And then my dad fell ill, and an acquaintance conspired to bump into me in the hospital, offering me his sympathies, showing care, only to con me into marrying him and bankrupting my life.

I wanted to gush all over him; I tried to keep my excitement under check but the fangirl moment was written all over my face. I still pretended to know little—rather nothing—of him but I could feel my face flush while looking at him. I had to snap out of it, lest I offended Simran, so I excused myself to help her in the kitchen.

The doorbell rang. Once. Twice. And many more times. People were trooping in. I didn't know I had been invited to a party. There wasn't one planned. It was Wednesday and, just like that, a ritual had developed over time for friends to drop by unannounced for a midweek rendezvous at Anand and Simran's place. Not just friends known to them, but friends of friends, models, designers, authors, photographers, and even actors and filmmakers if they were in town. Food and drinks were never in short supply. Volunteers cooked a big pot of biryani, and most guests brought along bottles and cans to add to the already overstocked bar.

It was a new world for me, a world I could have been a part of much earlier, a world where I might have been the centre of attraction and not one I would be looking at enviously from the sidelines. The house was on the top floor, and the living room opened into a sizeable terrace. The worst of summers and monsoons were over, and the weather at night was no longer warm or humid; it was pleasantly cool but still too early to put on woollens. Everyone seemed to be chatting with everyone at the same time; was anyone even listening? It was so effortless, so reassuring to be in the company of good people, happy people, all full of stories from the interesting lives they led. I may have felt like a queen bee in Bangalore, but this was alien territory for me. I really wanted to belong to groups like these. I hated Krishna even more in that moment.

I wanted a good friend in Simran who would be my bridge to this new universe. I didn't have to try hard at all. Simran took to me just like I did to her. She became my anchor in a new city just like Sabina had been in Bangalore.

❧

You should have been a model. You can still be one. I know one when I see her. That's what I get paid for. Your looks can launch a thousand brands.

I could not believe those words from none other than the great Anand himself. Simran had called me over but had to rush out to cover an unexpected story. Gun-Marie Fredriksson of the Roxette fame was passing through town on a private holiday; *Femina* magazine got an approval to interview the Swedish pop singer at short notice. I wish I could have gone along too; 'It Must Have Been Love' from *Pretty Woman* was one of my all-time favourite songs. Simran promised to be back soon, leaving me to chat alone with Anand.

I did not tell you earlier, but I had aspirations of being a model and a fashion designer before I got into my ill-fated marriage, I said.

I know your story briefly. You can't reverse the clock in your case, but I wish other young women get their own lives and ambitions sorted before committing themselves to regressive relationships, he said.

I try not to think much, only close that chapter of my life with a divorce. I will go mad if I allow regret to get to me.

It's not too late to pursue your dream occupation.

I no longer have the same spunk or the motivation.

You are very beautiful. Your figure is perfect. And your face can be a photographer's delight to capture on camera.

I could feel myself going pink all over. No one had said such words to me. Certainly not someone who mattered like Anand.

Thank you, I said.

Let me know if I can help. I can do a test shoot with you, he offered.

Can you?

Yes.

Let me think about it.

Sure. Come to Bombay when you have decided.

Bombay? Why Bombay?

I am moving there.

Oh, I didn't know that. When are you moving? Simran didn't tell me. I am really fond of her, I am going to miss her.

Simran is not going. Only I am.

Will she join you later?

No. She will not be joining me. And I will not be coming back.

You mean, are you splitting? Sorry if I heard you wrong.

Yes, we are. It's not working out for us.

But you look so good and happy together. You are such a power couple.

That's for the world. It's different in reality.

If you don't mind my asking, what went wrong? You don't have to answer if you don't want to.

Simran is not interested in me.

Is there another man?

No, another woman.

What?

Yes, her editor at *Femina*.

Then why did she marry you?

She was not aware of her orientation until a few years after our marriage. Only when she started writing for the women-only magazine, and spent time working with and reporting on women, did her attractions for the same sex came to the fore. She and I gradually moved apart in bed, even if we continued to be fond of each other as friends and companions.

Do the two of you still have sex?

Have not had for nearly two years now.

Wow. How do you manage? Sorry, you don't have to answer this either. I don't mean to intrude into your very personal life or make you feel awkward.

No, it's ok. I interact with a lot of women in my job. Some have been willing lovers. But I do love Simran, and I would not have been with other women had things been normal.

Does Simran know about the other women in your life?

Yes, she does. She only encouraged me to be with them. I guess it took the pressure and the guilt off her.

If everything is so open between the two of you, and you are so fond of each other, why don't you continue the current arrangement?

We can't. Rather, I can't. I can't lead this dual life. I know I will miss Simran, but I have no choice.

I feel so bad for both of you. Can I hug you?

Sure, I could do with one.

And I did. With my arms around him, I saw a tinge of sadness on his face and in his eyes at close quarters. He must have been really hurting. I could not help kissing him. A compassionate kiss turned passionate without any intention.

He kissed me back. His lips felt tender on mine, his breath sensuous on my skin. His hands felt warm on my partially exposed back, and his body clung to mine as if by a magnetic force. My thoughts were with Simran at the same time; she was my bestie and I was being intimate with her husband. But she had given him a pass to be with other women, so I was not doing anything to be ashamed of.

I was wearing a saree, and he undraped me with one hand without loosening his grip with the other arm. He was simultaneously kissing me on the neck, on my face, on my shoulders, and on my lips. He opened my blouse and unclasped my bra. We were lying on the floor by now, and he had one hand all the way up my petticoat. He took off my panties and shagged me with his fingers. I was embarrassingly wet.

He took off his shorts and briefs effortlessly but kept his t-shirt on when he came over me. My blouse and bra were still hanging loose on me. He raised my petticoat to my waist and penetrated me, big and hard as a rock. He moved fast, reaching deep within me, arousing all my sensitive bits; I came not once but twice. I was exhilarated. And then he came, inside me, without protection. Shit, shit, shit, I thought to myself. I wanted to feel worried, but I was revelling in the state of high.

He rolled over, and we lay panting on our backs, with bits of clothing hanging on us awkwardly. He stretched his arm to pick a pack of cigarettes and lighter. Simran does not approve of smoking inside the house, but I need one right away, he said. Would you like one?

Yes, I could do with one too, I said.

We smoked quietly till I had half-finished mine. I offered the rest to him, and he took it. I got up, threw the six yard long saree around myself, and went to the bedroom to wear it properly. The walls were decorated with photos of Simran and Anand on holidays, on their wedding day, at a picnic, at parties—and a self-portrait of them nude in bed. They looked happy together, the perfect couple. I would have felt guilty, or probably not gone so far with Anand had he not told me what he did.

I had not had sex with anyone since the trip to Kathmandu. I had been ok with it. But Anand reminded me of how much I enjoy sex. Why was I denying myself something I enjoyed so much? There was so much wrong in my life—if sex lifted my spirits and enhanced my mood, why should I deliberately abstain? Not that I wanted to be reckless about it, but if a desirable and willing partner came along, I should go for it.

I can't live with Anand. I am fed up of his philandering. His profession requires him to be in close proximity to some of the most beautiful and the sexiest women in the country. In an environment with few qualms, temptation hovers around men in all states of dressing. Anand is highly sought-after by these women; his camera and recommendations can make a difference to their careers. But this does not give him the licence to sleep with them as long as he's married to me.

Simran opened up to me when I asked about her and Anand splitting up. This tirade came as somewhat of a surprise to me. Anand had shown a very different picture to me. But you would have known he would be surrounded by these women when you married him, I said. Didn't that make you feel insecure at that stage?

I was young, and I found his life glamourous. I was a rookie lifestyle reporter, and I managed to get a lot of exclusive stories and scoops from his network. I will admit that helped fast-track my career to where it is today. I was smitten by him, and I felt flattered when he paid attention to me even though he could choose to be with a model or a movie star. I will be bold enough to say he was good in bed, better than any man I had been with. He proposed marriage, and I could not say no.

When did you decide to split up?

We have been having our share of fights with increasing frequency. Flare-ups would usually happen when I would accuse him of having slept with another woman, and he would deny it. I had no proof, only a woman's hunch. Gradually, his most lucrative assignments had been coming from Bombay, and he had been talking of both of us moving base there. I told him to go ahead with the move a fortnight ago but without me. I cannot live with his infidelities anymore, I will go mad.

But are you sure he has slept with others? I asked her. Even if she wasn't sure of the answer, I was. But I could not tell her without losing her as a friend.

That I am. He has admitted to a few indiscretions when he knew he could not get away with his lies. Even once is many more than is permissible in my book, and I cannot be forgiving any longer.

If I may ask, when did you last have sex with him? I asked.

She laughed and said yesterday, and almost every day he's been in town. You may find it strange, but we have both allowed ourselves to have sex with each other even during the worst of meltdowns. As long as he's around, why lose out on the pleasure he is so good at giving? Easier and safer than seeking other men to have sex with.

I gave a pretentiously wicked smile and asked if she was ever interested in women. While I was probing, I might as well seek the complete truth.

Are you interested in women? she replied with a question. If you are, then I would love to make out with you. I find you super sexy. I have actually visualized being in bed with you even though I am not a lesbian.

What about being with other women?

I will tell you, but it should stay a secret between us sisters.

Of course, I promise, I said. My heart was pounding.

I got drunk when my editor was over for dinner once, and we started kissing in Anand's presence. She is openly gay and was all over me. But nothing happened beyond the kissing and the fondling. Anand proposed a threesome, but we left the poor guy high and dry. I never gave another woman a thought until you quizzed me. Do you want to sleep with me?

No, no, I will stick to men only. For now at least, I said.

I was trying to make light of the conversation, but I was screaming inside. At Anand. The deceitful, lying, uncouth man. My hero fell from grace in my eyes. Why are men such bastards? I wanted to tell Simran everything and warn her never to warm up to Anand again. He was going, let him. He did not deserve her.

Men need to be taught lessons they will never forget. I was even more furious at Krishna. If he did not come to his senses soon and cooperate, I will make him regret whatever he did to me, I promised myself.

Zulfiqar was the eternal wingman, helping his friends find the loves of their lives. But he never promoted his own cause, nor did any of his friends. In Bangalore, he tried to make a match of Mahesh and me, but he never opened up about his feelings for me. I wanted him to, being fond of him myself—even though I was probably not ready to love anyone.

He moved to Delhi soon after I did. Was it a coincidence, or did he follow me by design? He called me a few weeks after he was settled in and we met for a Sunday brunch. So good to see you again. I didn't imagine we would meet anytime soon in life, I said.

Yes, this move was in the works for over a year, he said.

Over a year? How come you made no mention of it?

I could not. It was classified.

Really? What are you? Mafia? Spy? James Bond?

I can't tell you much, but I work in the ministry of home affairs. As an officer on special duty. Assigned to Kashmir. I will be staying in Delhi; I have been provided a house by the government. But I expect to be in Kashmir for extended periods of time.

Oh, that's a surprise. What do they want you to do?

The problems of Kashmir are all over the news. But I know my home state like few others do. I can move around almost invisibly. Our family is known all across; I can parachute myself anywhere and I can be sure someone will provide me a roof for the night and a hot meal with full discretion. I will be helping the army win the support of locals as they go about tracking terrorists who often use homes of locals to hide and to meet.

Isn't it dangerous?

Yes, it is. But someone has to do it. We have to bring peace back to my land, he said.

Your land? Not our land?

Best we don't talk about it. For both our sake. So how have you been? Found someone to marry?

Oh yes, I have a harem-in-waiting. I have heard the government will soon legalize polyandry; I will marry all the men I want to.

Jokes apart…

You seriously expect me to consider marriage? No, that's not an option on the table for me. For a while at least. Forget me, I can't help worrying for you already. Kashmir is not safe to be in.

Don't worry about me. I am in no mood to be a martyr. I have a long to-do before I pop off.

I hope playing Cupid for yourself is in the list.

What do you mean?

You are always recommending a match for your friends but never one for yourself. Unless you keep her the best kept secret in town.

Haha, I always get my share of love. Suits me not to be committed. Allows you to feel free. In any case, women are best advised not to give their hearts to those in my line of work.

You know you cannot hide what you feel from me. I know you well enough, Zulfi.

Anyway, got to rush now. We work seven days.

See, avoiding the topic.

Nikita, I know you care for me. And I really like you. But love is not an option for me either. The choices I have made make my life ephemeral at best.

You are scaring me now. What are you not telling me?

What I haven't told you cannot be told to anyone. You already know more than any of my other friends and family. I trust you so I told you even this much.

Promise me you will be safe.

I wish I could. But I will try. Will see you soon. I am getting text messages incessantly from the office. See you.

And he was gone. I sat at the table for a long time, staring after him. I felt like I was in love with Zulfiqar. God, please keep him safe for me, I prayed.

What do you say to a man who has a girlfriend, makes no secrets of sleeping around with other women, and yet proposes to marry you?

What do you say to the woman whose life is about all the dirty stuff hitting the fan, wants a normal life and yet says yes to such a man?

The man was Nakul. The woman was Nikita.

Simran had won an important book editing contract and decided to use a part of the fat advance to treat me at the upscale La Piazza at Hyatt Regency. I noticed a couple walking in and making a beeline towards our table. The guy bent to kiss Simran on the cheek, and both the newcomers sat at our table without being invited to.

Hi Simi, how are you? asked Simran looking at the girl. And how is my baby? she said, turning towards the man.

The girl smiled with a hi. I am good Simran, so good to bump into you here, the guy said.

Let me introduce you to Nikita, my bestiest bestie. Nikita, meet Nakul, the brother who came in late into my life. And that's Simi, her job is to keep Nakul on a leash, said Simran.

Come on, Simran, if I was half as bad as you make me out to be, I would not be able to show my face to anyone, said Nakul.

You know I love to tease you because I love you so much, said Simran. What are you doing here?

We wanted to have a tiramisu with coffee here. I cannot resist ordering it when passing by here, he said.

So let me order it for you, offered Simran.

No, no. I will leave the two of you to yourselves. I am sure you have stuff to talk about. I will catch up with you later, he said.

Later as in this Saturday, said Simran. Don't forget.

I won't. Will be there, he said and left to sit with Simi at another table.

He is such a cutie-pie. Half the girls in town hate him enough to want to kill him, and the other love him enough to want to marry him, said Simran.

What do you mean? I asked.

He breaks hearts like little boys break sandcastles on a beach. It's a marvel Simi has stuck around with him for as long as she has.

They make for a nice couple from what the eye can see.

They do. But Nakul being Nakul cannot stay away from other girls behind her back. But don't tell anyone.

How would you know what he does?

Where do you think he goes with them? He is constantly asking for keys to my apartment. I could give him a duplicate permanently, but he would run amok. I would be tripping over naked women sprawled on the floor when I return home.

Hahaha, you sure know how to conjure up grand possibilities.

You don't believe me? You will when you know Nakul better.

What's on Saturday?

Oh, I have been meaning to tell you, but I forgot. I have called a few friends over. To celebrate breaking up with Anand. Come over.

Has he moved out?

Yes, the day before. High time. I could not take it any longer.

Are you missing him?

Yes, I admit I am. But I was going nuts imagining him with other women. I would feel normal when he was around me but was in torment whenever he wasn't. The pain of his behaviour outweighed the pain of being without him.

Hang in there, Simran, I said holding her hand. This shall pass, and you will find a man you deserve.

Or a woman, she said and winked at me.

Oooh, what am I missing?

Nothing. Honestly. But seeing men and their ways, I should consider women. They will be more loyal and loving for sure.

Are you already with someone?

No, not yet. Don't even have anyone in mind. I don't even know if I would like to be. But such thoughts do come to me.

Don't let go of them. Maybe that's what will make you happy.

Yes, let's see. See you on Saturday. Anyway, it was a lovely lunch as usual. Thank you for coming.

I should thank you. And congratulations once again on your assignment. See you soon.

I was thinking of Nakul all the way back home. And for the rest of the week. I could not wait for Saturday. I needed to meet him. To figure out why he had captivated my mind. I had nothing to do with him. I could not have anything to do with the kind of guy Simran described him to be. And yet, my sixth sense was sending me messages, but they were too cryptic to decipher.

I had a chaperone on call for my social outings. There were two willing volunteers—Nakul and Zulfiqar. The wicked part? Sometimes I invited both together, one flanking me on either side. Neither took out the daggers for the other—yet—as each had been confined to their respective set of expectations.

Zulfi was the buddy around me. Not that his job gave him much time to himself. Even if he committed to meet me, things could and would change at the last minute. He had to leave me stranded at times. He was required to be on alert at all times of the day and night, and rush out at a moment's notice when called to. His phone had to be on and fully charged while sleeping, while in the washroom, while wooing a girl and while in bed with her. If the phone rang, he had to pick it even if he or his partner were on the cusp of an orgasm. Ok, I made up the last part but I am sure I was not off the mark.

He would call me whenever he was free and we would meet. For a coffee, a meal or a drink. One day, he just gave up alcohol. He said his religion did not permit him to. I may have been mistaken, but I noticed him increasingly sullen and withdrawn from that date onwards. He went totally mum about his work, not sharing even the few bits he would earlier. He gradually got more irritable and edgy too, far removed from his cheerful and positive outlook in life.

Nakul was on another trip with me. He just wanted to be around me, and I could never understand why. He would call out of the blue to say he was around my office, and asked if we could meet. I would avoid it, but relented at times keeping in mind his relationship with Simran. He would ask me to join him and Simi if they were going to a party, or for a drink or a meal. It would just be the three of us on most occasions. What am I doing between the two? I would wonder and feel stupid. When inviting me, Nakul was always vague about where we were going and who all would be there. My antennas would go up when he would take me—and just me—to a party. Does Simi know about it? I wanted to enquire but mostly did not.

What's between you and Zulfiqar? he asked once when driving to friend's place for a get-together. Simi was not there.

Why do you want to know? I asked. Two could play the game of being evasive.

Friends deserve to know.

Do they? Not everything. And friends fall in categories too.

What category do I come in?

Friend of a friend.

Really? After all this, you only see me as Simran's friend?

What 'after all this'? Nothing's happened between us.

Come on, we are friends in our own right.

Are we?

Of course.

Even if we are, I don't have to tell you everything. Or anything for that matter.

But I like you.

What do you mean you like me?

Like you as in like you. You know what I mean.

What's on between you and Simi?

She's my girlfriend.

What does that make me?

I don't know. I just like you.

Where is she tonight?

She could not join us, she is busy. He stammered a bit when he said this. He was lying.

I am sure she's not that busy. Let's call her. And pick her up.

No, no. It's ok. Let's not disturb her.

Why?

I want to be with you only.

Why?

Because I like you.

That's complicated. There is Simi. And then there is Zulfi. And we haven't discussed if I am interested in your company, I said.

Stop troubling me now.

I am troubling you? Your reputation precedes you, dude. A woman has to be careful around you.

Tell me now. What's on between you and Zulfi?

That's for you to figure out. Can we move the car now? He had stopped the car near our destination to talk to me longer in private.

There is a slight detail I missed out on, he said.

What?

The party got cancelled.

It got cancelled? When?

A little while back.

How little?

Yesterday.

And you didn't tell me?

I thought we could do something else since you had anyway set the time aside for this. Why should you have a boring evening?

Was there a party at all? Tell me the truth, I promise not to kill you.

No.

Does Simi know you are with me alone?

No.

Why?

Because I like you.

This is the umpteenth time you have said it this evening. I am not sure I like where this is going.

I will break up with Simi. And you can break up with Zulfiqar.

Can you drop me home?

The chill in my voice told Nakul to obey my orders and not speak a word thereafter. He dropped me off. Sorry, he said when I was getting out of the car.

❧

Nakul had a thick skin. That's how he got away with stuff he did and lived to tell the tale. A woman getting upset with him and asking to be dropped home would not ruffle his resolve one bit. It only made it stronger, and he was back to paying me the same level of attention as earlier. The snub was no more than a little speedbump for him.

Zulfiqar was mostly missing in action. We could speak only when he called; I was never to dial his number. Those were standing instructions by him. I looked forward to his company; I wanted to be around him. He made me feel secure, feel wanted. The closer I felt to him, the further he was physically. I missed him, and it hurt.

I was at a bar with a few office colleagues when I noticed Simi with a man. She was wearing as skimpy an attire as the law would allow. The two were standing in a corner, at close quarters. She was letting his hand have a free run of her body. To feel her breasts, to rub her back, to go up her micro skirt from behind and finger her between the legs. They were barely visible in the low light but I noticed everything from the angle I was sitting at. I could not help walking up to them.

Hi Simi, I said. I had to shout to make myself heard in the loud music.

She looked at me dreamily, took a patient drag on her cigarette, did a bottoms-up on her white wine, and said, Hi. Fancy seeing you here.

I should be saying that. I come here often but have never seen you before.

I rarely go to the same place again. I like to try new things.

She turned towards the man with her, smiled at him, pulled him closer to her, and kissed him on the cheek. He was the new thing for her tonight, I guessed. So, where are your lover boys? she asked.

What lover boys?

Your Zulfi and my Nakul.

They are not my lover boys.

Really? You mean they are lover boys for other girls, and you just help yourself to a few bites?

I don't know what you are talking about, but I don't like whatever it is you are trying to tell me.

Listen babe, I like to speak my mind and I will say this to you. You are the bitch who feasts on men and destroys their relationships.

You are talking nonsense now. I am trying hard not to lose my cool with you.

I don't give a fuck to you. After what you did to Nakul and me.

What did I do?

Look at Mother Teresa! I didn't do anything. I am so innocent. I am the Virgin Mary.

You can speak your mind clearly or I am ending this conversation, I said.

Ok bitch, then hear it. Nakul is so enamoured with you, he hardly pays any attention to me.

That's his problem, not mine. I don't have any interest in him. You need to talk to him directly and clarify things.

Then why do you hang around with him all the time? Why do you go out with him alone?

I don't. He hovers around me. And picks me up first and then tells me no one else is joining us. Anyway, if you must know, he is no saint. He has a reputation with other girls behind your back. And I know I have not crossed any lines with him. You are fighting with the wrong girl.

No baby, I am not. I know what he does with other girls. He's just pissing in them. Let him have his boyish fun with them. He would have got over that fetish eventually and then been mine only. But you are different. He wants to give you the life that was mine. You are so good at this, how do you do it? There's a word for women like you. Prostitute.

Go fuck yourself. I could strangle you right now, but I have to leave for Jaipur early morning tomorrow to meet my daughter. But you talk to me like this ever again, I will make you regret your words. Anyway, have a nice night with your lover boy here.

I could not help taking a dig at the man with her. I was fuming, but managed not to get into a catfight with Simi. I needed to leave. I walked out of the bar without telling my friends. But Simi did not give up, and shouted whore across the floor for everyone to hear. Sense prevailed, and I continued walking out.

You didn't tell me you have a daughter.

Nakul chose the worst time to have made that statement. He offered to pick me from Bikaner House, a terminal for buses to and from Rajasthan. I was having a terrible weekend. The Simi episode happened Friday night. On Saturday, I went to Jaipur only to meet Vani but Krishna did not let me despite agreeing to before I left Delhi. My divorce case was still in the doldrums. And then Nakul was late, and I had to wait in the dark, all by myself, starving and desperate for a smoke. My irritation was getting worse by the minute. His cell phone was switched off. Trust him not to keep his batteries charged.

He drove in just as I was about to go looking for an autorickshaw. No sooner was I in the car than he asked why I had not told him about my daughter.

I lost it. Stop the car right now, I screamed. Why am I supposed to tell you everything about my personal life? Why am I supposed to tell you anything at all? Who are you to me?

Cool it, I was just curious. Simran mentioned it to me so I was surprised.

Even if you were, what's this about why I didn't tell you?

Ok, sorry. I didn't mean it that way.

You and that girlfriend of yours need to get your act together. Where do I come in? Did she tell you anything? I am sure not. Let me tell you. She thinks I am a bloody whore who thrives on preying on other women's men. What have you been telling her about me? About us? What tales are you spreading?

I had never been so angry, at least not in Nakul's presence, let alone at him. I could see him looking troubled, and I could not help feeling bad and sorry for him at the same time. But my head was like a pressure cooker. A smoke and a bite would have helped to release the steam. His instincts kicked in at the right moment, and he offered me a cigarette just then. I accepted it even though I didn't want anything from him anymore. To his good fortune, I calmed down a bit.

I am sorry about what happened with Simi, he said. I don't know what exactly transpired between the two of you, I only heard multiple versions in bits and pieces. I want to know from you.

After what happened, I had resolved not to speak to you again. So don't feel pleased about being allowed to pick me up today. I called you to tell you about my encounter with Simi the other night. After today, I don't want to be dragged into matters related to your harem—real or imaginary, I said.

So what really happened?

I don't feel like talking about it any longer. It's in the past now; I have more pressing matters to dwell on. But if she talks to me once more the way she did, I will not be responsible for my reactions.

I will talk to her. And I am sorry on her behalf.

I could not let Simi off the hook easily. I had to play bitch, since she had anyway termed me one. Oh, another thing, I said. You may want to ask her about her other interests.

What other interests?

In men. The rich, flashy types. Ones whose fathers might be politicians, or shady businessmen, throwing money at their sons to snare innocent girls like your Simi darling.

What are you talking about?

What was she doing with another man in the bar? Nothing wrong in going out with male friends for a drink but is it ok for them to have their hand up your handkerchief of a dress, fingering your cunt in plain sight?

I could not believe myself speaking the way I was. I saw the colour change on Nakul's face. I know who you are talking about, he said. Why is she with that bastard?

Who is he?

Her ex. Loaded. She can't stay away from his money.

What are you complaining about?

How can she cheat on me?

I would have laughed had I not been starving. She is doing what you do, I said.

She promised not to see him anymore.

Fuck me! You are all the same, aren't you? I am suddenly not angry with Simi any more. I like her for making you miserable. So you know what women go through now? Philandering need not just be a male prerogative, what say?

Nakul went quiet. He did not speak a word till we reached my place. He dropped me off, and was gone. He did not even utter a goodbye. His mouth was still bitter from the taste of his own medicine.

❧

Zulfi is no more.

I was taking it easy at home after dinner, removing nail colour and figuring out which one to apply when the phone rang. I was surprised to see Mahesh's number. How come he is calling? I wondered. We had not spoken since I had left Bangalore.

He did not greet me when I picked the phone but straightway told me about Zulfiqar being no more. I froze.

What are you saying? I asked.

What you heard. We have lost Zulfi, he said. You are the first person he would have wanted me to call. You meant the world to him, but he never expressed it.

What happened? My eyes were already wet and throat dry when I said this.

I don't have the details, but the news reports are saying he was shot in an encounter.

Encounter? His job was not to go shooting terrorists.

I don't think you got me. He was shot in an encounter by the army.

What? That's not possible. He was assisting the army in their operations.

Who told you that?

Zulfi, who else.

Well, I don't think that was the case. He was very distressed after losing his brother and went back home to mourn. That's when he apparently became radicalized.

He lost his brother? How?

He was picked up by the police for routine questioning, not uncommon in those parts. The family did not see or hear from him for weeks. And then someone dropped his body outside their house late one night. It was discovered by the milkman the following morning who raised the alarm.

There has been a mistake somewhere. Zulfi was not like this.

The news says it. And I know they are right.

How do you know they are right?

I can't tell you. Zulfi was no less than a brother to me. He didn't need to say much for me to know what was going on in his life. I was in Delhi for an evening a few weeks ago and met him. He told me he was not going to live very long; the people who took his brother away were going after him too. I knew which side he was on then but there was no arguing with Zulfi about what he should do.

I feel so numb, it's just not making sense to me.

He left a note for you and asked me to read it out to you should something happen to him.

He did? What does it say?

Nikita, you are the only woman I have ever loved. If life had been any different, I would have asked for your hand in marriage. And made a home for us on the banks of the Lidder River in Pahalgam in Kashmir. But I could never admit my love for you because I know you would have accepted it, and returned it wholeheartedly. But I also knew I would not live long. I didn't want you to hurt. But in our next life, please be with me.

I lay in bed all night, unmoving, staring at the ceiling. I did not sleep a wink. It's likely that I did not even blink; an observer may have mistaken me to be dead. No matter what anyone says, Zulfi was a patriot to me. And the man I would have loved to love no matter what his truth was.

I have broken up with Simi. And I want you to know I love you.

Nakul rang the bell the morning after I had spoken to Mahesh. He started speaking the instant I opened the door—as if he had memorized a script and wanted to blurt it out before he fluffed his lines.

The house was dark with curtains drawn and the lights off. I must have looked like a silhouette to him; he could not see my eyes, red and wet with tears. I could only hear a babble trying to convey how sorry he was, what he felt for me, blah blah blah. I was not registering a word; I was still with Zulfi.

Nakul had never appeared at my door unannounced. Fortuitously, a universal force sent him when I needed somebody around me. I turned and went back into the house, leaving the door ajar. He followed.

Only when his vision adjusted to the dim lighting did he realize the state I was in. What happened? he asked. He sounded genuinely concerned.

My quiet tears turned into sobbing, bordering on the hysterical. He came closer to me, and I instinctively wrapped my arms around him. I buried my face in his chest and continued crying. He held me, gently yet firmly, patiently waiting till I had had my cry. I finally calmed down, and let go of him. I sat on the couch while he fetched me a glass of water. What happened? he asked after I had taken a few sips.

I mustered up the will to utter the words: Zulfi is no more.

Oh my God! How? When? Are you sure?

Yes, I got a call from Mahesh, his closest friend.

I still don't get it. Did he meet with an accident?

No. He was shot.

Shot? Why would anyone shoot him? Where?

In Kashmir. By the army.

Kashmir? What was he doing there? And what did the army have against him?

Nakul had no clue what Zulifqar did. He only saw him as a rival for my affections, but not with any malice. They had become good friends, cheerfully chaperoning me to parties and bars. I told him all that I knew, slowly, in a faltering voice.

This is so not believable, he said when I had finished. I can't get my head around it. Zulfi just did not come across as a guy who could go down such a path.

We don't know the truth, or the complete truth. I will never believe what they say about him. He was a good man who could not have harmed anyone. I am sure he has been sacrificed as a pawn in the game of politics, I said.

Can I get you something to eat? he asked. I was famished. He notched up multiple brownie points by offering to feed me.

Yes please, I said. I have not cooked anything. Can you order something? Or just go pick something up? And don't ask me what I want. Anything will do.

Sure. I will be back in half an hour. I know what to get.

He was back within forty minutes with Thai green curry and sticky rice. It was the perfect brunch for me. We made inane conversation to take my mind off Zulfi. We were sitting on a thick rug in my living room, and I dozed off on it. I woke a few hours later to find Nakul sleeping too, his arm over me.

I smiled. I slid closer to him, put my arm over him, and went back to sleep.

From the day I met Nakul, I wanted him for myself. But I avoided him, acted aloof, would blast him for even the smallest of transgressions because I was being overly circumspect. And I was scared. I did not want to reveal my feelings, give in to him, get emotionally attached, and then lose him. I had resolved not to be deeply involved with any man after Kenneth, at least not until I had sorted matters out in Jaipur. But I could not resist the pull towards Nakul. Despite his track record with women.

As I lay in his arms, I could not help analysing him in my life. What was drawing me to him? I didn't want to be hurt, and he was the master in going through women. My head would not let me be with him, while the rest of me wanted nothing else.

Why was he with me? I would exaggerate my weaknesses and problems with men to scare them—and to test them. No one had been put through the grind as much as Nakul had been. He believed in defying gravity and living his youth in the clouds, so why did he want to be grounded with the weight I carried on me?

My inner voice was telling me to wake him up, to ask him to leave right away, to say a big no to his romantic overtures. And yet, my intuitions were sounding me off about impending changes in my life, changes I had been determined to not allow. I had to move away from Nakul.

I did. At least for then. I gently pulled away and made two mugs of black coffee. I placed one near his nose to wake him. He blinked a few times, and looked at the coffee with a sense of relief. Just what I needed, he said. And good evening. Or is it morning already?

No, it is still a good evening, I said. I smiled. I was surprised I could. I was supposed to be grieving for a friend and was supposed to evict another half-asleep in my living room.

I hope I didn't do anything wrong like last time.

No, you did not. And don't sound so scared. I won't eat you up.

I am sorry I had no idea what had happened when I just started saying what I did at your door.

No, it's ok. You couldn't have known.

I still can't understand how it could have happened.

I know he's a victim of politics. I know he was not a terrorist or whatever he would be branded as. I would have known if he was. And I have seen him take calls; they were definitely from government offices. I could make out. If not, he would not have spoken in my presence.

I believe you.

Can we change the topic? I need to not think about him.

Of course. May I say something?

Yes.

You got me wrong the other day. Your past is your past. And I am ok with it. I was just a bit surprised, so could not wait to ask you. My choice of words when I did may have caused the furore it did.

That's fine. I had even forgotten about it.

Thank you. I really care for you. I really like you. Just say a yes to me.

A yes for what?

A yes to marry me.

What? I have not even been thinking about it. Forget marriage, you have not even made the cut as a prospective date.

Don't be in denial. I know you like me.

Really? Have I said or done even one thing to suggest so?

I just know. Can you deny it?

No, truth be told. I like you but I can't explain why I am saying no to you.

Simran warned me not to let you down. I promised her I won't. I don't want to be with anyone else. Please don't say no to me.

Today is not a good day. I need to be alone. I need to make sense of whatever's happened. But I will think about it. I promise.

May I stay with you longer?

I would have said yes, but you need to leave for now. We will talk soon.

Aye, aye captain. I will be back. To hear a yes from you.

Nakul left, obediently. My heart was throbbing like never before.

And then, just like that, Nakul became a part of my daily life. Unless I was at work, he seemed to be omnipresent around me. He would be waiting outside my office to drive me home, he made sure we socialized together, he volunteered to help with any chores, he called all day and all night to talk about everything insignificant under the sun. I let him; it helped to keep my mind off Zulfi.

He had only one sibling, a brother, Bobby. He was some kind of a finance wiz, and was much sought after by the banking sector after his master's in economics. He got a job with the Abu Dhabi Investment Authority, the sovereign investment fund headed by the head of the state himself. He had recently got engaged to his schooltime sweetheart, Kajal, and went around telling everyone about her being his good luck charm. Nakul was hosting a farewell party for him and asked for my help in putting it together. He had made me a co-host and mentioned so in the invites without taking my permission.

A friend of theirs was assigned to take photos for that evening, and he asked Nakul, Bobby and Kajal to come together for a family portrait. Nakul pulled me along and said the picture would have been incomplete without me in it. With everyone watching, he had effectively proposed to me. Just to make sure all those present understood what the photograph signified, he asked me to marry him in a booming voice so no one could miss it. There was a big cheer as it dawned upon all guests present: the playboy Nakul was finally reined in.

I told everyone not to take Nakul seriously since he was totally sloshed. After a while, I pulled him to the balcony and chided him for making a scene. You didn't even ask me before making such a big announcement, I said.

Ok, I will ask you now, Nikita. Will you marry me? Please.

Ask me when you are sober, so you know what you are doing and are responsible for the consequences of your actions.

He responded by pulling me close by the waist, going up on his toes to tower over me, tilting my head towards his, and planting his lips on mine. He kissed, passionately, for a long time. I let him. He had proposed in his style. I had given the answer in mine.

❧

I was scared. I had been betrayed in the past. I had made a promise to myself to never be vulnerable again, never leave any chinks in my amour to be hurt. And yet I said yes to Nakul.

Every time I got involved with a man, it felt different. So it did with Nakul too. But it was differently different. I could not even explain to myself how it was. I felt truly in love. There was no reluctance, no room for doubt, no impulse to pause and analyse. There was a certainty I had not felt for anything in my life. I was never so sure about anyone as I was about Nakul.

I wanted us to be a couple. I wanted us to be family. I wanted a home. I wanted Nakul.

I trusted him. And thus, the heart fractured into millions of fine pieces when he let down my faith. In him. In the idea of us.

❧

There was something very likeable, and lovable, about Nakul as a person. But he would make a hash of things when it came to managing personal equations and sensitivities. He insisted I meet his parents, and I relented despite my reservations. They were delighted with his choice; his mother even presented me with a gold coin to seal the match. But she—and others in his family—were not told about my daughter and pending divorce. When I threw a fit, Nakul was left scratching his head. He just did not get what the issue was.

His parents were coming to town to see Bobby off. They lived in Agra. Nakul wanted me to meet them, but I told him he was rushing it. I was wary about meeting parents, especially after my experience of meeting Kenneth's. Nothing will happen anyway till my divorce, so what's your rush? I asked.

A lunch was planned at his apartment; I agreed to join in when he promised to introduce me as just a friend. I was ready to leave when he came to pick me up, but disapproved of my attire. He fussed over a few dresses till he settled on an Indian suit. He was clearly going to introduce me as more than just a friend. But I didn't raise any last-minute issues and went along.

I may have been imagining it, but I felt all eyes on me through the afternoon. What were they thinking? What did they know about me? We were all lounging with cups of green tea to digest the heavy meal of biryani, seekh kebabs and naan when his mother came up and sat next to me. She opened her bag and gave me the gold coin. I am so happy for Nakul and you, she said. I am glad both my sons have found such good girls.

It was not right. I accepted the gift politely, excused myself, and went into the kitchen. Nakul followed. What was that? I asked.

What do you mean? he asked.

You know very well what I am talking about. Why is your mother addressing me like a future daughter-in-law? We had an understanding.

I didn't tell them anything. She just assumed.

Really? That's crap. What did you tell them?

I didn't. Kajal did.

You are lying again. All of you have obviously discussed this well in advance. Where did the gold coin appear from? Does she carry them around as currency?

Take it easy. If we have decided to marry, how does it matter when they know?

It's not about when they know. It's about what they know. Do they know about my other life, about the past clouding my future? Our future?

No, I will tell them.

And you think your parents will accept me with the same fondness as they did today?

Of course, they will.

No, they will not. They will feel cheated for being kept in the dark. You will never be blamed for it. They will look at me as someone who sneaked into their family on the sly. It will not earn me their love and respect. In all fairness, they deserved to know everything before meeting me. They might still have accepted me the same way as they did now, but they would have seen the complete picture and then made a choice. It's not fair to them, and it's not fair to me.

I know my parents, nothing will change for them when they are told everything. Trust me.

I want to go home. Now.

Please don't. What will I tell them?

That's your problem.

I went back into the living room, made an excuse about being called to office, thanked everyone for the lovely time, hugged his mother and left. I was scared again. What if they reject me when they learn the truth about me?

Grow up, Nakul, I felt like saying it out loud. And be sure you are ready to be someone's husband. Any marriage is a challenge, it will be excessively so with me given the baggage I will be carrying all my life.

Even after Anand went away, Simran would not say or hear a bad word for him. Her soul was still yoked to his; I am sure she was no more than a fading memory for him. But she was forced to call him the scum of the earth when he reneged on his commitment to pay the house rent till they came to a divorce settlement. With her limited budget, she had to move out of her relatively upscale accommodation. We agreed to take an apartment together.

It did not take much to adjust to each other; it just seemed a natural thing to do given our bond. The two of us took the apartment, but it seemed there were three in it. Nakul was almost permanently there. He would bum around in his spare time, going back at night only because I was not yet agreeable to sleeping with him. If I were to spend my life with him, I needed the distance to see him more clearly so I was sure of doing the right thing. If it were anyone else, Simran may have objected to his presence, and rightfully so; but she regarded him a brother and had to be fine with it.

Simran had always enjoyed playing host, and the partying continued in our house. Some of the big names from the fashion and film fraternity dropped out; they were Anand's acquaintances more than Simran's. Their place was taken by authors, journalists and publishers. Whenever some were over, I made a mental note to read more books to be an informed participant in their conversations. But my mind was running in many directions in the current phase of my life and I could not concentrate enough on the reading; I eventually gave up even trying to. I would catch up with it later.

Nakul was happy to be around me, but he would be looking at and following me like a forlorn puppy as the night set in. I knew what he wanted, and there were times when I wanted to lock myself in the room with him, but I needed to test him. I did not want infatuation for me to be mistaken for lifelong love. Nakul's elevated libido also needed to know marriage would not mean it could get what it wanted, whenever it wanted. It needed to learn restraint.

Regard me a friend or a foe, but pay close attention to what I am saying. You are making a big mistake with Nakul. Don't go by the attention and love he is showering on you. He does not know how to treat women right. And don't think I have any selfish motive in saying this to you. Nakul is history for me. I am joining my sister in Canada. She has secured a residency for me there.

I was enjoying a lazy Sunday morning, flipping through Simran's collection of old *Reader's Digest*'s over a bottomless cup of tea when Simi called. I was surprised to see her name flashing on the phone; my first instinct was to ignore the call but I took it anyway. A quick hi was followed by a monologue, warning me about Nakul.

Is this what you called me for? I asked when she paused.

Yes, I thought I should let you know, said Simi.

Why?

To save you from misery and heartburn in the future.

Why do you care about me? I thought you hated me.

I used to. I am indifferent now. Knowing Nakul better now, he was never going to be a permanent feature in my life. If not you, someone else would have come into his life and I would have been out anyway.

And what makes you think I will be miserable with him?

You will see for yourself. Mark my words. You still have time.

I have my own judgment of people.

I am sure you do. Even I thought I did. But we women are so gullible, we always get taken for a ride. We suffer at the hands of men no matter what we do. It is in their nature to cause us pain.

If that is so, then any man will hurt me. So let it be Nakul for now.

He's the worst kind. Look, he's a wonderful guy, that's why it was so unbearable to lose him. But he has a fond eye for women; someone scratched out the word fidelity from his dictionary. I would call him immature. He does not realize how his own follies will come back to haunt him.

Thank you for warning me, but let me decide for myself.

Don't say you were not warned.

Thank you once again. All the best for your new life in Canada. I am sure you will be happy there. I don't mean to sound rude, but please don't ever call me again.

Sure, ciao. She hung up before I could say a bye myself.

My Sunday solitude was shattered. Simi's words would echo for a long time in my head. It took two beers, a bowl of popcorn and a movie in the evening for me to get over her call.

Send me the papers. I will sign them. And will appear in court whenever the hearings are scheduled. But I suggest we don't mention we have a daughter. It will keep things simpler.

It sounded like a miracle. Krishna agreed to a divorce by mutual consent. We would file a petition with terms agreeable to both. All the court had to do was pass the decree since there would be no further disputes to be resolved. If things went as per procedure, we could be legally separated in six months.

Neither party sought financial compensation of any kind from the other. He had nothing to offer as alimony or to compensate me for the jewellery he had stolen. I wrote everything off. He was getting away with all the wrongs he had committed. Why don't you want to mention Vani? I asked.

It is mandatory for all children over three years old to appear in court for questioning. It will cause Vani unnecessary trauma, he explained. Cases where the couple do not have children are also disposed of quicker. You can anyway take Vani with you after the court issues the divorce decree.

I took the suggestion on face value. Since it was a straightforward case between consenting adults by now, I had engaged a relatively inexperienced lawyer with a modest practice to save costs. She did not give me the right advice about Vani. As expected, the judge granted the divorce without a fuss.

The day after receiving the order, I went to his house with my sister to pick up Vani. He stood at the door, his arms stretched as if blocking the entry to the house.

Hi, I said with a smile. I was so euphoric that day.

Hi, he said.

So here I am.

What for?

To pick Vani.

Pick Vani? Today? Did we discuss it?

No, but I assumed I could take her today.

You know we decide in advance when you can meet.

But I am not here to meet her. I am here to take her.

Take her where?

To Delhi, with me.

What for?

We agreed upon that. I will get her custody after the divorce.

He let out a laugh to make a clan of hyenas proud. It was vicious and ominous. You see that street dog out there, he asked pointing to one behind me.

Yes.

Everyone is careful of him. He's supposedly mad.

So?

This mad dog—or for that matter no mad dog—has bitten me. What makes you think I will let you take Vani?

He was mocking at me, humiliating me, making me feel small. But she is my daughter, and it is my right to have her, I said.

Really? But you told the court that you have no daughter.

That was for the court. We had an understanding.

We had other understandings, too. But you chose to abandon your husband and infant child to lead a life of revelry.

This is nonsense. You know why I left. But I continued to work hard. And send the money you would demand.

Anyway, go away. There is nothing or no one here for you.

He shut the door in my face. I was crying. I wanted to shout, break the door down but my sister restrained me. Take it easy, she said. He's played dirty. You cannot outmuscle him. We have to seek redressal from the courts only. We will consult a good lawyer and get back at him. It is best we leave for now.

And we did. I could not stop kicking myself for being so stupid. What was I smoking when I agreed to deny my daughter's existence in court? What could have been a more absurd thing to say? In another country, I could have been behind bars for lying under oath. But I wanted Krishna out of my life desperately, so I could start a new one with Nakul at the earliest. With Vani a part of it. I may have made things worse in trying to rush through the matter.

Go and get married. There is nothing you can do right away. But there is a lot you can do in due course. Even though you gave a false declaration in court, we will find a way for you to get legal custody of Vani. You cannot be denied. Remember, he also lied in court about a daughter. But for now, don't hold your life back.

I would have lost my mind if Simran and Nakul had not been around. They made me their top priority. They spent hours talking to me, consoling me, showing me hope. It helped. I gathered my wits within days and called Harish chacha, the hotshot lawyer in the family. I had avoided talking to him about my case after his recommended attorney had tried to take advantage of my vulnerability. There was no one else to turn to.

By then he was heading the bar council of the state, and no one dared take him lightly. Not even the judges. He set up a meeting with Daljeet Sahni, a kind looking Sikh with a brain famous—and infamous—for winning the trickiest of cases. His flair caused dread amongst the opposition, and evoked awe even in the most upright and nonpartisan of judges.

Daljeet heard me out, not taking his gaze away from me for even a moment while I spoke. He wrote without looking at his pad. When I was done, he reviewed his notes, thought for a while, and then told me to go ahead and get married. He advised me to stay patient and to not fret much. The law cannot deny me my right, he assured me. It was just a matter of time.

My life had been reduced to clutching at every straw of hope. I left the meeting with Daljeet feeling good. If there was someone who could win the battle for Vani, it was him.

❧

One day, rather night, just like that, without consulting me, Nakul was at my door. With two overstuffed suitcases, a couple of boxes, and some loose items. He looked more like a mobile flea market than my future husband.

What are you doing here? I asked.

I am here, to be with you, said Nakul.

What's the deal with these bags and boxes?

That's my stuff. All of it.

Why are you carrying it around with you?

I am moving in with you.

Says who?

Says my love for you. I cannot stay away any longer.

He walked through me, or so it seemed, and entered the house as if it were his own. He plonked himself, and all his belongings, in my room. Hey listen, I said. You just can't move in like this. You should have discussed with me at least. And even Simran needs to give her approval. It's not just my place.

I am sure she will be fine. And if we are getting married soon, she might as well get used to it, he said.

Simran heard us talk and came out of her room. What's happening here at this late hour? she asked. We stepped out of the room to show her.

Your dear brother is moving in with us, I said.

With us? Says who?

Says Nakul and his baggage, I said.

Nakul just grinned, went over to Simran, hugged her and said he won't be a bother at all. And will move out after we are married, which will be soon now that all obstacles have been removed.

Have you already fixed a date? asked Simran looking at me.

Not me, I said. If he has, I don't know. Maybe he has told some other girl.

Oh, come on Niki, said Nakul. Your divorce is through, there shouldn't be any delay now. No reason to.

We need to talk Nakul, I said. Sorry Simran, I had no idea he's coming in like this. If you want to throw him out right away, you can count on me to lend a hand.

No, it's ok for now. We will figure it out tomorrow, I am sleepy anyway. Good night, said Simran and went back to her room.

Let's talk, I said. I walked into my room, and he followed me like a puppy.

I have told my parents. Everything. My mother did not seem to have a problem with your past; she said she was fine with whatever I decide. My father asked why I was rushing matters; I may want to give myself some more time to think through everything.

Nakul knew I would not discuss any wedding plans till he told his parents all that they needed to know about me. And he blurted out their reaction without waiting for me to ask.

And they did not oppose our match? I asked.

They tried to, in their own way. I put my foot down. If I don't marry you, I will not marry anyone, I declared to them. Bobby can give them a daughter-in-law and a brood of grandkids, they should not expect anything from me, he said.

And have you thought through everything?

Yes. Why do you think I am here, like this?

This is not the same. Marriage is a different ball game altogether. I hope you know what you are getting into. Your father is right.

I love you, and I know I want to settle down with you.

You should know I will be fine even if we don't marry. You don't have to go through with this if you have any doubts.

I want to.

Getting Vani back and bringing her up will always be top priority for me. Everything and everybody is dispensable in comparison. I don't mean to sound harsh or heartless, but you should know this. I have battles waiting ahead.

I know. I will be by your side all through. Not just in getting her, but also in raising her.

You don't know what it is to raise a child.

Neither do you. We will learn together.

He was right. What did I know of bringing up a child? For that matter, what did I know of marriage too? There was nothing noteworthy about my previous one. I was on the defensive from the word go; there was never an opportunity to build a relationship between a husband and a wife.

I would have enough time with Nakul to. For now, he was despatched off to sleep on the couch in the living room. He may have moved into my house, but not into my bedroom. Yet.

Kenneth came back, pleading. Ravi called too, asking for my hand again in his usual dignified style. Sumit, a common friend, threatened to derail my plans with Nakul. Friends and colleagues did not desist from trying to hook me up with other guys; they did not expect my engagement with Nakul to last long. Men came or were thrown at me from all directions, but I swatted them away with amusement. My resolve to marry Nakul was set in stone.

Nakul knew of all the guys trying to get back with me—I had told him about everyone who had been a part of my past. He offered to tell me about the women he had been with, but I told him to let it be. The list would weigh a telephone directory, information I had no use of. I would handle the situation as and when any blast from his past tried to cause any trouble.

Kenneth sent me an old-fashioned postcard and a letter, apologizing profusely, asking me to wait for him, talking of how he screwed up and how much he misses me and loves me. I read and added them to my pile of personal papers. He called unexpectedly one day to tell me that he was in Delhi and wanted to meet me; I invited him home.

He was behaving like he was a few drinks down when he reached my place and readily accepted a beer when I offered. He enquired about my work, about Vani and about life in Delhi. He made small talk, evading the point of his visit. The alcohol level in his body reached the tipping point, and he lost a grip on himself. He started crying. I didn't know what to do, where to look. I just sat patiently till he quietened down.

I am so sorry, I messed up. I cannot live without you, he said.

You had your chance Kenneth, and I was all yours. Yes, you screwed up and no one is to blame but you, I said.

We can still be together. It is not too late.

It is. I am getting married.

You are? You never told me.

Was I expected to have? You are not even supposed to be here. But you just showed up.

Who is he?

His name is Nakul. He should be back any time now, you can meet him.

As if on cue, Nakul rang the doorbell. He knew Kenneth was over. I introduced the two of them, and went to the kitchen to warm up the samosas I had prepared earlier. I was hungry, and surely the others would be too. Anyhow, I wanted to create a distraction.

I served lemonade with the munchies; the bar was closed for the evening, or at least till Kenneth was around. The soda sobered him a bit; I wanted him to leave on his own before I had to ask him to. Instead, he asked Nakul to. She is mine, she always will be. She will never be happy with you. You should go away and leave us alone, he said. It was sudden, and unexpected. I was expecting the men to come to blows.

But Nakul kept his cool—at least pretended to. He laughed at Kenneth's words. Sorry buddy, he said, it's too late. I can't. It's your loss.

Kenneth didn't speak further. He kept looking down at his drink, as if hypnotized by it. And then he passed out. We let him be. Nakul took off his shoes, loosened his trousers and covered him with a blanket. He would wake up the following morning only.

He did, looking visibly downcast. He mumbled an apology for having drunk too much and being an inconvenience. We told him not to worry, everything was ok. No one brought up the conversations of the previous evening. We had breakfast and then he left. But not without congratulating us and wishing us a happy life together. Phew!

Ravi called a few days later; he was coming to Delhi and wanted to meet me. Would be tough, I said.

I wanted to talk to you, he said.

About what?

I will not mince any words. I want us to resume from where we left off.

It's not possible now.

Why? Are you seeing someone?

Kind of. I am marrying this someone.

Oh, he said and went quiet for a few seconds. I waited. Well, all I can say is congratulations, he said. I am truly happy for you. Your husband is a very lucky man.

And I am a very lucky woman to have found him.

Good one. When are you getting married?

In about two months.

Will you invite me?

No, might not be ok to.

I know, was kidding. Can I send you a wedding gift?

What do you want to send?

A television and a washing machine?

Are you my daddy?

No.

Then don't. Just stay happy for me. And find yourself a good girl to marry. You need to.

I found one but she didn't want to marry me. Anyway, all the best. And stay in touch.

Thanks, ciao.

Phew! This one passed smoothly too, I said to myself. What is it with these guys? Why were they suddenly crawling out of the woodwork to stake a claim on me?

Sumit was a different proposition altogether though. I used to meet him at Anand's parties; his job was to scout for aspiring models who wanted their portfolio shot by a top photographer for a fee. He would always try to cosy up to me, but I found him utterly repulsive. But he was not one to be deterred easily.

I was stuck without transport home late night once, and there was no one at hand except him to drop me. I agreed reluctantly. All through the drive, he tried to get me to invite him home but I kept declining as politely as I could. When we reached my place, he followed me up to the front door and tried to go in with me. When I blocked the passage in, he grabbed me and started kissing and groping me on the landing itself. I struggled, and tried not to scream lest I wake the neighbours. He left me with no choice but to strike him between the legs with my knee in self-defence; he withdrew in pain, and I rushed in and locked the door before he could regain his balance.

I bumped into him after months at another party where Nakul was talking boisterously about marrying me. I could feel his eyes on me all evening, and he cornered me finally when I stepped out for a smoke. Getting married I heard, he said.

Yes, I am, I replied.

What makes you think you will be able to?

What do you mean?

Do you think I will let you?

Who the fuck do you think you are? You don't matter.

You bet I do. I will make sure your lover boy Nakul does not marry you.

Go fuck yourself. This time I will not strike your balls, I will cut them, fry them, and feed them to stray dogs. Or maybe not. Those dogs have done no wrong to be inflicted your filthy bits.

You wait and see, you arrogant bitch. You will be sorry for this, he said and walked away.

Nakul's mother called two days later. We were in the car together when she did; he put her on speakerphone to avoid being booked by cops. Who is Sumit? she asked.

I don't know, Nakul said.

He called. He said he's known Nikita for a long time.

Yes, I have heard his name being mentioned. What about him?

He was saying things about Nikita I did not like.

Things like?

They are too disgusting to be repeated. But he was suggesting our family should not be taking in someone of her character. She will bring shame and ruin upon us, as she had on her ex-husband.

Come on, ma, you want to believe strangers?

I know, but we should not just ignore them either. Maybe you want to delve into this matter further.

I am not doing any such thing.

Then I suggest you get married soon. We don't want mischief-mongers running amok.

Sure, I am happy to be getting married sooner. I will talk to Nikita. Don't pick up calls from scoundrels like Sumit again. Bye.

He looked at me and laughed. Another jilted lover licking his wounds, he said.

No, another male whose ego cannot accept being rejected by a woman. A friend of Anand, each as disgusting as the other, I said.

Yeah, I know those kinds. Anyway, you heard my mom—she wants us to get married quickly. So let's do it.

You choose any date and let me know. I will be fine with it.

Even as I waited for the big day, friends were making last-ditch efforts to hook me up with someone more 'worthy' than Nakul. In fact, my elder brother Aman had found a match for me in Singapore; I must admit I was tempted to say yes to go further away from the toxic environment I was living in. When I told him about Nakul, he did not take it too kindly. He developed a dislike for Nakul even without knowing him, but he did become cordial with him by the time we got married.

Of course, I had no intention of being with anyone else but Nakul. The suitors were massaging my ego, and I was having the last laugh seeing the state of men like Kenneth. Life was entertaining me thoroughly even if it was not ideal yet.

❧

In all this, Simran was getting crabbier by the day. Her cheerful demeanour was cracking.

Our personal situations had flipped. While I was preparing to get married, she was getting divorced. If the separation wasn't bad enough for her, Anand was making it worse with his conduct. He was not sticking to his end of the bargain of sending her the promised moneys; it would come in bits and never as scheduled. Her lifestyle was plummeting as her own income was not consistent and never enough.

I knew Nakul should not have moved in; his presence was making it worse for her. He was sleeping in my room now, and our lovey-dovey selves was making her miserable. She was drinking more than usual, and would tend to snap at the slightest of provocation. We were fighting for the first time, as were she and Nakul. She would disappear from the house without informing me, and not come back all night at times. I would get worried, but she would say it was none of my concern.

Nakul finally took the matter in his own hands and offered that we move out. Of course, that was a problem because Simran could not afford the place by herself. Eventually, she herself opted to move in with a former colleague; it was perfect as we could stay put and do up the place as we wanted it to be.

It pained me to see Simran leave; she was a sister to me. But it was only sensible that she did. Her fortunes changed quickly for the better. The Internet boom was upon us, and start-ups were hiring any talent available at whatever price they demanded. She got a job with a portal as their features editor, commanding a salary far exceeding what Anand was expected to give her. She bounced back to her old self, and she and I were in love again.

I need not have despaired much on the Vani front. Her father allowed me increased access to her; I had a free run to spend as much time with her as I wanted to when in Jaipur. But I was under no illusions about a change in Krishna's heart; his hand was forced. He had no money to even pay for her schooling and had to ask me to cover the expense. Now that we were divorced, he could no longer arm-twist me and had to be 'nice' to me. More so after my new lawyer Daljeet Sahni had a strongly worded piece of advice for him.

If you are fancying yourself being a cunning fox in legal matters, then it would be a case of misplaced identity, the lawyer told Krishna. You are just a rookie in the game. The wrong has been committed by both parents so you cannot just usurp the mother's custodial rights to Vani. If she is not her parent for the court, neither are you. So if you do not want the police enquiring where you got a child from, then you better behave yourself with Nikita. And settle this matter in a reasonable and amicable manner.

Krishna tried to argue, but Daljeet advised him not to. When he gave advice, it was best to treat it as an order you should not disobey.

The higher frequency of trips enabled Vani to recognize me and bond with me as her mother. She was also spending more time with my brothers, my sister and her kids when I was not in town. Yes, Radha didi had got married again while I was away and gave birth to a boy and a girl with her new husband. She was bringing up four children—her husband had one from his previous marriage.

Of course, Krishna was not wired to play straight. I had been sending him money to pay for Vani's education but he was skimming part of it for himself. The school was threatening to take her off the rolls for the shortfall in payables. A few weeks before our wedding, Nakul and I made a trip to her school. Vani was moving to the first grade, and we had to buy her new books, supplies and uniforms. We made an arrangement to send the fees directly, and not through her father. All dues were settled by us.

We took her to my father's place after the school shopping, and Vani was gleefully showing off her new acquisitions to Raghav, her younger uncle.

This is lovely. Where did you get these from? he asked.

Mumma's boyfriend bought it for me, she said pointing to Nakul. I could not help feeling in seventh heaven hearing her call me mumma. She had been addressing me as her mother of late, but my heart soared every time she did.

How do you know he's her boyfriend? Raghav asked.

He's her friend. And he's a boy. So boyfriend, she said.

We all laughed. My girl will do fine for herself; she's a smart cookie already, I said to myself.

What am I doing? Why am I marrying again? Am I ready for it? What was my rush to bind myself to someone? Why was I mortgaging my hard-fought freedom?

I did not have any clear answers to my own questions, and that was unnerving. The first marriage was a nightmare I still had to wake up from; it would haunt me till I got custody of my daughter.

Even after I get Vani, will my problems be over? He may be showing a fondness for her but will Nakul adopt her as his own? Will his parents too? More so after I have children with Nakul. Will they let me have it easy?

Ours would be the first wedding in Nakul's family. They would want to do it with all pomp and show. But I can't ask my ailing father to put in the effort and money again given his precarious state. And any high-profile ceremonies in Jaipur would be a no-no. It will seem out of place, and I certainly did not want Krishna to assume I have come into wealth. His demands would go up, to be met using Vani as blackmail.

What about my professional ambitions? I made a mistake once. I gave up my aspirations to be in the fashion industry when I married Krishna. Was I being a fool in letting history repeat itself? I was already passing lucrative career opportunities to avoid any conflict with the life I was readying for with Nakul. I had an offer to head communications for an international chain of hotels; they had recently been licenced to operate in India, but I was required to relocate down south to Madras. I had another option to move to Hong Kong. If I stayed flexible and mobile, or single in other words, there would be no dearth of opportunities given my track record and the reputation I had built for myself within the hospitality industry.

I had choices to make. My head was bursting for days and weeks on end. I needed help. There was only one person who I could have turned to in the hour of dilemma: myself. I should have. I did not. I should have put on my hearing aids to amplify what my instincts, my gut, my experience were telling me. Instead, I stuffed cotton in my ears to drown out all voices.

I got dressed for the wedding without waiting for any answers.

I got married. To Nakul. And his mother too. That's what it seemed like, considering she parked herself on our honeymoon bed until the wee hours.

We finally settled on holding the ceremonies in Agra, Nakul's hometown. He took care of all expenses for a grand reception and got personally involved in the arrangements. The caterers left the guests licking their fingers. The musicians ensured the foot-tapping did not stop. The bootleggers stocked the bar with the finest of whiskies and wines from across the world to give guests a high they may have rarely experienced.

The party ended for Nakul before it did for the guests. Even as they danced and made merry, he lifted me off my feet and carried me to an open limousine rented for the evening. We sat on the back seats, and his mother plonked herself in the front. I figured she had to come along to perform the rituals to welcome the new bride home.

I was mistaken. She was not one for too many customs; I preferred it that way too. Nakul's room, the one he grew up in, had been decorated with flowers for the newlywed couple to consummate their marriage in. We went in, and my mother-in-law followed to check if everything was in order. She did and then sat on our bed. Maybe she just wanted to talk to us. I was right, she wanted to. All kinds of stuff, including gossip about relatives, her bridge club, their life when her husband served in the air force and any trivialities she could come up with. She finally wished us a happy married life, and left. At five in the morning. I fell asleep instantly in my heavy bridal wear.

I woke to loud knocking on our door; it was only eight. I had not even slept three hours. It was my mother-in-law. All the relatives are coming over soon, and they will be hungry, she said.

So? I asked.

It is tradition for the bride to cook the first meal for everyone.

You want me to cook?

Of course.

By what time?

They are expected by ten. And no one would have had breakfast in anticipation of the treat.

How many people will be there?

Around forty.

Forty? How will I cook for so many people? And what do you want me to cook?

Will you keep asking questions or go to the kitchen?

I am not ready yet.

Then what are you waiting for? Get ready quickly and come.

She left, and I turned to look at Nakul, still in bed; the commotion woke him up. I gave him a quizzical look. You never told me about the cooking, I said. And that too for so many people at such short notice.

Even I didn't know. I am sure you will manage.

You know I hate cooking. And I have never cooked for so many at one go. I am so exhausted, I can barely stand.

Come on now, don't fret. Best to get ready and go down without further delay. I will follow.

I freshened up, pretended to have bathed and put on a yellow saree with minimal make-up and no jewellery. Are you going to show yourself looking so plain? asked my mother-in-law.

I can't cook in anything heavier.

We all have when it was our time to. Why can't you?

I am not used to it.

Then get used to it. Anyway, change into something more appropriate before the guests arrive. Get the cooking done in the meantime.

I stood in the kitchen, my mind blank. I was tired. And irritated. Where do I start? I wondered.

An aunt of Nakul, who had stayed over, came in and offered to help. Don't worry, she said. We have all gone through this day. But someone always helps out. Come, let's do this together.

Relieved, I got down to the job in the right earnest. We prepared a big pot of mutton biryani along with sides of mint flavoured yogurt, salad, potato cutlets and kebabs. I changed into a bright green saree and put on a gold necklace and earrings before the first of the guests came in. There was no sanctity of time; the last ones trickled in only by two in the afternoon. We had to reheat the food multiple times.

When the last of the guests had been fed, my mother-in-law stood up to address them. It is so wonderful to have all of you over, it's a big day for us, she said. I know some of you would have liked a different meal, but it had to be prepared by Nikita as is the tradition. But she will learn of our tastes and standards over time. She has to for Nakul's sake anyway; he is very particular about his food. I can't send meals for him from Agra every day.

Everyone laughed, but I did not see what was funny. I ran to our room, and could not hold myself back from howling. Nakul followed and asked what the matter was.

How can your mother talk like this? I asked.

Come on, she was just joking. Didn't you hear everyone laugh? he said.

Laughter or mockery? I am sorry, but I don't subscribe to such humour.

You are making a big deal of nothing.

Really? Don't you see what your mother is up to? Why was she with us till early morning?

Come on, she loves me and must have been all excited with you joining the family.

There was so much I wanted to retort with but I did not want to slide into a quicksand of an argument. I gave in for then, and did not discuss the issue further. In any case, we were in Agra only for a couple of days. How bad could it get?

❧

My office colleagues had pooled in to gift us a three-day honeymoon in the luxurious Lake Palace hotel in the romantic city of Udaipur in my home state of Rajasthan. My mother-in-law came to me while I was packing to tell me she found the whole plan absurd and unnecessary, and should be cancelled. And while she was at it, she also tried to show me my place in the family.

I did not think Nakul had such a heart, she said.

Heart for what? I asked.

We never imagined he would marry someone like you. Considering your background, what your personal life has been.

What's wrong with my life?

You know it. The divorce, a child and all that. No amount of gratitude would be enough for his gesture.

I wanted to count till ten before I screamed at her. Before I socked her. Before I summoned Nakul to ask what he had been projecting to his family. But I kept quiet, and continued to keep stuff in the suitcase.

It's just been two days since you got married. What's your rush to leave? she asked.

It is peak season for us at work. Even the trip to Udaipur will be a squeeze, but my boss has been most understanding. The flights and hotel have been booked tomorrow onwards so we don't have a choice, I said.

You really think I will let you leave so soon?

What do you mean?

You want to take Nakul away for a honeymoon? I don't understand why it's so important.

It is important to us, we are starting a new life together. It's really been a thoughtful gesture from my colleagues; they knew we are really stretched for money and would not have been able to afford the trip on our own.

Why did you make Nakul spend so much on the wedding?

I did not, I wanted a simple affair. Even a court marriage would have been good for me. But he wanted it this way; I did ask him more than once if we could afford to indulge in such an extravagance.

The conversation was getting uncomfortable, but Nakul walked in just then. He asked what we were talking about.

Oh, I was just showing Nikita how to pack more efficiently for the trip. How to fold clothes in the suitcase, what stuff to carry and so on, said his mother. I looked at her incredulously, amazed at how quickly the chameleon changed her colours.

Ok, he said, and went about putting his work papers together to take back. I wanted to tell Nakul what we were really talking about, but stopped myself in the interest of peace. We are leaving tomorrow as scheduled, right? I asked him.

Yes, of course, he said. And we did. I managed to take the son away from his mother soon after the wedding, but feared for the unrest ahead. The mother-in-law was drawing battlelines but I had no clue what victory she was after anyway.

Whatever you do on the first day of January is supposed to be a harbinger for the year ahead. Or so the superstition goes. If that were so, then it would be best to spend the cold day under the duvet with Nakul. I could do with a less tumultuous period in my life.

And then the doorbell rang. My mother-in-law, Bobby and Kajal dropped in unannounced. With packed bags. It was their idea of a new year surprise. Did you know they were coming? I asked Nakul when we were by ourselves for a bit.

Nope, he said.

Are you sure?

Why are you getting edgy? You sound as if it's bothering you.

It is. I have no problem if they come to stay with us, but shouldn't they inform us? And it's just been two days since we returned from our honeymoon. What was their rush to be with us?

Why are we even discussing this? Anyway, they are family. We don't have to be formal with each other. They are here, let's make them comfortable, he said and left the room.

Nakul and I were still not settled in as a married couple. A lot of work was pending in the house. The pressure of work in office was not helping either. A sense of foreboding filled me. Bobby was returning to Abu Dhabi in a few days, and this was a kind of seeing-him-off visit. And also to discuss arrangements for his wedding with Kajal later in the year. The timing could not have been more inappropriate from my point of view. There was more to this visit than was meeting the eye.

Nakul's mother had dropped by a few times while we were living together before marriage. She had been the sweetest of souls then, asking after me, talking fondly about being a family, helping about the house, even packing my lunch for office. A different woman was staying with us now. She would not lift a finger, and did not have a kind word for me. I was a princess to her when I was her son's fiancé; as his wife, she had demoted me to a lowly servant. Nakul too was a transformed person in her presence. From being an indulgent partner when it was just the two of us, he would barely speak around his mother even when she was clearly in the wrong. He would make matters worse by berating me for my protestations.

She seemed to derive some kind of perverse pleasure by jumping into our bed whenever she could. She even slept off between us twice during that visit while we took an afternoon siesta. It got particularly weird during an early morning intrusion when she made herself cosy in our duvet and got chatting. A few minutes later, I felt a sensation along my leg. She was sliding my full-length night gown up with her foot. Just then, Bobby was passing by the open door and she called him and Kajal in with their tea. They sat on the chairs, facing us.

You should dress more appropriately when you have house guests over, she remarked all of a sudden. I had no idea what she was implying. I was covered head to toe to keep myself warm, in a satin gown she herself had presented me. Before I could respond to her comment, she threw the duvet aside to reveal my exposed thighs—her foot had pushed my gown up. See what I mean? she said.

I had never been so humiliated. I looked at her, then at Bobby, then at Kajal to check if they had seen anything before I covered my legs. I then turned to Nakul who just sat expressionless. I waited for him to say something, but he did not. I got up, and darted to the washroom. Locking myself in, I sat on the pot and cried. And cried and cried.

Where am I stuck? What kind of a family have I married into? Do I even know the man who is supposedly my life partner? Was history repeating itself? Should I have listened to my intuition and not committed myself to someone all over again? These questions kept swirling in my head, picking up pace like a tornado till I reached detonation point. I threw up, all over myself.

I could visualize my sister looking at me, glum, arms folded across her chest. She was not urging me to run, but she was quite disapproving of yet another mess I had landed myself in.

I must have been Nakul's lucky charm. No sooner were we engaged than he started getting calls from some of the biggest companies in the world. They wanted him to hack into and sabotage their computer systems.

That is what Nakul was trained for—find holes in technologies and plug them before miscreants broke in. While his clientele were mostly penny-pinching Indian companies before our engagement, it became increasingly international soon after. He began earning more in a day than he would in the entire month earlier. It took us a while to get used to the quantum of money he was bringing in.

But such career advancement was not good news for us as a couple. It would require him to travel, for weeks or even months at a time, to wherever his clients were. A big break with Siemens would take him to Europe for at least two months. We made the most of the three weeks we had together before he left. Even though we were both extremely busy with work, we made time to do stuff together. We splurged on shopping for the house with the advance payment from the contract, watched movies, enjoyed our date nights and revelled in phenomenal sex. Things were amorous and loving between us. I was happy.

The thought of being without him for an extended period was unsettling though, and I wanted to go along. He said he would be ok with it but I should realize we would barely have time together. He would be working day and night, taking breaks only to nap and to shower. I still wanted to go; it would be better than being in Delhi. Of course, I had my work too. I cut a deal with my boss to work seven days a week before and after the trip; he gave me three weeks off in lieu of the extra labour.

I was all clingy and weepy when Nakul was leaving, but gleefully joined him in Berlin within a month. It was a new world for me, something I had seen in movies only. Nakul had warned me about the time he would have for me but I barely missed him. I got busy exploring every nook and corner of the city with a public transport pass Nakul bought on the first day itself. I tried all the food and wine my budget allowed, and sprawled in gardens to read books despite the biting cold. I took trains to neighbouring towns and villages to get a feel of traditional Germany. You could have hired me as a guide to Berlin by the end of it.

We were staying in an apartment provided by the clients, and I would cook for us daily. We were trying to save every Deutsche Mark possible. Nakul was also glad for the break from European fare; nothing beat the aroma of Indian spices wafting through the tiny apartment. I would pack him something for the day too; he preferred that to the cafeteria meals. He must have shared some of the food in office; everyone loved it. About twenty of them got him to invite them to our apartment to savour more of it.

How will I cook for so many people? I asked Nakul. I don't have the utensils to prepare and serve in, nor is there space for so many people.

I am sure you will figure something out. Remember, they don't know anything about our food. So prepare whatever you can and they will have to relish it, he said.

I imagined myself in the shoes of one of the chefs back at the workplace: how would he manage such a situation? I figured. I went to an Indian store selling stuff I could use. I struck up a conversation with the owners while purchasing the required ingredients. I shared my predicament with them.

They offered, and I readily accepted, to lend larger cooking utensils from their home. And they suggested I cook in batches in advance and store in the freezer.

The dinner turned out to be perfect. We had given a time of seven in the evening, and everyone was there at the appointed hour. I was surprised with the punctuality for an informal evening. I loved the gifts they brought for me—wines, cheeses, chocolates, perfumes, a shirt and local souvenirs. The seniors in the company could not stop complimenting the wonderful and beautiful hostess who served them a meal they had not even heard of before. I had prepared yellow dal, chicken masala and rice, served with naan from the Indian store.

Thank you for the wonderful meal and for being such a gracious hostess, said Hans, a senior executive who directly sanctioned Nakul's contracts.

It was a delight to have you all over, I said. I tried to keep the spices mild, we didn't want any of you to develop a Delhi Belly.

What's that?

It's an upset stomach you would get if you are not careful with what you eat and drink when in India. Foreigners are quite susceptible to it, our systems have developed high tolerance levels for it though.

I am sure we are going to be fine. So what do you do back in India?

I manage communication for a hospitality brand.

Have you always lived in India?

Yes, this is my first trip outside the country.

Do you like it here?

I am loving it.

You should move here.

I would love to, but how can I? What will I do here? I don't even have work permits.

You could go to university here, and use the qualifications to get a job.

I doubt if I can afford to study here.

This is what is great about Germany. All tuition is free. You can easily cover your living costs by working part-time.

Really? That's a thought.

So when can we expect you to move here?

I will keep it in mind. I have to go back home for now, I have personal matters to take care of.

If you don't mind, may I ask what it is? You have a worried expression when you talk about personal issues. Of course, if you don't want to, you don't have to share it. And do pardon me if I overstepped.

No, it's not a secret. I have a daughter from my previous marriage. And I have to get her custody back from my ex-husband. A complicated legal battle is on.

These things can be tough. I am sorry to hear this. I do hope it gets sorted, I wish you all the best.

Thank you so much, I really appreciate it.

You are welcome. We should leave now. But if you need anything while you are here, please don't hesitate to call me or any of my colleagues. We would be happy to assist. Thank you once again for a memorable meal.

Nakul was beaming after they left. His stock certainly went up further with them; he was sure to get more lucrative assignments in the future. He did, the following morning itself. His stay had to be extended for another month at least.

But mine came to an end. The three weeks had passed in a flash. I howled again at the airport. Nakul asked me to stay on, but I had a job to go back to. You can quit, he suggested. We don't need the money. I can't, I said. It's not just about the money. It's about me never being dependent on anyone else's money and support again.

He looked confused. He did not understand the point I was making.

You are in my place. I have no idea what made Nakul say no to me. The families were agreeable, and plans for a future together were already on the drawing board. And then you came into the picture and ruined them.

Rina was dancing with me, and was blabbering away under the influence of alcohol. Or drugs. I was attending a wedding reception with Nakul's parents in Agra. He expected me to visit them every weekend while he was away, and my mother-in-law required me to doll up and tag along to her social engagements. No one would bother asking if I was interested in going or not; I was just expected to do their bidding.

She introduced me to Rina and her mother at the wedding. Nakul was supposed to marry Rina but you bewitched him before that, she said for all to hear as if it were a joke. Tact was certainly not a trait known to her. My father-in-law, a fine man, asked if I wanted a drink—as a courtesy, and to change the topic. I requested for a screwdriver. The evening was quite warm, and I did not take too long to finish it—and requested another one.

By then Ronak, Rina's brother, had joined us. He was visiting from the US. While his mother was trying to extol the great things he was pursuing in America, his mannerisms suggested he worked as a janitor or a taxi driver. He might not be but I was getting irritable and was in the mood to be mean to people—even if in my own mind without making an overt show of it. Ronak volunteered to get me my drink, and scampered off towards the bar before anyone else could.

Rina took my hand and led me to the dance floor, away from the oldies as she described the parents. That's when she started ruing about how she could have been the one with Nakul. I didn't react, focusing on my drink instead to avoid being dragged into any controversy. Through the corner of my eye, I could see my father-in-law's gaze fixed on me as if something was bothering him but I couldn't figure what.

Something did not feel right about my drink. The tumbler was three-quarters empty when I suddenly felt sick. I excused myself and headed to the nearest ladies washroom. I opened the door to find Ronak standing inside, grinning. Before I could make sense of anything, I passed out.

When I came to, I saw my father-in-law trying to comfort me and offering me water to drink. What happened to me? I asked and started crying. I don't understand.

I understand, he said. Don't worry, let's go home.

He helped me get up, and supported me all the way to the car. I threw up before we sat in the car, and thrice on the way. And a few times through the night. In all this, I could only hear my mother-in-law chiding me for not being able to carry myself after drinking, for embarrassing her, for sullying the family's reputation and giving the town something to gossip about. I had less than two mild cocktails; I can hold much more before I lose it. There was something else to it.

I had a train to catch the following morning to get to office on time. On the way, my father-in-law consoled me, assuring me I was not at fault. I will get to the bottom of this, he said.

I managed to reach home, but couldn't lift myself to go anywhere despite having important meetings scheduled for the day. I finally went to a doctor who took blood and urine samples. The reports showed the presence of a date-rape drug, referred to as horse drug at that time, in my system.

Ronak had fetched my second drink, and only he could have added something to it. I told Nakul and his parents but no one did anything about it. My mother-in-law refused to blame Ronak for it; he was her close friend's son and could commit no wrong. Nakul's father ordered everyone to break all contact with Rina and her family. He seldom gave orders, but no one disobeyed when he did.

A few years later, we heard Ronak had been busted in a drug raid in Los Angeles. From what we knew, jailers usually throw the key away when they lock up drug dealers like him. My mother-in-law would still not accept what he did to me.

What more did he intend doing with me? Rape me? Defame me to avenge his sister? What if my father-in-law had not kept an eye on me all through that evening?

Hadn't I told you to run? Radha didi's words were again echoing in my head.

It was the last flight of the day to Jaipur, and it was delayed. I was a bundle of nerves and emotions. The doctors had given my father only a few hours to live, and we were stuck at the airport during that vital period. Of all the days, why did the flight have to be delayed today? And then cancelled altogether?

My dad's health had been deteriorating rapidly for a few months, and the doctors only had palliative care to offer. I tried to spend as much time as I could with him while he was still chugging along. Despite knowing he would not be with us much longer, my mother-in-law would keep pressuring me to spend time with her in Agra. I would protest to Nakul, but he would barely open his mouth. Why did she want me around her when she only had barbs directed towards me?

I had taken two days off to spend an extended weekend with dad when I got a call from the office. I was required to go to Hyderabad for an urgent presentation; I was not given a choice. My father was not pleased, but he could not voice his concerns; he had no energy left to speak. I begged God to keep him alive at least until I returned. To his credit, Nakul offered to go along, seeing how distraught I was.

Fortunately, the presentation went well but we were scheduled to fly back the day following the meeting. Dad is sinking, Aman called to say. He might not live to see the morning.

I panicked. I needed to rush back. Nakul went down to the hotel's travel desk and found a flight leaving in two hours for Delhi. Only business class seats were available, but this was not the time to think about money. We swiped his credit card and also made a reservation for the onward flight to Jaipur.

While we waited at the airport, Nakul called his parents so they could comfort me. He had the speakerphone on so we could speak to his father together. We will come for the ceremony, let us know when, I heard his mother call out in the background.

I lost it. He's still alive, and he will come to your ceremony before you attend his, I screamed out. The whole airport must have heard it. Nakul disconnected the call promptly. He looked at me as if I were some kind of a witch, screeching the way I was.

And then the airlines announced the cancellation of the flight altogether. I might have strangled an Indian Airlines staffer if Nakul had not dragged me out of the terminal. Just then the phone rang. It was Aman again. No, no, no, I hoped that he was not calling to give me any bad news. I kept wailing and could not get myself to answer the phone. Nakul held me tight with his left arm, and used the free hand to take the call.

He only responded in monosyllables so I couldn't make out what Aman was conveying. He put the phone in his pocket when he was finished, held me close with both his arms, and said I am sorry, baby. He's gone.

I howled and howled into his shirt. He managed to get me to the cab stand and book one for Jaipur. And we were off. I was a zombie all through the five-hour drive; I knew this was one of those events when things would change. They did for me.

I took care of the funeral and prayer ceremonies in Jaipur. Nakul's father came. His mother did not. I couldn't care anymore. But I would never forget the disrespect to my father, a good and a kind man.

Ok, you can take her. As soon as the current school year is over. You can seek admission in a Delhi school in the meantime. And set up your house to accommodate her.

I took Krishna's call in the middle of a meeting—I never missed any of his for Vani's sake. He spoke gently; he always did. He won people over with that signature tone of his, leaving his victims in shock when a 'gentleman' like him stabbed them in the back. I think Vani may be better off with a mother than with me, he said. She goes into the second grade in about three months. You have enough time to secure an admission in a good school.

I was stoked. It had only been a few days since dad passed away, and this was just what I needed to snap out of the grief. I would have hugged and kissed Krishna had he been around me. In that moment, all ill towards him was forgotten. I forgave him for everything he had inflicted upon me. I called Nakul to share the good news. He sounded pleased, but could not match my exuberance. I didn't dwell much on the touch of scepticism in his reactions.

I got busy identifying suitable schools for Vani. My preferences zeroed in on Mother's International and Springdales. I needed her birth certificate and photos to apply though, and asked Krishna to arrange for them. He procrastinated on it. Every time I called to remind him, my tone sounded more panicky than the previous time. Application deadlines were approaching. But he would only laugh and ask what's the rush. He would promise to send them but never did.

With only days left, I found someone to make a fake birth certificate for her. But I still needed a photo. Seeing me distraught, Kamal, my junior, gave me photos of his niece to affix. How can I use these? I asked.

You have only one day to go. When someone points out the photo at the interview stage, just say you were travelling and had asked an office assistant to complete the form. He may have mixed up the photos with those of another colleague who was also applying for admissions for her child, he suggested.

I did so, and the interview calls came. I went to Jaipur to pick Vani up for the same, but Krishna refused to let me. When I insisted he keep his word, he let out the sinister laugh I was so familiar with. You really thought I would let you take her, he said. No way. She does not need you. I am getting remarried, and she will get the mother she needs.

I wondered what kind of a woman would marry a sadist like him. In all likelihood, one as gullible as I. If only there was a way to warn her about the mental and physical cruelty awaiting her. Unless Krishna had reserved such treatment only for me.

You bring out the worst in my son. That was the first thing my mother-in-law said to me when she saw me holding my bleeding forehead after Nakul struck me. My head was pounding, run Nikita, run. But where I do run to when every path is blocked by a wall?

My mother-in-law finally came calling about a month after my father passed away. But to our house in Delhi, not to any of the ceremonies in Jaipur. With her sister, her niece, Bobby and Kajal. And Nakul's father, of course. They were all going to stay with us for a week. Not that they checked with us before landing up. They freely invited other relatives to hang around too; at any given time, there would be over a dozen people in the house during that visit. That was her way of expressing her condolences.

I was the only one serving all the guests. With a bad back. Without any domestic help. Seeing so many people, the maid made excuses to not turn up for the week. I had taken a few days off from work to nurse my back, and to also get over the double shock of losing my dad and not gaining the promised custody of Vani. Nakul must have told his mother about my break from office; I am sure they made the plan realizing I would be around to wait upon them. And I did. I cooked, cleaned the house and did the laundry; no one raised a finger to help me. They would just sit around, chat, laugh, play cards, eat, drink and issue instructions. I kept my cool for as long as I could.

On the fourth evening of their visit, I was on the verge of collapsing. I had already prepared the dinner; I requested everyone to warm the food whenever they wanted to eat and went to my room to rest my back. Nakul followed and picked up an argument while I was brushing my teeth. That was rude of you, he said.

What was? I asked.

Telling them to serve themselves.

But I can't stand any more. I have done everything. They just have to warm it. I will do the clearing up and cleaning in the morning anyway.

You cannot treat my parents and family this way.

What are you talking? What more do you expect from me?

A bit of courtesy.

What else have I been doing all these days? Despite suffering from physical pain and emotional anguish.

It's always self-pity for you, isn't it?

Why are you talking like this? Can't you leave me alone for a bit? Don't I deserve some empathy?

Your attitude is getting increasingly intolerable by the day.

Listen, I have done what I could. And I would have been willing to further during their visit. But you and your family can take care of yourselves from now on. Don't expect anything out of me.

You make me look so small in front of others, he said. He struck a blow on my ear the moment he finished speaking those words. I lost my balance and hit my head on the wash basin. I must have screamed loudly; my mother-in-law and Kajal appeared instantly. They must have been eavesdropping on us to make such a quick entry.

You bring out the worst in my son, said my mother-in-law. Neither she, nor Kajal, nor Nakul stepped forward to administer first aid. I was holding up the bleeding with a towel. My vision was blurred, but I could have sworn I saw Kajal smirking.

My mother-in-law let her tongue run amok. Nakul has to be on the road so much, he's barely home. Why do you have to make it so difficult for him? Can't he have some peace while he's here? It's not easy living in hotels for months on end. Anyway, you will never appreciate what he's done for you. How many men will marry a woman with a past like yours?

Her words stung more than the wound. What was wrong with her? What was wrong with me? If he is so great, why doesn't he go around marrying a dozen divorcees and looking after them? Why doesn't he set up a charity for women with a troubled past? I wanted to say all this but kept quiet. I just wanted her to vanish in that moment. But she came wrapped in thicker skin.

I know how you snared him, she continued. You harassed him sexually, you unleashed your vile charms on his innocent ways till he could think of nothing else but marrying you. What do we have to show for it?

Just then my father-in-law entered before she could spit more venom. If the situation was not so serious, I would have laughed. He always seemed to come to my rescue when I was in distress in a washroom. He told everyone to shut up and took charge. He checked my gash, and said it's not as bad as it looks. I had a close call. He asked Nakul for the medicine box to clean and patch up the wound. He had been trained in basic medical care when employed with the armed forces.

After all the ado about serving food themselves, that is exactly what everyone did anyway. I stayed back in my room. No one asked if I wanted to eat. Just then my brother Aman called from Jaipur. It was a casual call, but he got concerned when he heard my sobbing. What's the matter? he asked.

Nothing. I was just missing dad, I lied.

No, there is more to it. I know you. Tell me.

It is what I am telling you, I swear.

I don't believe you. I am coming over.

No, don't. Please. I will be ok by the morning.

I am not listening to you.

Anyway, the house is full of people. Nakul's family is staying over.

Oh, so that's what it is. I can imagine where trouble has come from. See you in a bit.

He disconnected, and rang the doorbell at first light. He had driven all night to get to my place. My mother-in-law cornered him the moment he entered the house. Without offering even a cup of tea, she told him to have a word with me. Nikita needs to conduct herself more appropriately. She can be uncultured and rude, and does not know how to even dress decently with guests around. Our family is not used to such behaviour, she said.

Aman didn't even have to see my forehead to know who the villain of the piece was. To his credit, he maintained a dignified silence even as she raved on. I took him to my room to distance him from my mother-in-law, and served him coffee and cookies. He barely spoke, and offered to leave soon.

But you have just come, I said. You must be tired, driving all night.

It's best I go for now. You hang in there. We all have seen so much already. This too shall pass. But if things get bad again, just call me. Don't hold yourself back.

Where are you going?

I have a good friend, will go to his house. You might remember Prateek, he lived on our street. He's now in Delhi. I will finish some pending chores since I am here, and go back to Jaipur in the evening.

Ok, I would have asked you to stay longer but not today. See you soon. And drive safe.

Nakul came in a few minutes after he had left with his own rant. No apologies, no remorse, no mention of his actions.

What was last evening all about? he asked.

What do you mean?

Why did you raise so much hell?

I did? That's funny.

You should apologize to my mother. Touch her feet and ask for forgiveness. She has been crying since last night because of you. Her holiday has been ruined.

I didn't do anything. You know it. How can you even expect me to apologize?

I am not getting into any further argument. Do what I am saying. Or else …

Or else what? I turned deaf to him when he uttered those words. Not for the first time. It was always do this, or do that, or else. He played on my insecurities, threatening me with his or-elses, creating a fear of what would happen if I didn't. But a part of me always rebelled even if I submitted for the sake of peace in that moment. Not that time though.

I refused. I told him to do whatever he wanted to, but I would not be sorry. Or even admit to a wrong I was not guilty of. I continued to play host for the rest of their visit, doing what was required of me. But they were losing me. Slowly but surely.

Why was this happening to me? The beatings, the arguments—they were all back. Is this what I did everything for? Did I sign up for this? These questions were again resonating in my head. But I was still willing to stay put and see where it was leading. Nikita was not going to run. For the time being at least.

Vani is all yours. I am giving up all claims on her. Bring her up as you deem fit. Don't ever call me again. I will not call you or her. I am done. It's all over.

I never thought I could say those words. I never thought I could give up on my daughter. I never thought I could leave her with the monster her father was. But I did.

Seeing me slumped at my desk after the latest showdown with Krishna, my colleague Kamal took me aside and asked what the matter was. I told him.

I want to say something, and don't react adversely till I finish, he said.

Sure, I said. I have nothing to lose.

Are you fertile?

What kind of a question is that?

Just answer whatever I ask. I am coming to a point.

Yes, I am. It probably takes half a sperm to make me pregnant. High fertility runs in my family. I have to take extra precautions to prevent another unwanted pregnancy.

Then go ahead and plan another child.

What's that got to do with getting my daughter back?

Let go. Tell her father she's all his. Break off completely.

Are you nuts? Why would I do that? My struggles of the last few years have only been about getting her custody.

Don't worry, she will be yours. Just be patient for a while. Play this game. And work on conceiving another child.

I looked at Kamal. He was younger than me. He had trained under me. And yet, he was speaking with the conviction and wisdom of one who had seen much more of life. He had, at least of my life. He had become a friend, a confidant. We were buddies too, hanging around together outside of work. We would have meals together, and go out to pubs and movies. There were days when we cooked at either his place or mine, and watched television late into the night. He would volunteer to run any errands for me, even picking groceries and getting the car serviced. I took him along shopping; he knew my tailors, and he knew the sizes of my clothes. Including my lingerie. It may sound corny for him to have been that close, but we just became thick like that without planning to or realizing when we did. Nakul was travelling for extended periods of time, and Kamal and I got to spend the time together. I saw him as a friend who cared. He would joke about how he was my husband without benefits.

He was right. There were none. I kissed him a few times but never slept with him. Even on occasions when he spent the night at my place, or me at his. But I knew one thing: he was hopelessly in love with me. And would do anything for me. He would openly express his feelings for me, but would tell me not to feel pressured for not reciprocating. He was satisfied with the unrequited love for me as long as he got to spend time with me.

I knew he cared. And he was smart and sensible about things. That's why I took his advice seriously. I made another trip to Jaipur.

She's your daughter, right? I asked Krishna while looking directly into his eyes. I did not blink, I did not look here and there. I used to be, but was suddenly not scared. Of anyone, or anything. And certainly not of him. When you are willing to give up something most dear to you, you get wings. You develop an inner confidence to do things you may have found inconceivable earlier.

Yes, he said. I could hear his mind ticking, wondering what the conversation was leading to.

Then I have a gift for you. Your daughter. She is all yours. I will never call her or you again. I will not try to meet her. I will not send any gifts. I will not pay for any of her expenses. You and I are over.

How can you do that?

Why can't I? I thought you would be happy to hear this. If your new wife is agreeable to being her mother figure, then let her be. I don't want Vani confused. She should have only one mother.

But you have responsibilities towards your daughter.

Ha! What I am hearing is I have responsibilities to send money to her good-for-nothing father. I know you by now. You are thinking about the expenses of bring her up. You don't fool me.

We have to share her burden. It's only fair.

You want to talk fair? Let's talk what's fair. To me. I am sick of you. I will not let you mess with me anymore. I am still in my twenties. I am married. To a good man. We will have more children. I will focus on them. I will miss Vani, but destiny seems to have a different plan for her and me. This conversation is over. You can leave now.

I could not have said what I did but for a newly developed inner conviction. Krishna once had the power to intimidate me, but no longer. I was playing a game with him, and there was no guarantee the dice would roll my way. I had bet everything, and was willing to lose my daughter. I needed closure, one way or the other.

The timing of what you are saying is so strange, he said. I was finally willing to give her up. And now you don't want her.

I don't believe a word you say. You just seek sadistic pleasure in my misery. I will no longer fall for it, I said.

You have to believe me this time. I mean it. Ask my mother, I confided in her.

Ok, I will try to believe you but you have to prove your intent. I will not take her just like that. You will go to court and admit to the false declaration about us not having any child when we separated. You will allow my husband, Nakul, to legally adopt her as his daughter. You will give up all legal rights to her, and never try to meet her. She will not accept Nakul as her father otherwise.

It sounds a bit extreme.

The terms are not negotiable. Accept them or keep Vani. She will have only one of us as her parent, not both.

Let me think about it.

Sure, take your time. Call me when you have decided.

I left to spend the night with my brothers before returning to Delhi the following day. He called the same night. You can take her now, he said.

No, not this way. We will do it the way I told you. If all my conditions are agreeable to you, call Aman and let him know. Go to my lawyer with him, and draw up an agreement to be presented in court. Only then will I come and take her. Not before that. I am going overseas with Nakul for a month. You have until then to make up your mind firmly and prepare the legal papers.

I hung up and called my lawyer. I apologized for calling him late, and told him everything. You are doing the right thing, he said. Hold your ground, and don't give in no matter what. This is a masterstroke by you, and you will win.

I was beaming all night while I slept. Soundly. After a long time.

Krishna has agreed to your conditions. He signed the papers today. We will submit them in court and request a date for a hearing whenever you can be here.

I was in Hay-on-Wye, a small town in England popular for its massive stores selling second-hand books, when Aman called with the good news. The floodgates opened for me. I could not hold back any longer. I had to catch the first flight back to India. Nakul was at a client site in Birmingham.

I rushed back to my bed and breakfast to pack my bags. I had paid to be there for another two days but I couldn't be bothered. I called Nakul while packing, and gave him the good news. I needed him to reschedule my flight to the next available. And he had to go along with me.

But I can't just drop everything and leave baby, he said.

Nothing matters more than this. Don't you understand? I said.

Why don't you go ahead and I will follow in a few days?

No, I need you. I can't do this by myself. What could be more important?

I will lose all my fee if I leave the project hanging.

You will lose me if you are not there for this.

I meant it. I could, and I would, leave him if he did not come along. He believed me. He got the flights organized and packed the bags while I drove to Birmingham. We left for Heathrow the same evening and took off for Delhi at midnight. We had dinner with Aman and Daljeet, my lawyer, upon arrival in Jaipur to discuss the way forward. Nakul was sullen throughout but did not pick any arguments. I bore no guilt on his account.

Krishna met up with us the following day and tried to add a twist to the proceedings. He wanted a clause where Vani's custody would revert to him if I bore another child. The lawyer advised me against accepting the condition; this was Krishna's way of asserting control, he said. We disagreed politely first, and then told him to keep Vani and fuck off when he insisted. He blinked. He agreed to all our terms in the presence of the judge. A decree was passed in my favour the same day. I was allowed to pick her up in three months so she could complete the current school year without any disruption.

I resigned from work the day I returned to Delhi. I would be required to serve a notice period of two months. It would give me ample time to prepare for Vani's entry into our home. Her home.

❧

How do we explain Vani?

My mother-in-law could think of nothing else when she learnt that Vani was coming home. Not a word of congratulations, not a gesture of happiness for me. She had not told the extended family and her social circle about my daughter from the previous marriage. How should she explain her presence in our life now? People will have to be told.

She proposed all kinds of ideas as face-savers. Vani was adopted by us. She was a love child Nakul and I had but kept under wraps. She was Nakul's love child from an earlier relationship. I chose not to get into such absurdities with her directly; Nakul was the go-between us.

It's not my problem if she did not believe I would get my daughter back, and thus did not tell anyone about her, I said when Nakul conveyed his mother's concerns.

But let's understand her predicament. I am sure we can come up with something plausible for society, he said.

You disappoint me, Nakul. I didn't expect you to even suggest anything along the lines of what your mother is saying. You are concerned about the world? But you are ok with me bringing up my own daughter as an adopted one, or as one born out of wedlock? What will that do to her psyche?

I am not disagreeing with your point. But what do I tell mom?

You deal with it. They are your family. If they are so ashamed of my daughter, or of me, then you all decide what you want. I don't want to be a party to your dilemmas; there are none in my opinion. I will bring up Vani with all the love and dignity she deserves, and expects. And don't ask me to go to Agra with Vani till your parents accept her as my daughter, and as our child.

I dug my heels in. I had seen the magical effects of being assertive when you are in the right. It helped me get my daughter back. Vani would not get to meet her new grandparents for over three months after moving in with us because of the stand I took. She did only after my parents-in-law accepted her as my daughter, and their granddaughter.

I had my daughter. Now what? I was under no delusions of the challenges at hand, but they need not have been exacerbated by my mother-in-law. And Nakul too. He was guilty too on many counts.

I invited my sister to stay with us for a while since Vani had spent time with her in Jaipur; the familiarity would put her in a comfort zone. Radha didi agreed—and came over for the duration of the summer vacations with her four kids in tow. Yes, she gave birth to two in quick succession after her second marriage. The one from the first was the big brother to all. Her husband had one from his first marriage; he had lost his first wife to breast cancer when she was only twenty-six. My sister's match was arranged for by tai, Aman's adoptive mother; it was her good deed just before she passed away.

Vani would take time adjusting. She was not used to the presence of so many people around her, and the absence of the only people she had known closely since her birth. She missed her father and grandmother, and would pine inconsolably for them. She knew me to be her mother by title, but she was yet to grasp the meaning—and significance—of living with one. She addressed Nakul by name for many months. If she got into crying fits, we just had to stand by patiently till she calmed down herself; there was little we could do to pacify her.

Feeding her was another issue. She was malnourished. Vegetables and eggs were strange food to her. Her diet had mostly been milk, toast and rice so far given the state of Krishna's finances and the callous attitude of his mother. It took some coaxing for her to eat healthy. I was making progress, slowly but surely. Despite Nakul and his mother. I need not have had to deal with unreasonable adults when I had a difficult child to manage.

From resenting Vani's existence and denying it too, my mother-in-law did not take long to assume the role of a doting grandmother. But her affections were reserved only for the child. She would buy her clothes and toys, take her out for ice-cream and other treats, play with her at home and in the gardens. She took her along to meet friends, and showed her off as her own. She made efforts to get Vani to eat well, and results were there for us to see. You had to give the devil her due. Even if she spewed fire at me.

I did not know what it took to be a good mother, or so I was reminded by her frequently. I did not know how to handle a child, how to talk to her, how to groom her, how to keep her clean, how to school her, how to feed her, how to entertain her, how to shop for her, how to look after her health, how to manage her sleep, how to bring her up. My mother-in-law could find faults in everything I did, and she let it be known to all. I heard her telling Bobby and Kajal too on the phone about the poor parent I made. Nakul was not even called to trial; he was the benefactor who had given refuge to a distressed woman and her daughter.

She should have made a career in diplomacy or theatre though. The face she had for me in private was not the one for public appearances. I was introduced to her society as the daughter she never had; there was never a harsh word for me in their presence. Or in Vani's either. She also wanted to keep us close. She requested, cajoled and demanded we spend every weekend with her; she could not bear to be without her grandchild for long. I was to be tolerated as a part of the package.

She was drawing all attention to herself when I needed to spend time alone with Vani. How else would I build a bond with her? My mother-in-law's behaviour started taking a psychological toll on me. Self-doubt crept in about my ability to be a good mother but I could not figure what more I could do. I was anyway struggling to bridge a gap of six years, critical ones when Vani was opening her eyes and mind to the first impressions of her world; I was missing in those pictures.

I felt like I was being watched, being judged all the time by my mother-in-law. She would not desist from stigmatizing my past, one she forced me to reflect upon repeatedly despite all my efforts to put it behind me.

❧

Vani moved into a house of strangers. I was one too for her. My efforts to bond with her and to establish my authority as a mother were undermined by the continuous interference of my mother-in-law. Vani took to defying my instructions as if trying to make a statement. She would either not do what I told her to, or would do the exact opposite. Reverse psychology might have worked had I tried it. The child in her was rebelling—I felt she had no just cause to. I should have been more patient and understanding of the turmoil within her. But I was frustrated, I was exasperated, I was exhausted. There was pent up anger within me. It needed a release. I found one in Vani herself. By beating her.

It started with a slap when she was refusing to go to bed on a school night. It worked, even if she had to cry herself to sleep. I was shocked at my behaviour, and I too cried myself to sleep. Not that it held me back in the future. I had found my vent and a tool of discipline. For years, I would hit her, often at the slightest of provocations. I unleashed an arsenal on her. I would whack her, wallop her, spank her with my hands. And a stick, a scale, a broom, a shoe, and even a rolling pin once.

The more I was judged and criticized, the worse my behaviour got. The worse my behaviour, the more I was judged and criticized. Much of the adversity, the negativity, could have been prevented if, and only if, Nakul had acted a bit more responsible. If he had stood up for me. If he had told his mother to back off. If he had asked how I was feeling. If he had enquired about my health. If he had offered to go that extra mile in support. He did not ask the reasons for my tears, he did not check if I had eaten, he did not take me out shopping, he did not invite me for a date. He never did any of these. Never as in never. He was just a bystander, not even looking in my direction.

If only he had held me close, given me warm hugs, kissed me lovingly, told me he was with me. I needed to hear we were in this together. The assurance would have been enough.

I might not have asked him to do anything, I might not have made him do anything. But I just needed to know he would do it if I asked him to. But he did not. I ended up learning to live with myself even though I had a family.

Vani's entry into my life brought along its own set of frustrations, its own set of insecurities. I had my daughter, one I had been struggling to get since the day I walked out on her father, but I felt alone, and lonely, all over again. I just needed someone to talk to, someone to talk to me. That someone could only have been Nakul. But he stayed silent and aloof.

Maybe I was to blame too. I should have asserted my rights; my right to be treated better. I should have told others to let me be, to let me be the one to decide how to bring up my daughter. I should have told them cordially first, and then aggressively if needed to. If they had still not got the message, I should have opted to live with Vani by ourselves. I might have been happier for it.

But the fear of fending for myself forced me to compromise the quality of my life. I only had myself to blame if I was unhappy.

I think we should have another child. What do you say? We wouldn't want Vani to be by herself after we are gone, would we?

The suggestion from Nakul surprised me. He had reacted indifferently when I had broached the subject of children of our own in the past. So what changed? Did it have anything to do with Vani being with us? Were his paternal instincts wanting a biological child of his own? Was his mother prodding him in the background? I wanted to ask him but didn't want to sound a cynic when discussing such a tender subject.

I had always wanted another child with Nakul, irrespective of whether we had gained custody of Vani or not. I was ready to plan one whenever he was ready. Of course, there was a minor matter to be taken care of. We needed to have sex with each other. I don't even remember when we last hugged or kissed, or went out on a romantic date. Lovemaking had been ripped out of our lexicon. Not that we didn't have sex at all; we did, sometimes. But the process was too mechanical to give us anything to look forward to.

I agreed but I needed a go-ahead from the gynaecologist considering my history of aborted pregnancies. I was in poor shape too. The stresses of the recent past had led to poor sleeping patterns, an unhealthy diet, excessive drinking and chain smoking. I was also running out of time on my biological clock. Or so I thought. Nonsense, said Dr Manchanda, you are good to have babies for at least another fifteen years if you take care of yourself.

He ran some tests and gave me the green signal—with a long list of dos and don'ts. I needed to be careful lest I suffer from any physical or mental trauma. I wanted to strike gold in one try. I did not want to go through the anxiety of trying every month. And, to be honest, sex with Nakul was already a bit of a put-off for me. I got the doctor to explain how the ovulation kit worked to improve the odds of becoming pregnant with minimum fuss in the sack.

I should have paused to reflect upon what I had set out to do. If I was already abhorring the father of my future child, should I even be planning one with him? What if we are not even together after a while? Even if these thoughts crossed my mind, I dismissed them. Life had ceased to be about love and care and family. It was just a series of tasks you carried out. Having another child was one of those.

I did all I could to rejuvenate my soul and heal my body. I went on long walks, stuck to mostly a Mediterranean diet, consumed wine in moderation, smoked only when I was desperate, attended concerts, read books and indulged in shopping therapy. Nakul and I tried to be affectionate, and to have sex with a bit of heart in it.

Only when I felt I was ready to carry a child did I propose we try to conceive one. But home would not be the right place for it. We both needed to be away from distractions and irritants. His next client assignment was taking him back to Germany. We planned to be together for a part of the trip, coinciding with my ovulation window. I joined him when it was the right time of the month to.

While he worked, I entertained myself to feel relaxed. The moment the kit showed I was ovulating, I called him at work and insisted he drop everything and come back to the apartment. He asked for the reason but I did not tell him. I dragged him to the bedroom as soon as he was home, took off his clothes, let my gown drop on the floor and made him have sex with me. It was over in twenty minutes. What was that about? he asked.

Nothing, I was feeling lovey-dovey, I replied. You can go back to office now.

I winked at him, put on my clothes and left for the public park nearby. I intended to pick up a chocolate ice cream cone, lie on the grass and listen to music. I had sex twice more with him before returning to India.

Are you sure you were not pregnant before you left for Germany? Nakul had been in Berlin for over a month before you joined him. Anything is possible.

I showed no reaction to my mother-in-law's words. I had become used to the most absurd and derogatory of insinuations from her. They used to hurt earlier, but no longer. I had learnt to be immune to her. In fact, I would enjoy seeing her getting worked up when she failed to rile me up.

I was in Agra when I ran the pregnancy test, and she was the first to know the results. I expected her to hug me and show me some love; her son was going to be a father for the first time, biologically, and she a grandmother. Rather than put me on a pedestal for the child I would bring into her family, she cast me as the whore by doubting the paternity of the foetus. She had sunk to a new low for me.

It was a tough pregnancy. I did not feel like eating much, and I seemed to be throwing up more than I was taking in. Where was the extra coming from? Were my innards falling out? I was being treated for haemorrhoids, and would also suffer from high fever every few weeks. These symptoms only left me weaker by the day. I got a scare in my third month; I thought I had miscarried but it was a false alarm. The medical fraternity could take me up as a case study in pregnancy-related complications.

Since he was the one keen about it, I thought Nakul would spend more time caring for me, and looking after Vani too. He had to travel, and more than usual. His work was project-based; he could easily have declined some to be home. Even when he was in India, he would go off to Agra every few days, leaving Vani and me to fend for ourselves. Why was he shirking his responsibilities? Didn't basic human decency demand he be a bigger help to his wife during that period?

Kamal stepped in to fill the vacuum created by my husband. He was around as much as he could to look after me, taking care of even the smallest of things. I felt guilty for using him like that, and for not returning the love he had for me. But what was I to do? I could not get myself to develop any romantic feelings for him despite our proximity. In any case, I was married and had not yet given up on Nakul.

Was I thinking of? I must admit I had been. But mostly in passing. The prospect of being on my own was too daunting for me to dwell long on any such possibility. Especially with a second child on the way. Ours was supposed to have been a relationship founded on love and passion, but it was sliding into one of mutual need and security. And that too could not be taken for granted considering how little I saw of Nakul when his physical presence was needed most.

His mother continued being her incorrigible self. She would call me daily—and not a day passed when she did not—to play mind games for reasons known only to her. Unless she played mischief for the sake of it. She would express her inability to be by my side during the delivery, and to look after Vani and the newborn while I recovered. Not that I was inviting or expecting her to come. In fact, I hoped she did not. She continued to seek updates on how I was caring for and bringing up Vani, and would have a critical remark no matter what I said. She was driving me nuts. I would rather she shut up and not call at all; it would be easier to manage the situation. But only Nakul could have told her to leave me alone. Fat chance!

Did he really want a child? Was my hunch correct? Did he suggest we have one at his mother's insistence? If that was their desire, why were they not being kind and loving towards me?

Do you realize your foetus is already six months old? Are you sure you want to abort it?

Nakul had been back only two days from his latest trip when we had a big argument over his mother. Her constant interference and criticisms were getting to me, and I had requested him to do something about it. Rather than trying to understand my point, or being empathetic towards my pregnant situation, he blew his top.

You persist with raising issues where none exist, and always getting mom wrong. Her intent is to only help and care, he said.

Then you have not seen the true picture. She conducts herself as you describe her when there are others around. But you should observe like a fly on the wall when it's only the two of us; her behaviour is nothing short of obnoxious towards me. You will then understand what I am so disturbed about.

You should consider yourself lucky to have a mother finally. You never had the good fortune of being raised by one.

I have tried very hard to accept her as my mother, but what do I do if she is always like this?

She is always what? You are still making an issue. If she had a problem, she would not treat Vani as her own. You should be grateful for that.

Grateful? Is that what both you and your mother want me to be? She wants me to be grateful to you for accepting me. You want me to be grateful to her for accepting my daughter.

Is this what it is for the both of you? Is it a transaction? I don't think we are making a family here. And if we are not, what am I doing carrying your baby? Or should I be grateful for being impregnated by you? By the way, you may want to convince your mother it is your child, and not someone else's.

Before Nakul could reply, I picked my bag and left the room. And the house. I hopped into an autorickshaw and directed it towards my gynaecologist's clinic. I called Kamal to tell him where I was off to.

Somehow, he managed to be at the clinic before me. I had not asked him to come over, but he did. I was not surprised. The receptionist told me to wait as the doctor was busy with a delivery. She took me to a room where I could lie down. Tea and biscuits were offered and I accepted.

It was over an hour before the doctor could see me. I told him I wanted to abort the child. He cautioned me about doing it at such a late stage but I was adamant. You will have to sign an undertaking assuming all risk. And we will have to run tests before we can take a final call, he said. I gave my consent.

Kamal said he had work to do, and would be back shortly. He apparently went out and called Nakul to tell him what was happening. He did not take my permission to, knowing I would not let him.

My blood pressure was abnormally high, making the procedure riskier. The doctor was conducting an ultrasound when Nakul reached. The nurse brought him in and he stood in a corner and watched silently. I didn't realize he was there.

The screen showed the shape of a fully formed male. I started crying seeing the image, and realized I would be murdering a child if I went ahead. Nakul stepped forward and sat beside me. The doctor excused himself, advising us to discuss the matter as parents before a final decision.

I can't have the child, I said. I am not fit to bring him up.

Says who? he asked.

You know who, and everyone else.

This is not the time to get carried away with emotions. We have to be rational and do what's right.

What is right?

We should go ahead and have the child. I am sure we will be glad for it. Anyway, it's too risky at this stage. I am not even sure if it's legal.

It was borderline legal. The doctor would have to justify the late-stage abortion but he would have managed. It was risky no doubt. If things went awry, I could even lose my life and the doctor would be in serious trouble with the authorities. I decided to keep the baby.

On the way back home, Nakul didn't say much. I am hurt that you confided in Kamal and had him by your side and not me, were the only words of significance spoken by him.

Nakul didn't get it. The only person I wanted by my side was him. And he was not there as I would have wanted him to be. He was hurt. So was I.

I was already gearing up to bringing up two kids by myself if Nakul continued to disappoint me.

Nakul left Vani and me in a restaurant and told us not to come home. Ever. The due date of delivery of his son was just a week away.

This wasn't the first time he had done it. When he lost his cool, he could tell me to leave home. And leave home there and then. He had done it a few times already. He had even ordered me out of the car on the highway to Agra once. He did not turn back or call me. If I didn't have some money in my handbag, I would not have found my way to Simran's place. I mustered up the courage to go home after two days after giving up on any hopes of Nakul calling me to apologized. Incidents like those instilled the fear of him going away for good. I was not prepared for another struggle at that stage of my life.

Our argument started over his mother as it often did over dinner; it was likely to be our last outing for months since the baby could arrive any day. I didn't want her around for the delivery; she had already conveyed her unavailability for the same. I had been glad to hear that; her toxic behaviour would cause too much stress. Nakul got defensive of her as usual, chiding me for demonising her. I was the trouble-monger according to him. The argument went out of control, and he walked away warning me not to follow him home.

I felt a nervous breakdown coming. What if something happened to the baby with the anxiety? We were in the Hyatt Regency hotel. I managed to get to the reception to check if a room was available; it was. I almost booked myself into one but decided otherwise.

The concierge helped me get a cab home; a pile of bags awaited outside the main door. Nakul had packed most of my clothes and other belongings, including photos, into bags. I cried and begged him to let me in, fearing the worst for both the babies. He relented eventually, but we did not speak anything meaningful for three days. I went into labour four days after I almost became homeless.

Although we survived the unsavoury episode, a switch flicked off within me. I went through the motions for years to come, but the marriage ceased to mean what I wanted it to. I stopped caring or worrying about everything falling apart. I refused to be treated like shit anymore.

❧

A woman's stock is supposed to go up if she bears a boy. I hoped mine would and my in-laws would treat me with greater respect and love. I assumed Nakul would be happy too—for being father to both a son and a daughter. My optimism was misplaced.

I had urged the doctor to try for a natural delivery but stress-induced complications made caesarean section the safer option. It was the first surgery of any kind on me; I had not even received stitches for a wound as a child. I did not take to it well. I was in immense pain and discomfort, with nobody to put me at ease. I would have liked my sister to be around, but she could not come. Maybe her reasons were genuine; she had her own brood of kids to manage while holding a day job. Or she was just being moody. I could never be sure of her responses. She had been like that since that fateful night we never spoke about. I never grudged her; many in her position would have given up living a long time back. But she was a fighter. And an inspiration. And my hero.

The mother-in-law was in Delhi for six days after the delivery, but I wish she had not come at all. She tortured me throughout—and this is not an overstatement. It started with naming the newborn. I was keen to call him Amar, but Nakul insisted we name him Kabir. His mother always dreamt of a grandson with that name, so that's what it should be.

Not that she developed any fondness for me after her dream came true. I was unable to nurse Kabir; he had to be formula fed from the day he was born. The mother-in-law had the choicest of words to criticize me for it, again reminding me how unfit I was to be a mother. I was barely conscious during my stay in the hospital, but she insisted I make the effort to wish Kajal's parents on their silver jubilee anniversary. Why the fuck would I care to wish them? Not just forty-eight hours after the birth of my son, but any other time as well. But she had her way, even as Nakul looked on.

Their presence did not provide much physical comfort either; they would barely move to help. I had to summon the nurses for my medicines and meals, to check on Kabir and to feed him. I had to wait for an attendant to arrive before I could even use the washroom; I had to rely on a bedpan for the first four days. Vani was being ignored too at home, and would throw fits. Instead of pacifying her, they would scold her and get her even more worked up. What if I had died during the delivery?

I almost did a few days later though. I had been home for two days when Deepa, my closest friend and confidant at the time, came calling. I could have relied on her to be by my side in the hospital if she had not been in Thailand for an extended wellness holiday with her boyfriend. She came home straight from the airport and was shocked to see me so weak and sickly.

She's running a very high fever, she told Nakul the moment she touched me.

Is she? he asked.

Didn't you realize it yourself? What the fuck have you been doing then?

She did not like Nakul. And would mince no words when she had to be nasty to him. In fact, she liked to use expletives in general and with him in particular. The thermometer showed six degrees Fahrenheit above normal. Were you conspiring to kill her? she asked Nakul.

Why would I want to do that? he asked.

It seems so going by your irresponsible attitude. You just needed to touch her forehead, or any part of her, to know that she's burning.

I would suggest you don't speak to me like that.

I would suggest you pick up the bloody phone and call the doctor.

He cowed down, and made the call. It was clearly a case of infection in the stitches, figured the doctor. I was prescribed antibiotics on the phone, and told to visit the clinic in three days for cleaning and to be stitched up afresh. The misery was only prolonging itself.

The doctor lost his father on the morning of the procedure but he still came to the clinic just to fix me; I would be eternally grateful to him for it. He left for the funeral only after he was satisfied everything had gone fine. I was required to get the dressing changed daily for a fortnight, and then every alternate day for another fortnight. It was an hour's drive one way, every bump on the road causing a spike in the pain.

Kamal and Deepa took turns to take me. Nakul would be busy hacking away on his computers. I had a part-time help to take care of the kids; he would check on them only if he felt there was a crisis while I was away.

I could not comprehend the reasons for Nakul's behaviour. Why had he pursued me the way he had? Why did he take a strong stand against his family to be able to marry me? Where did it all go wrong? Who was the real Nakul?

It was my thirtieth birthday, and someone sent me thirty bouquets. I have no idea who it could have been. I would never know. Nakul passed a few snide remarks, but he soon forgot about them. Or chose not to make a further mention. We were all busy organizing a party for me.

The celebration was an aberration to the life I was leading. I had become indifferent to everything. And everyone. My screens went blank. I remember little from that phase. Except arguing with Nakul incessantly, no matter where he was.

The disgust set in eight weeks after Kabir was born. Nakul had to travel—for four months. He had never needed to be out so long. The timing could not have been worse. I know he could have put off any trips for a while; I had seen him service clients from home. It was almost as if he was trying to run away from home, from me, from the children, from everything. I was probably not off the mark.

I was angry. At myself. At everyone. I blamed everybody for the mess around me. I was yet to fully come out of the trauma of my pregnancy and delivery; that was the time when the family could have made itself count with all the support they could extend. But none was forthcoming. Everyone vanished. There was no one to handle Vani and Kabir, to administer my medication, to fetch me water, to clean the wet beds, to do the laundry. I had to drag myself for everything. I ended up being sleep-deprived, exhausted, cranky, sick and fat.

I would have make-believe squabbles with my late father for letting me marry Krishna. What did I know of people and life then? Gosh, I was barely nineteen. He had seen the worst—at home, amongst the royals, in people in general. Why didn't he call upon his experiences in life when it came to marrying me off? Why didn't he check Krishna and his family out before it was too late? My adult life got off on the wrong foot with the first marriage. I was still groping for a sense of normalcy. My life was in shambles. Where do I start cleaning up?

I needed to distract myself from the thoughts pulling me down. I turned my attention to the children. I didn't feel like talking to anyone. I only socialized with Kamal and Deepa, mostly at home. They became my extended family. The weight I had lost before my pregnancy came back, bringing a few extra kilos with it. I detested the person looking at me from the mirror. The worse I looked, the deeper a hole I dug for myself. Within months, I could not recognize my own self. I felt alone. I felt I was not being of any use to anyone or to myself. I became melancholic. I had not felt so low even during the worst phases of my life with Krishna.

And yet, an inner voice kept urging me to stay positive. To not lose hope. To live up to any promises I had made to myself. Promises of a life to be lived well. To not despair. To not forget that I was just thirty, and there was time to do so much more.

The affirmations started showing results. My mother-in-law surprised me by proposing a thirtieth birthday party for me. Nakul took it upon himself to make it special. All he asked of me was to turn up, and leave the rest to him. He booked an entire open-air restaurant in Mehrauli overlooking the iconic Qutab Minar. All our friends had been invited. I worked on my appearance in the meantime. I starved myself over the fortnight leading up to the big day. I meditated, went for long walks and got masseurs to pamper my body. The results showed, even if there was no miraculous metamorphosis. I managed to fit into a few of my old dresses. My skin was glowing—I attributed it more to my inner joy; if only Nakul would realize what little it took to keep me happy and energized.

I walked into the party and could have shed tears of ecstasy if I wasn't worried about ruining the make-up. Scores of friends were already waiting to raise a toast upon my arrival. The decorations were exquisite to say the least. The feast was fit for a king, or queen since that's who I was feeling like with the attention and the gifts. To my delight, Nakul had flown in Seby and the Wings from Goa to entertain guests with retro music—rock and roll as well as romantic Bollywood from the black and white era.

It was close to ten when Nakul proposed we cut the cake. Let's wait a bit, I said. I am waiting for Kamal and Deepa.

Are they coming? he asked.

I wouldn't know. You said you will take care of all invites.

Oh, I didn't invite them.

Why?

I thought you would. They are your friends.

We did speak about inviting them, and you reiterated that I should leave it to you. There are others here too who are just my friends and you only invited them.

I guess it's been a blooper then. Anyway, can't do anything about it now. Should we cut the cake?

I said ok but knew this was not an oversight. He did not invite them deliberately. He behaved cool about it, but their proximity—and influence—to me was not lost on him. He resented it. My birthday would have been a celebration had they been the only two guests attending. And since they were the only two missing, it no longer was.

I took out a plastic smile and pasted it on my face. And let go. I had been disciplining myself to drink moderately, and only while socializing. But I downed more than a bottle of wine, on an empty stomach. I wanted to be sick. And I was.

Nakul had to carry me home and put me to bed. I woke up the following morning in my silk dress, jewellery and shoes. Nakul would grudge my revolting show at his meticulously planned party for years to come. And would remind me of it whenever he wished me happy birthday in the future.

It is ok to pursue interests outside of your marriage. You cannot keep moping about the state you are in. Go and get a life.

Deepa did not need to be told why my closest friends were missing on my birthday. Unable to hold back any longer, she took it upon herself to prod me to seek pleasure and respect from others if my husband was falling short of my expectations. Simply put, she was condoning extramarital affairs for damsels in sexual and emotional distress.

She had a boyfriend. The fourth one. She had not known what it was to be in a relationship with a man until she married. At eighteen. To a fabulously wealthy man. Her marriage was a non-starter; her husband was a creep of a character, a philanderer who made no secrets of the women he was involved with. He was older to her by ten years, and they never got along. I could identify with her plight; maybe that's what drew us close to one another.

I opted to walk out of my first marriage but Deepa chose to err on the side of pragmatism. She stayed put. Her parents had effectively got rid of her and had little to offer had she gone back to them. She did not want to face the financial struggles of a single woman; with no higher academic qualifications or work experience, it would have been a grind for her anyway.

She gave her husband a wife to show off and someone to manage his house. They had sex too, once in a while. For him, it was just a release. She did it to satiate his desire when he had no one else to be with, even though she found the process painful. She was always dry and would be sore for days after he had been inside her. She suffered from frequent bouts of infection too, compliments of the women her husband had been with. He was not a fan of protection, even with women of liberal integrities. Deepa allowed him to get his way because he paid her bills—and any excesses she indulged in. She was ok with the compromise.

She thus had no qualms, or guilt, in being with other men. She crossed the line on their third wedding anniversary. No celebrations had been planned; he was not even in town on the day. He was in Kerala, in a houseboat. With his mistress, Rhea. Deepa had seen the flight tickets by chance a few days before he was scheduled to leave on the 'business' trip. She had sensed something was amiss for a long time, and the evidence confirmed her suspicions. Rhea was a part of their social circle, and there was no reason for her to travel with him for work.

All of twenty-one, Deepa opened herself to other men. Society would have branded her life a lie. To her, there was no other truth to choose from.

She was beckoning me to follow her on the same path.

I was not ready to cheat on my marriage yet—even though I had begun to seriously ponder Deepa's advice. It might be prudent to test the waters with my toe first to figure out if I would be inclined to dive deeper. It was time to start going out again and meeting new people.

As if it were a sign, I found someone very efficient and trusted to look after the children in my absence. Dinah was a trained nurse from Kerala and an experienced governess. She had worked for expatriates only so it was a coup to get her to work in an Indian home. She took a liking to the kids and me, and the affection was reciprocated; we all got along like a family from day one.

I had been used to the pub culture in Bangalore, but it was a relatively new phenomenon in Delhi and its suburban town of Gurgaon. A large swathe of the population took to the pubs like parched travellers coming upon an oasis in a desert. The new joints emerged as the places to meet, to be seen in and to find partners—especially for one-night stands and illicit affairs.

I needed to look—and feel—better before stepping out. I worked hard to lose weight by watching my diet, going for brisk walks and sleeping well. Dinah had a way with kids—she would have them asleep by nine every night so others in the house could get their rest too. I joined meditation and Buddhist chanting groups to calm my mind. I found a good masseur to come home twice a week. He was gay, and I had no qualms in stripping to my birthday suit for him to work his magic on me. He was by far the best in the trade, and an acquaintance of Dinah. I was his only non-expat customer. And he only took on women clients. I asked him once if he was really gay or if it was just an act to get women to shed their clothes for him. Oh darling, you are so naïve, he said. I use women to get to their husbands.

Should you ever expand your preferences to include wives too, you know I will gladly be yours sweetheart, I said trying to imitate his effeminate style.

Done, so let's seal it with a kiss, he said. He pouted his lips, and I did likewise, and we kissed. We had a deal.

Mahesh had moved to Gurgaon recently, and we reconnected. We had barely been in touch since we lost Zulfiqar. We were a group of drinking buddies in Bangalore, and that's what we became again. He was still single, he was not dating anyone, and he still had the hots for me. These were the first bits of trivia he shared with me when we met.

Even if I was interested in Mahesh being anything more than a friend, there were barriers between us now. Nakul was the biggest one—I was still not ready to wrong him. And then there was Kamal. Deepa was insistent of me jumping into bed with him. I can't, I said on a day when she sat me down with the agenda of deciding this way or that way with him.

Why can't you? she asked. He adores you; he's head over heels in love with you. You are the epitome of beauty for him. He's always by your side, doing whatever you ask of him. And more even without being told to. He would gladly wipe your ass every morning.

It was true. And everyone knew what he felt for me. His parents, our common friends, his office colleagues, even Nakul. Mahesh noticed this fondness for me over our first outing together; he preferred not to be a part of any race to get me. As other men did. When they realized what Kamal felt for me, they assumed I did likewise for him since we looked inseparable—and happy together. He did not have me yet, but he kept competition—and pesky men—at bay.

The idea of having flings, the sinful types, may sound titillating but I wanted to probe what Nakul really felt for me, for us, before I embarked on any such adventures. Was he possessive about me? Did he cherish me, value me enough to stop me from being involved with anyone? I needed only the faintest of positive indications from him to be able to tell Deepa to stop peddling my morals.

I sometimes wonder what you think of Kamal, I asked Nakul.

Think what about him? he asked back.

Everyone knows he's really crazy for me. We may joke about it when we sit in a group, but we all know he's serious.

That's ok. It is normal to be attracted to others, even if they are forbidden fruit. We can't ostracize such people, especially when they are good friends like Kamal.

So you are ok if someone desires me and lets it be known too?

Nakul did not reply. He continued to treat Kamal as he always had—a good friend of mine. Was it trust? Or negligence? I think the latter. Nakul made light of too many things except his work. If only he put in the same thought, the same effort in personal matters as he did in professional, we would all have been happier for it. At least we would know where he stands. I only wish he had not neglected to show his love for me.

But he did. We did not engage in meaningful conversation; we spoke as if in bullet points to one another. He was always on a short fuse with me. I had to badger him into even talking to me when he was travelling to client sites for extended durations. I desired for him to be physical with me; I needed to be hugged, to be kissed, to be made love to. I wanted to shake him, holler in his ear and warn him to get a hold of his wife lest he lose her; Deepa was keeping the engines running to whisk her away if he did not act.

He did not. I was left with no choice. It was time to move on. I would not be leaving Nakul, but I would allow myself to be with someone else if he was right for me. I would not be desperate, I would not compromise. I wanted a man I would want to love, and have sex with. And he should reciprocate with the respect I deserved and the passion I desired. Deepa insisted that Kamal made the cut. But he did only because he was handy, he was explicitly vocal with his feelings for me, he was safe, and he was blocking the door to other men.

But here's the thing: Kamal was a good and trusted friend, and I could not get myself to see him as anything more than that. Cupid couldn't be bothered to play broker; I just did not feel romantic towards him. I tried to visualize myself in bed with him, and the idea held little appeal. Maybe I was thinking too much. Once I allowed myself to be close to him, sparks would fly and a fire would be lit.

I never got to test my theory—call it bad timing, at least for him. And maybe good for me since my heart was a reluctant participant in the possible affair with Kamal. He had been under pressure at home to get married. Just when I was on the cusp of taking our relationship to the level he had been chasing me for, he broke the news of his engagement to Antara.

What was I to do? Good sense should have told me to heave a sigh of relief. He would finally be off my back, and I was saved from getting into a relationship I did not really want to be in. But what did I do? I threw tantrums. Like a woman scorned.

I wanted to believe I was in love with him, and it was his duty to love me too. I only ended up creating confusion for him. He was committed to someone else now, but his heart still beat for me. What was he to do? Breaking the engagement would bring the ire of his family upon him, and break Antara's heart. Staying put meant he was hurting me, and also giving up on the one thing he had prayed for day in and day out for years. He picked the worst option: he let the wedding arrangements proceed even as he tried to get into a relationship with me.

Kamal should have spent the months leading up to the wedding day with Antara—for the two to get to know and understand each other better, to develop affection for one another and to make plans for their future as a married couple. Instead, he spent most of his available time with me. Our conversations would just play in a loop. He would apologize for what was happening, and would ask what he should be doing. I kept moping about the distress his actions were causing. He even offered to call off everything to be with me; that would not be the right thing to do, I would emphasize. Because, despite my behaviour, I never wanted to be with him. Not before he got engaged, nor after. I was being melodramatic to no end.

I reserved the worst of my outbursts for the morning of his wedding. I cried incessantly on the phone, telling him how I would miss him, and how I wished that he wasn't getting hitched to another woman. I turned my phone off after speaking to him, and did not switch it on again until the following morning. In the middle of his wedding vows, he called Deepa multiple times to ask if I was ok. She made it worse by telling him off for causing me all the anguish.

If it wasn't an Indian wedding with all its societal pressures, Kamal would certainly have run off from the big stage before they could be pronounced man and wife. I wouldn't have known what to do with him had he done so.

Kamal marked his first wedding anniversary by consummating his marriage. He stayed celibate for a year lest he be seen as unfaithful to me—to no one else but to his own self. I was overcome with guilt and shame when I learnt of it—and resolved to distance myself from him. For his sake. And for the sake of Antara, his wife.

Even after getting married, nothing changed for Kamal with regard to me. In fact, he was around me even more than usual. He would meet me three to five times a week to take me shopping, drinking and even picking up and dropping off the kids when needed. Nothing else happened between us. It was never supposed to have. He was chasing hope when there was none; I was clinging to a desire I did not have. He showed me off as a trophy he had not won; he was a convenience I did not want to lose by posing uncomfortable questions. He was delusional, I was selfish. Neither wanted to wake to reality.

I wanted to ask him what his wife thought of him hanging around with me so much. Before I could, she only asked what I was doing with him. She had discovered a photo of me in his wallet and called me.

What is on between you and Kamal? she asked.

What do you mean? You know we are all good friends, I said. Antara and Kamal socialized with Nakul and me sometimes, and had even come over to our place. She knew Kamal helped me out with chores when Nakul was travelling, but could not be sure of when and in what way. Any woman would be irked if her husband was abstaining from sex with her but Antara did not know the reasons why Kamal avoided her in bed. My photograph in his wallet gave her clues to investigate further.

If he spends more waking hours with you than with his wife, then something is clearly wrong, she said.

You have to ask him, I said.

What do I ask him? It seems your presence in his life is ruining our marriage.

Listen Antara, let me clarify. I am not involved with Kamal in the way you think we might be. I am not only married, but I have no desire or inclination to get messed up with anyone. He's a very good friend, a buddy, and a big help to me. But nothing more.

It seems he regards you as more than just a friend.

I can't help it if that's the case. Not that he has tried anything, but I know where the lines are drawn should he have any intention to wrong two marriages. You can rest assured we are not involved in anything to jeopardize your relationship. You should talk to him, not me. He has to act responsible, I said.

She must have had a talk with him. Maybe the families too. The frequency of his interactions with me went down overnight. But he was still doing everything with me as earlier, only lesser of it.

Kamal had to drive into a truck while drunk for us to finally break up.

We had gone out clubbing and it was well past midnight when he dropped me home. I just flopped into my bed without even changing and fell asleep instantly. I woke up to the incessant ringing of my phone. It was from an unknown number. Who would call at three in the morning? My head was throbbing; I didn't want to pick up the phone, but I did.

Nikita? a male voice enquired from the other end.

Yes, I said.

I am Kamal's cousin, Neeraj.

I was suddenly awake. Something was wrong. Is everything ok? I asked. I could feel myself shivering in anticipation of hearing the worst.

Kamal met with an accident. It seems he fell asleep at the wheel and hit a stationery truck from behind.

Oh my God! Please tell me he's ok.

He's not. He's badly injured. The doctors are preparing to take him into surgery. But he's insisting on seeing you before that.

Where is he?

He's at the Max Hospital in Saket. In the emergency ward.

I am coming. Tell him.

How will you come? Should I come to pick you?

No, I will drive. I will be there as soon as possible.

I woke Dinah and quickly apologized for doing so before explaining the situation. I drove out in the tight jeans and cropped top I was still wearing from the evening before. The roads were clear, and I was with Kamal within thirty minutes of Neeraj's call. His wounds were covered with temporary bandaging before the surgery; his clothes were soiled with blood. He was in pain but tried a smile when he saw me. His parents and his brother were by his side.

What did you do? How did this happen? Are you all right? I was blabbering all sorts of questions, as if he could answer them.

He asked everyone to leave us alone. When he noticed their reluctance, he tried to shout at them. He was gesticulating more than speaking. They left.

I am going to be all right, don't worry, he said. Every word he spoke caused his body to twitch in pain.

Of course you will be. Please stay strong, I said.

I will. I got you after trying for so many years, I will not let go now. I will live.

Don't think all this, we will talk when you are fine.

Do you love me?

Please don't speak. You need your energy.

I need to know. I will not go into surgery without your answer.

I didn't know what to say. I looked into his eyes. They were imploring. With hope.

Of course I do, I said.

He smiled. And then passed out without another word. I ran out in panic, looking for a doctor. Neeraj said he will do the needful and returned with the surgeon a few minutes later. The doctor examined him, and told the nurse to take him to the operating theatre.

His mother had been sitting with moist eyes all through but burst into tears when they wheeled her younger son away. I sat her down and held her close. She finally spoke up.

He was out with you? she asked.

Yes, I replied.

Why?

We had gone out for a drink.

I am not asking that. Why was he with you? Why so late?

We often do.

He's obsessed with you. He's ruining his life, and Antara's too. It's not fair to anyone. It's not right.

What do I do? He insists on meeting me.

He will not back off, but you can. You are more mature. You are older than him. I am praying he recovers fast. But I beg you to go away from his life.

I did. In that instant itself. I got up and left the hospital. He would survive the accident. But he would survive me only if I distanced myself.

There was nothing sexual or romantic between Kamal and me. But that did not make it any easier to be away from him. I was fond of him, and wanted him around me. I agreed with his mother though: I had to go away from his life. I needed a distraction to avoid thinking of him. It was time to heed Deepa's advice and find someone to fill the voids in my life.

Kamal was hospitalized for just under two months. I did not call or message him even once. I could not anyway. His phone was in Antara's possession. With access to all the messages we had exchanged. She must have been hurt reading them; he had expressed his love for me many times, but I did not send even a single message suggesting I felt anywhere close to what he did. Because I actually did not, even if I was forcing myself to believe I loved him. It might have been small consolation for Antara though; I felt bad for her. I kept tabs on Kamal's progress through Neeraj.

Deepa and I started going out more often, scoping out men. Her standards were very different from mine. For her, a man was acceptable unless he gave strong reasons not to be. For me, every man was unacceptable unless he really appealed to me. Our respective moral compasses also created different levels of barriers. She had long crossed over to the territory where there was no guilt, no shame, no fear in what she did outside of her marriage. I was still tiptoeing around the borderline.

We would talk for hours, exchanging notes, sharing updates. We knew everything about each other. What we were doing, what we were planning to do, what we were feeling, what we were eating, and even the colour of the underwear we had on at any given time. She would share graphic details of what happened in bed each time she made out; she would call me the moment she was done with the guy, even if it was two in the morning. I was expected to listen in, pay attention and masturbate with arousal when she did. I did not but lied to please her.

Deepa would get upset with me for being so picky; I rejected whoever she introduced me to. I would sleep with each and every guy you rejected, she would tell me. So go ahead, they are all yours, I would reply. She thought I was finding faults in each guy because I had no intention of sleeping with anyone yet. You only have to hook up for sex, not marry him, she would say.

I know, and I am ready to, but only if I meet the right guy. I will not compromise, I would tell her.

I had to pretend I was drunk to let myself be kissed sensually by another man for the first time since I married Nakul. I was not able to overcome the barriers created in my head otherwise. Deepa was more relieved than I was.

Only when Kamal was out of the picture did I realize what an impediment he was to my socializing. I finally felt free—the way I had in Bangalore even though I was married now. I had grown wings again. I went out and allowed myself to meet new people. Including Manan.

Someone in our group brought him along and introduced him as his cousin. He came across as a sweet, soft-spoken guy; he was six years younger than me. With a sense of humour leaving us in splits all evening. He must have been actually funny to have made us laugh even before we were tipsy. The evening ended with our stomachs hurting from the laughter and our heads hurting because of the liquor. We all went home, sobered up eventually and went back to our day-to-day existence. Then my phone rang a few days later.

Hi, this is Manan, he said.

Manan who? I asked.

The joker in the pack at Strikers last weekend.

The joker?

I was with you all, the guy cracking the jokes, trying to tickle you oldies.

Oh yes, of course. How are you? I must say I am surprised to hear from you. How did you get my number?

There are enough men on the way to martyrdom in your love. One of them shared your number in his dying statement.

Isn't that a bit cheesy?

Let's try coffee then.

Coffee?

Yes, I would like to meet you for a coffee.

Why?

I suppose that's a decent enough setting when you want to meet a girl for the first time.

Have you asked the girl?

I am asking her now. Would you like to meet me for coffee?

No.

No? As in a straight no? Without even thinking?

I did think about it.

When? You replied even before I finished my sentence.

No, you asked a few moments back also. I had time to think.

Why are you saying no?

Why should I say yes?

Because I am a nice guy.

I don't have coffee with all nice guys.

I am nicer.

If you say so. But it's still a no for now. We will see later. Anyway, I am an oldie like you said. So go pick someone your age. Ciao, kiddo!

I hung up, added his name to the list of rejected suitors and updated Deepa over text. But I didn't realize I was up against a spunky character who would not take no for an answer. He called me every few days, and texted me daily. Always conducting himself in a nice, rather nicer, manner. He was persistent, but in a dignified way. I had to say yes eventually. Just to tell him that his pursuits would be in vain.

So we met. Not just once as I had planned, but many times. At a regular frequency. For coffee. And pasta and wine. And drinks. And movies. I liked the weepy, tragic ones but he preferred rom-coms. We agreed to alternate between the genres. We watched live theatre too. I enjoyed going on long drives with him. He took lots of photos of me wherever he went; he was inept at the art, shooting unflattering portraits, but I let him.

We did everything. But we did not hold hands. Or kiss. Sex was not even on the cards. He was letting me be till I was ready. He played the waiting game and he played it right.

Deepa was being impatient though, as usual. It was almost as if she was going to hop into the bed with us when we did.

But her urging me on was as a friend. What's stopping you? she asked when we were lazing over beer in her house.

I am not mentally ready to be unfaithful to Nakul, I said.

Who said you were being unfaithful?

What else is it?

It would have been so if Nakul was caring, loving and sexually active with you. But he's not. One can understand the compulsion to be away from home for long stretches, but what about the times when he is home? Does he make you feel like his beloved, his lover, his sweetheart he could not wait to get back to?

Still …

What still? Stop being the old-fashioned wife willing to be her husband's doormat. And what do you think he does when he's in Europe?

He works, what else?

He is a man. You really think he would not be with someone out there?

Who could he be with?

Anyone. But definitely someone. Could even be a whore in Amsterdam. If he wasn't, he would devour you first thing after putting his bags down every time he returned.

But he's not emotionally involved with anyone, he does not love anyone.

You don't know that. Maybe he's not. Anyhow, who's asking you to get sentimental with anyone, babe? Just go and do your thing. In any case, you don't want lovestruck men following you home.

You must understand that I am seeking love and companionship more than sexual gratification. I will be driven to do what you are asking me to only if I can fix my loneliness, my heartburn. I can't keep it casual. It's different from my earlier flings. I wasn't seeking men because I was pained, so there were no expectations and no guilt in being with them and in walking away from them. I did not let my feelings get out of hand even when I had a kind of a long-term relationship with Ravi. But I will get deeply involved with whoever I am with, and it will only lead to greater torment since it will not be for keeps.

Listen, worry about that when you get to that stage. Just lower the pants for carnal pleasures for now.

I will never do it if you make it sound so crass.

You were not doing it when I made it sound like an honourable thing to do. I can put it the way you prefer, but say yes.

I will feel so awkward the first time. I might run away. Or I might laugh. Worse, I could think of Nakul and start crying. And what if I don't like it? What if I don't want to do it again? I will lose a good buddy like Manan.

Just kiss him for now.

But I still can't get myself to cheat.

Kissing is not cheating.

What else is it? You also know it won't stop at that.

You are painting too many scenarios which are mostly inconsequential to the decision making. I will tell you a trick—it works every time. The next time you go out, pretend you are drunk. And let him kiss you. Don't go beyond that. If you like it, then take it to the next level. If not, pretend to have no memory of the evening.

I gave in. Let Deepa have her way for once at least. I will check Manan out. I did not admit it, but I was really looking forward to being held, to being kissed by him. I just hoped he would take the bait.

I had been meeting Manan at least twice a week of late, so it wasn't long before we went out again. We were spending more of our time together in night clubs and lesser in the pursuit of other interests. The darkness, the music, the dancing, the drinks made for ideal ingredients for an aphrodisiac, building a wall of sexual energy between us. It was drawing us closer physically but we were resisting the pull. Deepa was wasting her breath to persuade me; it would have been just a matter of time before Manan and I came together in a sexual union. The force would have been irresistible.

It was the evening to finally give in to the inevitable. I drank a lot, or at least made it seem like. I had to give an impression of being high while maintaining a grip on my senses. I should witness, and recall, whatever he does with me. We followed our usual routine: he picked me up, we drank, we danced, I laughed at his jokes, left the club around one, and got into his car to go home. That is where I tweaked the script.

I reclined my seat, indicating a desire to hang around longer. He put on the air-conditioning and lay back himself. We spoke gibberish for a while, faces turned towards each other. He took my hand to stroke it gently. He took it to his lips and kissed it. Once. And then a few more times. There was no resistance from me, so he pushed his luck. He took my fingers in his mouth to suck them, one at time and then two or three together. He shifted in his seat to be close enough to kiss me along the arm. I kept my eyes closed, humming to the music from the stereo as if I had no inkling of what was being done to me.

He got bolder, but only because I wanted him to. He leaned over to kiss me on the cheek, then on the forehead, and then on the chin. His lips felt warm and moist when he locked ours together; he moved his tongue in my mouth, simulating the sexual motions of a man inside a woman. He was on fire, and I was burning. I wanted more. But I could not ask, or demand, anything. Alcohol had supposedly made me oblivious to his stimulations.

His lips stayed planted on mine even as he took his hand behind my back to unclasp my bra. I had deliberately worn a short, flimsy and string shoulder dress to make it easier for him to navigate my body in the restrained space of a car. He lowered the dress along one arm and felt my breast. He took the nipple in his mouth, sucked at it gently, rolling his tongue at the same time before biting me all over the breast. He tried to take the breast fully in his mouth, and I was surprised he managed quite well; he sucked deep and hard, raising a frenzy in my nerves. I was drooling between my legs. I wanted him inside me, and I wanted him right then.

He raised my dress to the neck and kissed me all over the abdomen, giving the other breast its due pleasure too. He then turned me over to kiss and lick me on the back. I prayed that he would strip me fully, penetrate me, hurt me, make me come. He did not. Not that day.

He flopped back to his seat, eyes closed, breathing hard. I opened my eyes a wee bit to see him smiling. He was looking so sweet and cute. And sexy. Damn! I was in love. Just the thing I did not want. I shut my eyes. I was smiling too. All of me was. I kept my lips straight though. I could not give away anything for now.

If the men I married had planned their first nights with me like the way Manan did, I might not have had the problems I had with them. Not only would they have made me feel special and loved, but it would have been a reflection of the kind of men they were. If I was still single, Manan would have been the one I would have married. I would have been faithfully his. Forever.

He booked us a suite at the Sheraton and heaped it with all the works. Candle lights, flowers, decorations, music, champagne, butler service—if such an amorous setting did not get a couple into a wildly romantic mood, nothing would. He got me a sexy dress for the dinner, and sexier lingerie and shirt for the night. Not that I would be wearing anything after the butlers had left us to ourselves.

Manan had God written all over him. No one had given me as much pleasure as he did that night. He knew how much conversing mattered to me, and that's how he started. He talked, he joked, he expressed his love all evening over the bubbly. He whispered sweet-nothings and erotic-everythings in my ears before his lips felt me. From head to toe. And between my legs. He went down on me, taking me between his lips, running his tongue on the outside and then pushing it inside. He was soaking in my wetness, giving me head I had not known was possible.

He massaged my back, my shoulders and my thighs. He took his fingers down, probing till he discovered my erogenous zones. He felt the area—gently at first, then vigorously. He did not have to be inside me to give me an orgasm; his fingers did the job very well. The suite was located at the far end of the corridor; other guests and staff were spared the disturbance my moaning and screaming would have caused.

My high state had clouded my senses, but I vaguely remember begging him to penetrate me, but he stretched the tease longer. He finally took me, with me on top. I came, and so did he. We did it again, with me sitting on his lap. And then he came in from behind; he had come prepared with lubricants. He wrapped up the madness by taking me in the missionary position.

I could make out the first light of dawn through the thick blinds by the time he was finished with me. He rolled over and slept. And so did I. Did it actually happen, or did I dream it all up? I woke hours later and turned my head to see Manan still asleep. There had not been a lovelier sight in my bed ever before.

Kamal finally healed. And went out looking for me. He tried to get me to meet him, but I evaded him. He took to stalking me, being fully versed with places I frequented. He eventually cornered me in a pub and ended up getting bashed in a brawl with my friend Prateek who was there with me. Why was Kamal reducing himself to such a sorry state?

I had not communicated with him while he was in hospital. There were a few exchanges of text messages and a couple of brief calls while he was recuperating at home, but were limited to updates on each other's lives and his health. His phone was being monitored by Antara. But he did get out of bed eventually and was able to move around town. His priority was to see me. I had promised his family that I would stay away, and intended to keep my word.

It couldn't have been very difficult for Kamal to track me down; he always joked about me being a creature of habit. My movements were predictable; until the accident, he had been the one taking me around. He hung around shops I picked up daily supplies from, my preferred salon, Vani's school, the gym, my favourite cafes—but he always missed me. But not at Strikers.

I was sitting with my usual group of friends when I saw him approaching our table. I got up and walked towards him before he reached us. What are you doing here? I asked.

I have been trying to reach out to you for weeks. Why haven't you been responding? he asked. I could smell whisky in his breath.

You are fretting too much. You should be worrying about your health and family right now.

Don't tell me what to do. I know what I want.

So do I. We are both adults. You know what I mean.

You can't do this to me.

Do what to you?

Treat me like this, ignore me. I lose my head when you don't talk to me.

Listen Kamal, there is nothing going on between us. If something had to happen, it would have by now. But it didn't. I think it's best we move on. And stay good friends.

I can't. I love you.

But I don't. I tried. I just don't feel it.

You are lying.

I am not. You should go home now. You should not be driving at night anyway after drinking. You still need to be careful after what you have been through. I will talk to you tomorrow. Let me go back to my table now. Bye.

I turned to leave but he held me by my arm. I tried to free myself without creating a scene but his grip was very firm. It seemed everyone in the pub had their eyes on us. Before I could figure out how to tackle the situation, Prateek walked up from our table and pushed Kamal away from me.

What followed was typical of what men do. Each pushed the other a couple of times before coming to blows. They were both tall, bulky men and made for quite a sight. Kamal took a fall, and hit his head on a table. There was no blood fortunately. He charged at Prateek but he got entangled in the arms of a bouncer. The latter kept a tight hold of him and dragged him out. I wanted to follow them to see if he was ok, but my friend Lara held me back and advised me to return to the table.

I was ruffled and irritated. Lara ordered a double whisky for me. I mumbled a thanks and a sorry to everyone. I wished Manan was around, but he was stuck at home with his parents.

A few blows were not enough to dissuade Kamal from pursuing me. He continued investigating into my affairs and learnt about Manan from common acquaintances. He followed me for days till he spotted Manan and me at the Kunzum Travel Café.

Nikita is the love of my life. I want her, I cannot live without her, declared Kamal. He was cheeky enough to walk in and say what he did, never having met Manan before.

She might be, but you have to ask the girl what she wants, replied Manan.

When I didn't say anything, Kamal understood and finally backed off. It was heart-rending to see him walk away, dejected. I wanted to hold him and cry, but our relationship needed to go under the guillotine for him to get his family life in order. He stopped calling me and messaging me. He must have finally given his wife a husband, for they soon had kids. Two in three years.

Manan continued to love me, to pamper me, to spoil me. We grabbed every opportunity to go out of town. It could just be a day trip to a resort near town, or further away to even Singapore and Istanbul. I got creative with reasons to justify the need to travel. And he with letters.

He would write long ones, and then read them out to me before handing them over. I used a photo album to make a scrapbook of the letters and some of the terrible portraits he shot of me. To go back to again and again. He had a special talent to make me laugh wherever we were. And scream when in bed. He could turn invisible when required. He would drop by at home at times, but spend the night in my room after giving an impression he had left. In a bold move, he once stayed over when Nakul was home too. We were as energetic and wild as we could get away with. We were like teenagers with one another, without a care in the world. I felt unleashed despite being shackled in marriage. And I was emotionally invested in a way I had not been with anyone.

I had stopped feeling guilty long back. I did not care even if we got caught. Nakul treated all my male friends the same, never questioning why some—and one in particular—hung around at our place excessively. I still could not fathom what was in his mind and heart, why he continued to be so negligent about us.

And yet, no matter what I felt for Manan emotionally and physically, and even for those I was in relationships with after him, I would always see myself as a tramp seeking the comforts and security of a home of my own. With Nakul.

Manan was a toy I didn't want to let go of. But his parents obviously did not see him the same way; he was a man they were pressuring to get married. He wanted to marry me, and I would have been readily agreeable, but I needed time to get a divorce. Or that's what I told him. Truth be told, I was not ready to leave home yet and was buying time till I was sure about what I wanted, despite being in love with Manan. But he could not wait much longer.

It should not have been unexpected for me. He came from a business family where it was a norm to be married by one's mid-twenties, or even sooner. His parents gave him an ultimatum: bring home someone you like, or be agreeable to one they do. He could not take home a married woman, so he said yes to a girl they arranged for him.

He broke the news to me in bed after an afternoon of passionate sex—in the same suite in Sheraton where we had had a honeymoon night of sorts. I blew my top. How can you get married to someone else? I asked.

What choice do I have? We have had discussions about being together for life, but it's not possible till you get a divorce.

I will get one. I just need time.

How much time? We have been together for over two and a half years. Nakul has no inkling of your intent to leave him.

I need a suitable opportunity.

There is never the right time for these things. It's a surgery one has to go through. Without anaesthesia. It will be painful, and maybe ugly too, whenever you do it.

You can't put me under pressure to do it. I will fail.

Honestly, I am not even sure if you will ever leave your husband. And I don't want to live with the uncertainty.

How dare you doubt me? Can't you see how much I love you?

I can see that. You are older than I am, and have seen much more of life. But I know it will not be easy for you to live with insecurities once again after broaching the subject of divorce with your husband. It's not a kind world out there for divorced women. You have seen it already.

But I won't be single. I will be with you.

Yes, you would have been. But only if you had taken timely steps for a divorce. Even if you tell him tonight, it will take years. You might have been done with it by now had you acted sooner.

What are you trying to say? Your mind is made up about marrying someone else? I asked.

You cannot leave a person only if you have someone else waiting for you. You should want to leave him because you cannot live with him anymore. What if you split up with him and don't find me waiting?

Why would you not be waiting?

Let me finish. I love you, and I love you very much. I would have married you today if you were single. Even if I was willing to wait and you initiated the process today, things might change between now and your legal separation. What if we are no longer together?

You still have not answered my question. Have you decided on marrying someone else?

He paused. He looked at me. I could feel him breathing for a long time. And then he spoke. Yes.

What is all this then? A final fuck before you go off? Break-up sex? Does your fiancée know where you are right now?

You don't have to talk like this.

Why not? You are moving on, but also want to have your pleasure with me.

You are seeing it all wrong.

Go fuck yourself. You are just like everyone else. Go all over town dropping your sperm into any hole you find, but marrying the woman your parents tell you to. Having a big dick on steroids does not make you a man. The way you treat women defines the man you are.

Aren't we being a little extreme here?

Extreme? Me? I feel so humiliated. I cannot even get myself to come out of these sheets to change. I don't want you to see my body anymore.

This had to happen one day if you were going to stay married.

I don't want to discuss this anymore. Can you do me one last favour? Please put on your clothes and leave the room for a while. I need to get dressed, but not in your presence.

He tried to say something but stopped himself. He lifted his naked body from the bed, picked up his clothes which were strewn around and went to the bathroom. He came out after fifteen minutes to find me lying on my stomach, still covered, my face buried in the pillow. I could feel my skin burning but I was not crying. I will be in the coffee shop, he said. Join me there or call me back up. I will be waiting. Let's talk.

I heard the door open and close when he left. I got up, took a shower, put on my clothes, dabbed light make-up, mustered up whatever dignity I could and left the suite. I went straight out to the porch of the hotel, hailed a cab and went home.

Manan called me the same night. And then the following day. And every day after that for weeks. I would take only a few of his calls, never returning the ones I ignored. He begged me to meet him. I didn't want to. But I did. Not every time he asked, but when I felt too weak to stay away. We would fight, we would argue. I behaved like the spoilt child; he tried to pacify me, console me, but I could not be assuaged. I would cry, and he too would. Every rendezvous would end in angry sex.

There was nothing sweet, or loving, when our bodies were entangled. Not much was said to each other; he didn't even attempt to make me laugh. We knew our relationship was terminally ill, on ventilator support. The gaps between our meetings kept going up, till it reached infinity one day. We met for the last time. There were no parting hugs, kisses or sex. We just sat with each other; I don't remember a word being exchanged. He got married the following day.

I felt rejected. I felt alone all over again. I was upset. I wanted to get drunk everyday, but my survival instincts stopped me, lest I again disfigure the body I had restored with immense effort and sacrifice. I did not feel like looking at the children. I stayed aloof from Nakul more than ever before. I missed his calls and took forever to reply to his messages and emails when he was away. I would insist that he have sex with me when he was home, but I did not sleep in the same room as him. I needed to smoke to be rid of his taste and breath after he had been over and inside me. I hated him; I would have been laughing with Manan but for Nakul's presence in my life.

Manan was great for my ego; he was a confidence booster. As were Kamal and the other men when they wooed me and fought over me. I did not expect to be sought after in my thirties, married and with two kids. I didn't even try to be discreet about the relationship with Manan; all our friends knew we were a pair. I didn't give a damn if Nakul got to know; in all likelihood, someone might have squealed on me. But he never brought it up.

Was Manan the love of my life? He might have been. But he was definitely a need, to transport me to a utopia I had never been to. I didn't want to lose that. But I had to. I had to wake up from my dream, to face reality. The reality of motherhood, the reality of an insipid marriage, the reality of the raw deal I was getting in life, the reality of living behind a cracked facade.

In hindsight, Manan was the adult between us despite being much younger to me. Even when we spoke about marriage, he knew it would not happen. There might have been too much resistance from his family. Nakul would not have let go of me easily either. Even though I hated him at the time, I thanked my stars later for the maturity and wisdom with which he handled the situation.

Not that I was done with men. Even if I wanted to be, Deepa would not let me. Move on, she said. This is a game where men will come and men will go, but you cannot leave the field. Keep playing.

If I was a prostitute, Deepa would have been my pimp. She took it upon herself to set me up with men. I met almost everyone she proposed. I rejected everyone I met.

There was Jai who took me out for a drink. He was slurring after the first glass of wine. He threw up after the second. I had to drop him home. He called to apologize later, and pleaded to meet again. I agreed. He was out by the second drink again. I could not be with a man I had to carry home.

I met Manan's namesake. I was drawn to the name more than to the man. By the second meeting, he was miserably in love with me. He was texting every few minutes, for days on end. He sent me letters, cards, flowers and cakes—there was a delivery for me daily. It was getting embarrassing. I tried to talk him out of it, but he asked me not to be furious at the overt display of his affections but to consider the sentiment behind it. I relented. We went out a few times. I had sex with him. But only in the dark. I was trying to be with the Manan I yearned for, not the one in my bed. I had to keep the lights off so I would not see his face, only imagine the one I wanted to see. When the lights came on, I would feel repulsed at the Manan fawning over me. He made for an ugly sight. It was not going to last. I was over him in three months.

Deepa fixed a blind date with Gopi; he owned a chain of garment stores. He picked me up on a weekday afternoon but we didn't know what we were going to be doing together. We made small talk, and then he said I smelt like a freshly baked bun. I had no idea how to react. Should I take it as a compliment or as an insult? I don't know why Deepa wanted us to meet, I finally said.

You don't like my company? he asked.

It's not that. I am not in the frame of mind to be with anyone. A few personal issues, and I am also setting up a business of my own.

You are? What's it about?

It's a label of nightwear for women.

That's interesting. Who's doing your designing, production and distribution?

I am still figuring. Let's see.

You can supply to me. I have my own stores. I would be happy to stock them.

That's real nice of you. Thanks.

Since we are out anyway, would you like to have lunch? Do you like Thai?

I would like that. I have not had Thai in ages.

I know a good place near my office itself. We can go there.

That's what we did. I had not heard of the place, but it was a good recommendation. I made a note to go back there the next time I had a craving for Thai. I wanted to use a clean washroom when we were leaving and he suggested the one in his office. We walked across and he guided me to the one attached to his own cabin.

It was a relief to use a spotless bathroom; it said something about the owner. But it did not say enough about him. I found Gopi standing just outside the door when I opened it to step out. He grabbed me and was kissing and groping me before I could fully fathom what was happening. He tried to kiss me on the lips and shove his tongue inside my mouth. He had one hand squeezing my bum and another my breast. I was cornered but not defeated. I wiggled till I made room to raise my knee and smash his nuts. He had to let go of me, clutching himself between the legs, writhing in agony.

You are a worthless piece of shit, an asshole. Go fuck yourself, I screamed. I could not care who heard me in his office. I walked out and hopped into the first autorickshaw I saw and called Deepa to tell her to stop being my 'agent'. I was done with men for now. Or at least the ones she sent my way.

Gopi was bad news. I should never have been in touch with him again. But I must be a sucker for those who talk sweet, even if their past conduct had been criminal in my book. I forgave him, and he paid me back with an introduction to Angad.

Deepa and I were out on a bestie evening at TGI Fridays when Gopi walked up to us. I looked at Deepa with an expression of 'what's he doing here'. She ignored me and greeted him with a peck and a hug.

I know I am intruding, but I requested Deepa to let me come and see you for a few minutes, he said. I stayed expressionless while he continued speaking. Don't be angry with your friend, I made life hell for her. I wanted to apologize to you. I have no idea what came over me that day, and I have only felt miserable since.

You deserve to, I said.

Can you forgive me?

What if I do? What do you want?

I just want to know that you have accepted my apology, so we can be friends. Nothing more, I promise.

Ok, I will not hold anything against you. But don't expect me to meet you or call you.

You don't have to one on one. But allow me to when we meet in groups.

I don't know what that entails, but I will not grudge your presence if there are others around. And I will not talk to you if I don't want to.

Thank you so much. It's a big load off my head. I promise to make it up to you if I ever can.

Don't bother, you won't be able to. But take a chill pill and rest easy. And be careful in the future. Other women might be more spiteful should you try any hanky-panky with them.

I promise to conduct myself properly. I have learnt my lesson.

Good. I have to leave now. You can pay my bill as the penalty.

Gladly, he said. He was all smiles. The predator was suddenly looking docile. I actually forgave him.

He left us alone to go to another table where a man was already sitting. I had not noticed until then, but he was looking continuously in my direction. He did not look like someone I would want to remember. But he was eyeing me as someone he would not forget. He did not.

❧

Gopi broke the first condition of his parole by calling me. He wanted to introduce me to a friend—the one who was waiting for him at the other table at TGI Fridays. Why would I want to be introduced to him?

No reason, he just wants to know you, said Gopi. I agreed for a brief phone call.

We spoke, but it wasn't a long conversation. It was more about what he does and what I do. He called again a few days later. We chatted longer this time; he was curious about my new venture. The third time he called was to tell me about his real estate network, and how he could help me set up my own stores. I had not been thinking of that option yet; I was looking at supplying to existing ones. Having your own shopfront will enable you to establish your own brand and design identity in the market, he suggested.

And then we met. I invited him to join our group for drinks and dinner. He looked worse than what I remembered of him from TGI Fridays. He was downright unattractive if I could be rude enough to say so. He had the top buttons of his shirt open, his gold chains camouflaged under heavy chest hair. He was wearing gold bracelets, rings and even a stud in his right ear. I tried to imagine a woman in bed with such a character. I almost threw up my drink at the visual I conjured.

But he was soft-spoken in a gentlemanly kind of way; he was ever willing to fetch drinks for us, and was always leading ladies to dances. He moved well on the floor in his shiny, white leather shoes. I still had my reservations; I was curious to meet a woman who was willing to kiss him. I would, before the evening was over.

He offered to drop Deepa and me home when we were leaving. She whispered in my ear to not worry, he's a safe guy. We dropped her first and were on the way to my place when I asked him to pull over. I needed fresh air; I had a drink too many. I could do with a smoke too. We got talking.

Why did you ask Gopi to connect us? I asked.

Just like that. I saw you at TGI Fridays and I was drawn to you. I just wanted to know you better, he said.

If it's about having a thing with me, I would advise you not to get your hopes too high.

I just want to be friends.

Come on, you liar. You would not be wasting your time if that was so. Won't you like me to take my clothes off for you?

Which man wouldn't? But I don't have any such intentions.

You guys crack me up. Anyway, I am in a bad place right now. I am married with two kids. I have had relationships outside marriage. I am still to recover from the last one; it has been tough for me to accept the break-up. I have thrown myself at some men on a rebound, and hated myself more than them for it. If you touch me, your hands will get gooey with the mess I am in. Judge me if you want to. And I don't know what I am blabbering, I am sure I am drunk right now.

I can wait.

Wait for what?

For you.

But you just wanted to be a friend.

I am sure you can do with more than just a friend.

I know what you are after baby. You look like such a lamb. Come to momma!

And then I did something I had never done before. I pulled him close to me and smooched him. Long, wet and rough. I pushed my tongue inside his mouth and bit his lips. He did not flinch, but let me do what I wanted to. He kissed me back gingerly but did nothing more. I wondered if he had ever shared a passionate kiss with another woman. By the looks of him, I doubt any woman would be willing to. Except me.

What made me kiss a man like Angad?

❧

Angad fell in love with me. Rather, he assumed I was in love with him and it was only right for him to reciprocate. Just because we kissed. He interpreted the evening to suit whatever he wanted to believe. An evening I have only a blurry memory of, and no justification or reason to have done what I did. It just happened. But he issued a licence to himself to play a leading role in my life. And just then, Kamal too came back into the picture, all the way from the USA.

I got a call from an American number out of the blue; it was Kamal. I was surprised to hear his voice; I could recognize his exuberant self anywhere. Despite whatever happened between us, I was delighted to hear from him. He had been my comfort zone, and was just the person I needed around. Even if he was halfway across the planet.

Kamal stayed true to who he had always been. He got an opening when I took his call, and he tried to wiggle in as much as he could. He would call frequently, sometimes even twice a day—for a good morning and for a good night. The wishes were inverted though due to the time zones. I was glad for the distraction; it gave me an excuse to avoid Angad's calls. I would deliberately tell him about being on a call with Kamal and how close we are. I knew the revelation of Kamal being in love with me perennially would bother Angad, but I needed him to back off a bit. I underestimated him.

I want to meet you, said Kamal one day. I have already booked my tickets and will land the following Monday.

There was nothing I could do about it. His timing was cunningly planned. I had casually mentioned when Nakul would be leaving the country again; Kamal was landing two days after that. He also knew that the kids would be in Agra for the vacations. I offered to pick him up from the airport. I could make out how happy he was to hear that. I became a bundle of nerves though. I feared for what would happen. We had been talking about all kinds of stuff for the past few months, even a bit of tender-loving stuff. I felt there was no risk in such flirting; we were separated by the seven seas and I could get away with it. I had forgotten what Kamal could be like when it came to me.

We greeted each other with big smiles and hugs like friends separated since childhood. Are you staying with your mother? I asked.

Didn't I tell you? My brother got a job in Kathmandu; mom also moved with him.

Did they? Even Raghav, my younger brother, found work to his liking in Nepal. Our siblings should connect. So where are you staying?

I don't know yet.

You landed here without a place to stay?

It didn't even strike me. Let me figure something out.

You want to stay at my place, for at least a few days?

Yes, that would be lovely. Let's go.

My blood pressure must have dropped to zero. I didn't expect him to accept the invite offered as just a courtesy. I assumed he would not find it proper to stay with me in an empty house, and would offer to check into a hotel or stay with a friend. My hands were cold and my head hot as a stove by the time we reached home. He checked to see if I was ok; I was not. I was running a fever four degrees above normal. The stress had made me sick.

It took five days for the fever to subside; he played nurse to me all those days just like he would have in the past. If he was expecting to be close to me during the visit, he could not have imagined it this way. I had a million missed calls from Angad while I was bedridden; I didn't have the strength to talk to anyone except with Vani briefly.

Angad went nuts. He knew Kamal was staying with me; I had casually mentioned it while we were driving back from the airport. He assumed all sorts of things happening between Kamal and me in the privacy of the house. Why else would I be ignoring his calls? He didn't know how sick I was. He would have come home to check things out for himself, but he was in Ahmedabad for work. I finally returned his call when I could, to hear him ranting at the other end.

Why didn't you take my calls all these days? he asked.

I could not, I replied. My voice was still subdued with weakness.

Why? Just because Kamal is over?

No, because I have been running a very high fever.

Why didn't you tell me?

I had no energy. I have not touched my phone in days.

Who looked after you?

Kamal. Who else?

Can I ask you something?

Sure.

Is there something going on between you and Kamal?

As much as it is between you and me.

That's not right.

What's not right?

You can't be involved with the both of us.

Ok, you did not understand what I meant. There is nothing on between you and me. And there is nothing on between Kamal and me. You are the same for me: good friends, that's it.

I could sense his relief on the phone. He could live with me not loving him for the time being as long as I did not fancy anyone else in the meantime either.

I am back tomorrow. Can we meet? he asked.

Let me feel better. Then we will, I replied and hung up.

It felt like I was sitting in a pool of mud. Or shit. How do I manage to make a mess of things? Why were Angad and Kamal trying to appropriate my life? Who was giving them the right to? Did they take permission from me? One guy was trying to erect a wall around me to keep other men out. And another had come all the way from America to woo me all over again despite all that had transpired in his life over the past few years. They refused to accept my rejection of them. I wouldn't miss them for a moment if they both vanished from the face of the Earth.

The best tactic under the circumstances was to take on one challenge at a time. It was just a matter of four days before Kamal flew back. I decided to play the gracious host and entertain him while he was there. Angad could be tackled after that.

Kamal achieved nirvana within his lifetime. He had sex with me.

We stayed home mostly even after my fever had subsided, stepping out only for him to shop for things to take back. I didn't want to eat out or go drinking for fear of a relapse. We talked endlessly; in those four days, we managed to update each other about our respective lives.

There was no fire in his marriage, as he put it. Life followed a set routine. Both he and his wife held day jobs, dropping the older kid to a playschool and the younger one to a creche on the way to work. Their social circle was only people of Indian origin. He was learning to play golf on weekends, while Antara cooked and stored the food in a deep freezer to be consumed over the coming week. They had pledged to have sex at least twice a week. They were lucky if they managed thrice a month. She was still to experience an orgasm with her husband; she didn't even try to fake it.

I told him everything about the men who had been in and out of my life. I assumed that he would abhor me for being involved with all those men, but nothing could have been further from his way of thinking. He got jealous and wanted to possess me even more than before. On his last night in town, he opened his heart up.

I have not loved any woman except you Nikita, he said.

I know, Kamal. And I have always been fond of you. But I could not reciprocate with so much happening in my life. When I tried to, the timing went awry and you got married, I said.

If I had not got married, could we have been together?

I don't know. But I was trying to get closer to you. My heart was dragging its feet, but I did make an honest attempt.

I wish I had not got married.

Don't say that. You don't know what you have got. Antara is a very good girl, one who will keep you and the family grounded. You might not find it a fiery marriage, but many would gladly exchange their lives for yours. Having a stable and a trusted partner is an invaluable gift in times when relationships have become so ephemeral.

I know, but what do I do? I can't stop missing you.

I am just an infatuation for you, something the little boy in you has not been able to get his hands on. I am sure you will not feel this way if you had got me. You would have been long over me by now.

I disagree.

We can't prove it now, it's too late.

We can.

What?

Still test your theory.

How?

Allow me to kiss you.

You have kissed me in the past.

Those were not kisses of passion. And we kissed only when high, more in jest than as a prelude to seduction.

But the kiss will not establish anything.

It can. Allow me to kiss you. All over.

I looked at him. He was looking straight at me, unblinking, with the intensity of a man who wants to take the woman in front of him. I had not seen such a look in him before. He had grown up. At the same time, a part of his eyes were imploring me to do something. I did not want to disappoint my truest friend, even if it threw our future into uncertain waters.

I was sitting on my bed and he on a stool next to it. I extended my arm to take his. I pulled him closer till he was sitting beside me. I put my arms around his neck and my lips to his. We kissed. And then we kissed more. We rolled over to lie next to each other. We continued kissing even as I unbuttoned his shirt and jeans. He tried to pull my top off but he couldn't without my help. No sooner were our clothes off than he was inside me. Neither bothered about nor desired foreplay. I was having sex with him out of a sense of gratitude. He was having sex with me as a stamp of victory. He did not use a condom, I didn't ask him to. I let him come inside me. I wanted the experience to be complete for him. I did not come.

He lay on his back beside me when it was over. There was no afterplay either. We had sex because we should have had it long back. Kamal would have stopped chasing me then itself. But he got his closure only that day. And then, just like that, we both went silent on one another. We barely spoke till the following day when I dropped him off at the airport. There was nothing left to say. The pressure had been released.

I had always felt guilty for messing with Kamal's mind and heart with my tantrums after he had got engaged. The load was finally off my shoulders. I had paid my debt. I would never see Kamal again in my life.

It was time to get a handle on things with Angad.

Angad had no ego. He hovered around me no matter how I treated him. He just wanted to be close to me physically, if not emotionally. To be able to do things to please me. Sometimes he tried too hard. I would find it pesky, but I just could not shake him off.

He offered to invest in my business. I declined. I could have used the money, but not his. He insisted. And offered unsolicited advice continuously. To my ears, he made sense. I was a first-time entrepreneur, still learning the ropes. Everything was new to me; he made himself sound very intelligent. You have nothing to lose if you take my money, he kept saying. It is my loss to bear should things not work out.

I relented and he made a hefty bank transfer. I wasn't even sure if he had that kind of money to spare. I hoped he was not stretching himself to impress me. He didn't stop at that. The kids were now staying with me, and he stepped forward to share the responsibility of minding them so that I would have more time for other work. He volunteered to drive them to wherever they needed to be, help them with their projects and even entertain them in the new malls that were opening up. But I drew a line there; I would not trust him with my children without me being present.

He invited me often to go out, but I would find excuses not to unless there were others present. Whenever we did, he made sure he picked me up and dropped me off. I wish I had not accepted his money. I could then have been rude if I wanted to be, but I was stuck. Maybe that's what he had wanted. He bought my politeness even if I had to force it.

He finally proposed. Not to marry but just to date him. He was over at my place to discuss business plans. When we were done, he asked for a beer. I poured myself a whisky. I know what you feel about me, Angad, but I am not able to respond the way you want me to, I said.

But you made me believe you are interested in me, he said.

How and when?

You hang around with me so much. I don't see you doing it with others.

Yes, but that's because you are so insistent about it. I am not always comfortable.

Why did you kiss me on the highway? And you also told me you loved me.

I never said that. If I did, I must have been drunk. Just as I was when I kissed you. We are both adults. We cannot cling onto such things. They happen, but are meant to be forgotten.

This talk was stressing me out, more so since no one else was home. He had me cornered. I didn't realize I was drinking very fast and was already on my fourth double. I could feel my head swim; his presence in the house was freaking me out. I wanted to ask him to leave, but I don't know what I actually said. Whatever he heard encouraged him to come close to me, hold me and kiss me. He was groping me, taking my clothes off. I wanted to push him away, but I kept melting in his body. I passed out soon.

When I came to, the lights were still on. My head was throbbing. I looked at the wall clock to my left. It was around three. Something told me I was not alone. I felt scared. My heart started beating faster. I slowly turned to look on the other side of the bed. I saw Angad. Sleeping. Without any clothes on. That's when I realized I was naked waist down and my bra was open. Shit!

I wanted to scream but managed to keep a lid on my nerves. Maybe nothing happened. I looked around, and across him. And then I saw it. On the floor. A used condom. I sank back into the bed. My eyes were wet. If I had a knife, I would have stabbed Angad in the chest right then and there.

There was nothing I could do but feel sick. I slunk out of the bed, wrapped the duvet around me and went to another room. I locked myself in and tried to sleep. Surprisingly, I could. When I woke up, I looked at my phone. Angad had messaged to say he was leaving, and will talk to me later. The message ended with the icon of a heart and a smiley. Groan!

*I told you to run*, Radha didi was back in my head. *But you don't listen. I was raped because I had nowhere to hide, no one to save me. But you had a choice, Niki.*

The name matters. It would have been tough to be out with a guy called Markandey. I met such a man. Fortunately for us, he hated his name too. And thus called himself Mark. Now that's a name I could love. Rather, I could love a man with such a name. I did. I fell in love. For truly the first time in my life. With Mark.

I was introduced to Mark at a tech conference I was attending with Nakul. Mark was heading the software operations of IBM in North India. He was one of the many people I got introduced to but I did not care to remember anyone. I was bored as hell, but Nakul had insisted I accompany him for the cocktails session of the event. Sporting a beautiful wife is good to draw attention for profitable networking. Fortunately, I survived the ordeal without giving Nakul any reasons to complain.

A few days later, Deepa and I were invited to a party at a farmhouse hosted by an acquaintance of her sixth boyfriend. She was late, and I didn't know anyone there. I found a safe spot by the bar and got a martini to keep me company. I preferred to be alone, but two men came up in quick succession, trying to make small talk. My responses were colder than my drink, sending them scurrying for cover. I was anyway irritated with Deepa for leaving me stranded at a place I knew no one, and these men only made it worse. I resisted the temptation to order a large whisky to calm down.

And then suitor number three walked up. I think I know you, he said.

I have had enough for the evening, I said.

Excuse me?

I have never met you, I have never spoken to you, I don't want to know you.

You are getting it wrong.

Why? Did you just drop an original pick-up line and I failed to catch it?

He started laughing. I am not trying to hit on you, I am not trying to pick you, he said. I have been trying to place you for the last ten minutes before I remembered. We met at the conference at the Taj Palace last week. I am Mark, and I work at IBM.

I jogged my memory but could not really place him from the many I had met that evening. But I pretended to recall somewhat. Thankfully, he told me his name again so I didn't have to feel awkward about asking him. I am so sorry, I said.

It's just that a lady cannot have a drink by herself in this city without men making clowns of themselves around her. Two already came by, I thought you were the third.

That's ok.

You were in formals that day and in casuals now. So I didn't make the connection immediately.

You are Nikita, right? Nakul's wife?

Yes. Do you know Nakul well?

Yes, I do. Independent consultants like him are important to us; their recommendations swing deals for us with clients. So we have to take good care of them. And offer our company if their wives would allow us to.

Of course, it would be a pleasure. Are you here alone?

I was, until now.

Can I get you a drink?

I thought gentlemen asked that question. But since you offered, I would not mind a martini too, he said.

I requested a server passing by to get us one. Mark and I agreed we were misfits at the event; we kept ourselves entertained by observing others present and judging them on the basis of their looks. We laughed like crazy at our own silliness but managed to kill the boredom. Deepa finally walked in, boyfriend in tow.

Introductions followed, and Deepa said we needed to leave. For an impromptu bash at Gopi's farm. This party already looks boring, she said. Right, after I had been suffering for a good part of the hour. I figured it may be best to leave. I thanked Mark for his company, and we exchanged numbers.

Sorry for breaking up your little private party with the dude, but I am sure you will not regret it, she said on the way.

Gopi has promised a shindig like nothing we have never been to before. I shrugged. I couldn't care less.

I forgot all about Mark but he made sure I did not for long. He called a few weeks later. Even though I had his number saved on my phone, it took me a few moments to place him before I answered.

I think I know you, he said. I caught on and laughed. Yes, I remember you this time, I replied.

How have you been? he asked.

I am good, thank you. And you?

All good. I called for a reason, so I will get straight to the point. Would you like to have lunch with me?

What's the occasion?

Nothing; inviting you just like that.

Ummm, I am not sure. I am really busy at work and just don't know if I will be able to make time.

No problem, I thought of asking. I enjoyed talking to you the last time we met before your friend abducted you. I have not had such fun with anyone in a long time.

Did anyone tell you I like good conversationalists? I asked.

No.

Now you do. We will meet because I liked talking to you too. Can we fix our date in a few days? I am up to my neck with work, literally. I am surrounded by cartons filled with the first lot of my nightwear line. I need to sort and index these, and repack them to ship out to retailers.

Of course. Will check with you next week. Should you need me to, I can bring lunch to your warehouse and help out too.

Sure, thanks. Ciao.

I would actually have liked Mark to bring me a meal to the workplace but for the omnipresence of Angad. Ever since he had spent the night with me, he assumed he was the man in my life and was all over me. No matter what I was doing, if he got to know about it, he would turn up to be a part of it. Including the times I was with the kids. He tried to shower me with gifts—shoes, perfumes, dresses and even a diamond set. I rejected most; I did not want to encourage him further by accepting his gifts. In any case, he had utterly poor taste in such stuff. I did not hesitate to express my dislikes; I had no feelings for him, so I did not care if it hurt him.

He would come home unannounced and hang around even if I was not there. Nakul's presence did not deter him either. Angad behaved as if he were my other husband. He went about introducing himself as my business partner and assumed the role of one too. He would come to the office whenever he felt like, throwing his weight and advice around. He would interact with the staff, customers and vendors without consulting me, often creating confusion. I should have listened to my instincts and not accepted his money.

I should also not have softened up to Gopi and forgiven him; I think he introduced Angad into my life as some form of revenge for the snub I gave him.

I managed to evade the hawk-eyed Angad to spend time with Mark.

We met for lunch—I got breathing space a good three weeks after he first called to invite me. I made up for it by agreeing to meet him again. And we did. Frequently. Over meals, coffee and an occasional drink. He had not climbed the corporate ladder for nothing. He deserved it, for the depth of his knowledge and his overall intelligence. It was rare to know someone with whom I could have highly engaging conversations. A day did not pass when we did not talk. We could be on the phone with each other for hours daily.

This went on for nearly a year. And yet, in all that time, Mark did not express any romantic or sexual interest in me. Not even a hint. It was beautiful, and relieving to have such a companion. God knows how we both needed one at that stage of our respective lives. I wanted to stay away from men, and he was the ideal foil. He was going through a divorce himself, and found solace in my friendship. With benefits of the platonic kind.

He missed calling or messaging me one day. And for another four days. At first, I didn't make much of it, but something started knocking in my head then. Why had he not called all those days? Even if he had not, why was I thinking so much about it? He's just a friend; all my friends don't call daily. What was I getting so anxious about? Why couldn't I get a grip on myself? If I am so edgy, why was I not calling him to check?

His name flashed on my phone eventually. I am so sorry I was missing all these days, he said. But there was no commitment between us to call the other, I thought. Why was he apologizing? But it felt nice, very nice, to hear his voice.

No, you don't have to say this. It's fine. I am sure you were caught up with something important, I said.

Yes, my mother had to be admitted to the hospital for a chest infection. She was in intensive care. I was too frazzled to think straight. The only person I wanted to call was you but didn't want to bother you.

I felt sorry for his mother, and sincerely wished she recover soon. But it was a relief to know he was not with another woman. But why was I even letting such thoughts come to me? Why couldn't Mark have been with a woman? He and I didn't weren't seeing each other. We were just great friends who had not given any indications of wanting to be more than that. What was wrong with me?

Please don't hold yourself back from reaching out to me ever, I said. I am really sorry to hear about your mom. How is she now?

She's back home and is feeling quite normal. It was a scare but there are no long-term consequences of the infection thankfully, he said.

He promised to call again soon and hung up. But my head was still raising a storm. Why was I feeling happy knowing he was not with another woman? Such thoughts were really bothering me. I was falling in the trap again. What if I was just a friend to him and nothing more? Will that break my heart?

For the first time, I was paying attention to a man. It had always been a case of them being after me. It was a strange feeling for me. No matter how hard I tried, I could not push Mark out of my head. And heart.

I drink, therefore I do stuff I regret later. Consumption of alcohol should thus be made illegal for me. Mark would disagree though.

I was treating myself to a fine champagne Nakul had procured during his last trip. I had the television on but I was not registering anything playing on the screen. I could only see Mark's face. The more I drank, the fuzzier my head got. Mark stayed put. I saw him clearly through the mist in my eyes. He was smiling at me, holding his arms out. I stretched my arms but could only grasp air. I needed to talk to him.

I took out my phone to call him, but it was already past midnight. Not a good idea. I messaged him. I sent out a series of texts. I don't remember when I dozed off.

It was eleven in the morning when I woke up. It was Sunday, so I didn't fret. I was lazing in bed, thinking myriad things when something dawned upon me. I sat up with a start. And looked for my phone. It was under the pillow. Shit, shit, shit! I hope it was all a dream and I actually didn't do it. I looked at my phone. There was a missed call from Mark. No, no, no! I went to messages. I navigated to the sent folder. Nooo!

There were at least a dozen messages to Mark. I went scarlet all over. What was I smoking the previous night? My Marlboros, but they had never got me into any trouble in the past. Must be the champagne. I had written about how adorable he was, what a gentleman he was, and how he was the nicest man I had ever met. What was the need to tell him I had no marriage, that my personal life was a farce? That I felt at home around Mark, that he was family to me even though we were not together. That I loved him.

I tried to look for an undo command, to delete messages from Mark's phone, but in vain. He must have read them anyway. Why else would he have called on a Sunday morning? And just then, he called again. I moved my thumb in slow motion, taking my time to press the answer key.

Hello, I said. My voice was a squeak.

Good morning. How are you? he asked.

I am fine, I replied. I could barely hear my own self speak.

I got your messages.

You did?

It's a big load off my mind.

What do you mean?

I have been meaning to say the same things to you but could not get myself to. It would not have come across as appropriate considering your marital status and the professional acquaintance I have with your husband.

I am hung over. Maybe I didn't know what I was typing. So ignore whatever I wrote.

Now that we are talking about it, I want to tell you how attracted I am to you.

What if I didn't mean what I wrote?

It's too late now. I have been keeping a lid on my feelings for too long. The wait has not been easy. You can't back off now. And be honest with yourself: why would you write what you did if you didn't mean it?

Now what?

Let's meet for lunch.

❧

I was hopelessly in love. With Mark. I may have felt in love before, but this was the real deal. I could do anything for this relationship. I should have done everything for the relationship.

We got close effortlessly, as if our union was preordained. There were no fireworks between us. We did not get drunk and make fools of ourselves. We did not scream from the rooftops. We did not write letters to each other with our blood; we never wrote to each other with any kind of ink on paper. The sex was good but did not bring the house down. Or break any beds and office desks. Nothing was in the extreme; the average gave us a semblance of normalcy. Neither had ever felt such calm in our lives.

Being with Mark was nothing short of sublime. If I had to choose only one man in this lifetime, I would pick him without batting an eyelid. I have never had such certainty about anyone. I did not let Nakul touch me for over three years, even if he got angry and violent in frustration. I allowed myself to belong to Mark in the truest sense possible.

We would have been together for the rest of our lives if only our actions had spoken louder than our words of love for one another.

❧

I would have walked out on everything for Mark. I just needed him to wait five years. He was not willing to. My condition and his refusal left us both angry and bitter despite our respective justifications for the stands we took.

His divorce proceedings were taking longer than he had expected them to. Why was he rushing me then to get a divorce? We were together anyway, in the same boat. And happily so. Why don't men understand it's more difficult for women to just walk out of a marriage than it is for them? Manan had not handled it right. And now Mark was approaching it wrong too.

Mark was willing to wait but he found me unreasonable by asking for five years. He was confident of his divorce coming through much sooner than that. Why can't you set the ball rolling at your end too? he would argue. You have already drafted the obituary of your marriage, so why are you holding on to its carcass?

And yet, I never believed that Mark and I would be separated. The bond was too strong to come unstuck over disagreements of little consequence in the bigger scheme of things. But human beings have a special talent for overlooking the vital to favour the trivial. Mark allowed his gaze to wander first. In the direction of Tulika.

He had dated her in university; it was a teen romance, and was over before either reached their twenties. They reconnected on Facebook and exchanged notes as long lost friends do. She never married. He told her about his impending divorce and his relationship with me. She provided the first spark to rekindle the fires that had gone cold between them.

She desired him back, but he was besotted with me. She took to stalking him on social media. His phone pinged with her calls and messages at a steady regularity. He should have pushed her back, but he seemed to be deriving adolescent pleasure in the attention he was getting. He was careless with his phone, and I could not help peeping in. Tulika would send him flirty messages, and he would reply in jest. She persisted, seeing his humour as a sign of interest in her. Married women can never be more than a passing infatuation, but old flames never die, read one text from her. If you are right, then I shall seek warmth where you say it awaits, but it is my lady love who matters for now, he replied.

I did not doubt his commitment to me but could not help losing my cool seeing such exchanges. What do you think you are doing? I asked.

Come on, there is nothing to it. She's an old friend and we are just making light of our kiddie love in college, he said.

Don't be daft. You are not teenagers any more. You are both in your thirties for God's sake. She is clearly trying to woo you.

She is not. Even if she is, it does not matter. She knows, and you know, where my loyalties lie.

But do you know?

Of course I do. I love you.

She will snare you and you will not even know when the trap closed around you.

You are being paranoid, she's just a good friend.

I suggest you break off contact with her.

Why would I do that?

She is not a good influence.

I am not a child.

You are a man, you will slip.

You live with a man. You could give in to him too. Maybe you do.

How dare you accuse me like that?

How dare you doubt me like that?

Why do you give in to her flirtations?

Why do you continue living with your husband?

I have my compulsions.

And I have my friendships.

You can talk to her, or you can talk to me.

Don't blackmail me, it will backfire.

Try me.

Ok, then don't talk to me.

I didn't. For three weeks. I threw myself at the deep of my work to keep my mind off him. Eventually, he only called first. To apologize. He cried when he did, and asked me never to go off like that again. We met, we hugged, we kissed, we cried again, and we made love. But our bodies told us that something had changed between us.

I don't feel anything for you; you are no more than a good friend and a business partner for me. Why don't you understand? And unless you have been sleeping under a rock, I am sure you have seen me with Mark. I really love him, and cannot even think of being with anyone else. I don't even let my husband touch me.

I had to spell it out in so many words to Angad. I must have wasted my breath for he did not want to listen to what he did not want to accept. Rather than respecting my choices gracefully, he went off his rocker. I wouldn't have been bothered with him had he not stayed a sinister presence, forcibly, in my life for over a decade.

He tried to talk me out of my relationship with Mark without offering any plausible reasons to. When that failed, he tried to scare me. He got people to keep tabs on Mark and would tell me his whereabouts. I would check with Mark and the information would hold up; Angad was not bluffing. If I know where he is, I can even cause him harm, he would threaten.

Why would you do that? You will still not get me, I would retort.

Why don't you pay attention to what I am trying to warn you about? He's just out to have good fun with you, he's not to be trusted to be yours the way you him to be.

You are wrong. He's told his parents and sisters he intends to marry me.

That's just words. Why do you want to wait till your heart breaks into many more pieces than if you put an end to it now?

Let that be my problem.

And how do you explain him meeting Tulika?

How do you know about Tulika? And he doesn't meet her.

Should I arrange for photographs the next time they meet?

Yes, that would prove the liar you are.

Suit yourself. But the photos won't make for a pretty sight since the two of them would be in bed.

They don't meet anyway. And you are trying to tell me they have sex too? That's the most far-fetched scenario you could have come up with.

You will find out for yourself. Don't forget to say thank you when I am bandaging your heart.

You won't need to. Any bodily harm comes to Mark, and I will chew you till you are unrecognizable to even your wife.

You will kiss me one day.

He was blackmailing me, and sowing the seeds of suspicion in my mind at the same time. But I refused to be swayed. Even I did not want to listen to anything I did not want to accept.

I want out. Return the money I have invested. And do it without any delay. Even if it means shutting shop and selling everything to pay my dues.

When other tactics failed, Angad turned the financial screws on me. He demanded his investment back. Not that he needed the money, but he just wanted to torment me. He stooped low enough to even ask for the gifts he had given me. Especially the hideous diamonds; I had turned them down but he had insisted I keep them. I gathered all the gifts I could find and handed over a bagful to him. He accepted them without an iota of self-respect.

He did scare me initially but I realized I had nothing to lose by standing up to him. I will pay up when I find a buyer for the business or for my share, I told him.

But I want the money now, he said.

I don't have it. Anyway, you forced me to accept your investment. You did not give the company a loan, you bought shares of it. You are involved in the business fully so you figure the funds and keep them.

I wouldn't have asked for the money back if you had not misled me.

Misled you about?

About loving me.

When did I ever say I love you? Just because we have been spending time together, and did something foolish in a drunken state, does not mean anything. Not my fault you want to interpret things to suit you.

No, you found Mark so you dumped me.

Why do you go on and on about Mark? What's it to you what I do with him? Or with anyone else for that matter? And you only dump someone when you have a thing with them in the first place; there was nothing between us.

You cannot toy with my feelings.

I am repeating myself: I do not feel anything romantic for you. For the sake of argument, even if you got the impression I ever did, I no longer do. It is over.

What about all the investment I have made?

What does that have to do with our personal equations? Take it back when we have the money. You manage the accounts, find the money to pay yourself. If need be, we can shut the business down. Or I will quit. You can transfer all the shares to your name and run it your way. I will find something else to do.

He behaved like a jilted lover for months. We didn't meet except in the office. The air was frosty between us and would not have gone unnoticed by employees. He would send lewd messages, accusing me of being an opportunist, using men for my needs and pleasure. You will never find your peace, he cursed me. He raved about how much he had done for me but I had no gratitude to show for it. What will you do when Nakul knows about your doings? he threatened.

He sought perverse pleasure in engaging in verbal bouts with me; I gave him none. I ignored him steadfastly. It didn't strike me to ask how his wife would feel is she read the messages he had been sending me. I couldn't get such vicious thoughts in me. That's how he and I were different, and thus could not be together. But he refused to get it.

The breakup did not happen overnight. The flame went out one lumen at a time, taking several years to extinguish. But never fully. The wick is still warm when I touch it. My soul has not given up, it never will. I will always love Mark, always wait for him to come back. I can, and I will, walk out on everything to be with him now. If he will have me. The five years I had asked for have been long over.

The frequency of our meetings, our calls, our messages to each other went down gradually. There was a time when he and I couldn't converse enough, but that link slowly came apart. All that was left between us was sex. For weeks, for months, for years, no matter when we met, or what was happening in our respective lives, Mark and I had sex. Actually, if there was no sex, there would be no reason to meet. We didn't know what to say to each other. We stopped the pretence of a coffee or a meal together too; the time would just drag. An unspoken understanding was forged between us. If either proposed we meet, it was to figure a time and place to have sex.

He didn't admit to it, and I didn't probe, but I am sure Tulika eased into the space I was vacating in his life. Angad was willing to give me evidence of it, but I did not want it. It wasn't about confronting Mark with it. I could not grudge him if he was with her. I did not want to grudge him. Not until I walked out on Nakul and released myself from the suffocating grip of the devilish Angad.

And overcame my fears.

Fear is the mother of all fuck-ups. It makes you take decisions you don't want to, and it can end up ruining your life.

If I had not allowed it to get the better of me, my life could have been so different. It could have been what I had dreamt of growing up. Each time I found myself at crossroads, I allowed fear to have not just a say in the deliberations but the casting vote too. When I found myself at the most critical juncture of my life, I should have kept fear out of the room. Because I knew the right calls to make. My past experiences had given me the wisdom to. But not the courage.

The courage to challenge Angad for his threats to harm Mark. The courage to prioritize the personal over the professional. The courage to let my love win. The courage to call it quits on my marriage and live with Mark. The courage to marry for the third time. The courage to bring up my children in the face of any societal stigma. The courage to start all over again to prove my mettle as a professional. The courage to face up to and be responsible for my decisions.

Fear consumed me. I took decisions I knew were not right. I did not give myself a choice, even if the world had. I left my desired destiny stranded on an island as I rowed away.

I had started my business with immense passion and ambition but Angad was chipping away at it. He had first coerced me into taking his money, then he muscled his way into its operations. He extended this dominance into my personal life too. I was exasperated, and set to throw in the towel. He could keep everything if I never had to see him again. Just then a major retail chain approached us—they were willing to not only stock our products but also allocate space to be a store-in-store. This was the break we had been waiting for. The timing of it created a dilemma for me.

If I walked away as I was threatening to, either the brand would die or Angad would reap all the dividends. If I stayed put, I would have to tolerate Angad. It was too much for me to leave on the table, more so since I was emotionally invested in what was my first start-up. I decided to continue working if I could get him to be reasonable. I had to play my cards smart.

I am willing to let you own the business fully. You can buy out my share, I offered.

Our balance sheet is nothing to boast about. The valuation of the company will be less than what's already been put in by me. So you may have to end up paying just to exit, he replied.

He was not wrong. The company held a promise of doing well with the new tie-up being offered to us, but we were still tiny if measured by current sales. He was a tough cookie; he would not be checkmated easily.

How do we do this then? I asked.

Let's continue working together. Without your design and production inputs, I can't run it anyway, he said.

There is something you should know and accept. I am going out with someone. Even if I was single, don't have expectations from me; I cannot be in a relationship with you. More so since it might affect the work we do together. If you are agreeable to us being business partners and no more, then we can stay business partners.

Who are you with?

That is not important, I just explained to you.

Ok.

That was it. We got back to work together. I didn't discuss anything further in detail. I did not want to give up on my venture. I needed the work, and the money when it came. I was the sole founder, and I was not going to let someone usurp it without earning their due or giving me mine. More than anything else, I wanted the brand to be successful and I wanted to be the one waving the victory flag.

I assumed Angad had made peace with my point of view, and he would deal with me purely on professional terms.

After the truce came the pincer manoeuvre. Angad became an integral part of my life, at work and beyond. And took control of the oxygen supply to me.

He wanted to know what I was doing every minute and tried to make himself a part of it. He joined me to shop for vegetables, he waited while I was in a salon, he even went along to buy tampons. If he wasn't doing it with me, he would volunteer to do it for me. I allowed him to do small things for me initially for the convenience—there was too much work, and I needed every possible minute for the children. I do not remember the moment when the takeover of my personal life was complete. His omnipresence came in the way of even casual socializing with my friends, and I barely remember going out with any after a while.

Fortunately, business was doing well. Our products were moving faster than we could produce. There was no competing brand of note in nightwear for women, and we raked in the money. My forte was training and processes, and these assets helped build an efficient organization.

Not that I saw much of the financial windfall I was expecting. I had left the accounts to Angad, but he would keep complaining of losses or low profitability. I was too involved in the rest of the operations to interrogate him, but I would wonder how we could possibly not be making money if we were selling so much. I needed the money to pay my bills and feel independent; we had agreed on a salary for me, but it was a pittance compared to what I could have been earning in another job. I hung in there for the big payday when someone would buy my shares for a hefty premium. Till then, finances stayed a sore point between Angad and me; every raise came my way only after fighting and begging for it.

Through all this, Angad never desisted from trying to get close to me but I was resolute in my snubs. He would pass snide remarks if I was out and he didn't have an inkling of my whereabouts. I did manage to shake him off at times, usually to be out with the children; I did not want his presence in their lives. He would be downright derogatory in his insinuations about my dalliances with other men even when there were none. The only man I would meet behind Angad's back was Mark, and that too with increasing rarity.

Despite the undefined nature of our relationship, meetings with Mark always put me in a happy state of mind. We had hooked up in a room in the Marriott on one such occasion, and a friend of Angad saw us coming out of the hotel. He snitched on me but I was unaware of it. I went home, took a hot shower, poured myself some red wine, curled up in my bed and put on jazz on the music system. I was shaken out of my reverie by a call from Angad. Where are you? he asked.

At home. Why? I asked.

Come down.

Come down where?

I am in my car outside. I want to meet you.

At this hour? Who died?

Just come down.

But what's the matter?

I will tell you when you see me.

I am not coming. I am not even dressed to step out. And I am tired.

Come down.

Don't order me like this.

If you don't, I will come up. Take your pick.

The door is locked.

You don't want me banging on it and waking the kids up.

Knowing him, he would not go away till he had met me. I quickly put on a pair of blue denim jeans and a white shirt and went out, still holding my wine glass. He was sitting in his car, face puffed up. I recognized that angry look so well.

Did you meet Mark? he asked as soon as I was seated inside.

Why would you want to know who I meet and who I don't? I asked.

Did you meet Mark?

Did your spies tell you something? So what if I did?

You told me you don't meet him anymore.

Did I? Maybe I did, but I don't remember.

How dare you meet him?

Whoa! Let's get this straight. I told you very clearly I will do what I want to, and it will not be your concern. That was a pre-condition to us resuming work together.

I never accepted the condition.

It seemed like you did. Even if you didn't, what I do outside of work is not your business. And I repeat, I am not interested in you. Why don't you get it?

What is Mark's number?

Why should I give it to you?

If I see you with him or any other man again, I will not be responsible for what happens to them.

His words were building a pressure in my system. The top of my head was throbbing, and it could rip any moment. My heart was beating faster. I was having trouble breathing. I wanted to scream, and to cry, and to beat him, and to jump off a roof myself. Since I could not, all the energy got channelized through my hand and onto the wine glass. It broke in my hand. There was blood all over in an instant. The glass cut through the skin, busting some arteries. Our discussion ended right there, and Angad sped off in panic to the nearest hospital.

I have to give credit where it is due: when it comes to handling crises, Angad can be your man. If he had not collected his wits right there and then and rushed me into emergency and woken the best surgeon to come to my aid, my left hand would have become useless for life. It was my dominant hand.

It would take three months and multiple surgical procedures before I could sign my name again. I was recommended plastic surgery for the scars but I wanted them to stay. As a reminder, and a metaphor, for what my life had been.

I am not a flagbearer of religious or traditional ceremonies. I don't think I have ever gone to a place of worship by myself. And I couldn't be bothered with most rituals practised in Indian homes.

Only Karva Chauth mattered to me.

Not because I believed fasting on the day would ensure the health and longevity of my husband. Rather, it was symbolic of a family I have always aspired for, a family I missed growing up. No one could fill the void left by my mother. I never saw my father happy and healthy. A brother was given up for adoption, and another physically and psychologically scarred for life. The sister forced into a cocoon after being ravaged by the elders entrusted with the task of being our guardians.

I wished ill on my first husband, even if I put on a pretence of caring for his well-being. I wanted to make Karva Chauth count for Nakul, even though he was travelling mostly, leaving me alone to observe the occasion. He would play along for my sake if he was home but I could see that his heart—and belief—was not in it. He did surprise me once though, in the sixth year of our marriage. He booked a romantic dinner on the rooftop of the Maurya hotel; it was a big deal for me. I got nervous with excitement like a teenage girl being asked out on a first date; I suffered wardrobe malfunction and my hair went all frizzy while getting ready for the evening. I was in tears when Nakul got home; he laughed at my plight, got me tucked into a pair of silk trousers and a matching shirt, fastened my hair with a scrunchy and half carried, half dragged me to the car.

It was one of my happiest evenings in a long time. Being out with Nakul was enough to intoxicate me; the wine on the table was only as potent as water in comparison. My husband was with me on an important day of the year. Even if he was erratic in his affections for the rest of the year, even if he barely felt like a part of my life anymore, even if I was no longer the faithful wife.

For those who practice it, the ritual also requires the woman to present her mother-in-law with a gift. Despite our differences, I ensured she got one every year. I would pack it well and compose a letter thanking her, in all sincerity, for everything, especially for Nakul. Over the years, I sent across sarees, shawls and even jewellery when I could afford to, but she was invariably indifferent to them. There was always something she did not like in what I sent. I collected the returns in a trunk, and they are still there. But I did not stop the practice for as long as she was alive.

It may seem hypocritical to the life I was leading but I made Karva Chauth count. It was a day of hope for me. A hope for a home, a family, a life I was still seeking. It was a day when I shut my doors to every human being, to be spent with myself. Or with Nakul if he was there.

❧

For as long as Nakul and I were cohabitating, I pledged to make home a place we would want to go back to. To eat, to sleep, to play, to be one. To be the sanctuary for our weary bodies and souls.

No matter what was going on in his life or mine, with each other or with other people, I made sure home felt like home. I did it up elegantly even if not opulently. Cleanliness and tidiness was sacrosanct; no one dared leave anything lying where it should not have been. Meals were wholesome, fresh and served on time. Guests would always comment on the warmth and positive vibes they felt in our home.

Nakul and I did not socialize much together, but I stood by his side as the ideal wife when we did. We could be hosting, or we would be out, and no one would find anything amiss in my conduct. Because there wasn't. Just being with Nakul was enough to flush my face with smiles and my eyes with sparkles. All genuine. Because that is how I truly felt from within when I was with him.

I wanted no one else. Being with other men was just an escape for me. Away from the Nakul who did not pay me the attention I sought, did not say the things I wanted to hear, did not love me the way I desired he would. When he was home, he was lost in his work, his music, his movies and his books. He would ride off on his superbike impulsively, sometimes as far as his parents place in Agra. He would call from there to say he will be back only in a day or two. I would not have grudged him giving time to his side of the family and his hobbies if only he was giving his wife and children their due share of the attention.

I had seen the caring, the affectionate, the loving, the passionate side of Nakul before we got married. What changed in the transition from being his live-in girlfriend to being his live-in wife? Was there someone else in his life? He certainly could not be surviving on the quantum of sex he was having with me. He had an appetite and desire for much more. What he did outside home did not rankle me. What he did within did. When he was home, I required him to be the man his wife had been longing for and his children had been waiting for. He had to be a good man, a family man and feel truly so from within.

I was certainly a good mother. There had been strong crosswinds for many years after Vani was born—things quietened down only after Kabir became a part of our lives. I directed my energies towards making up for lost opportunities with my daughter, and ensuring Kabir never suffered like his sister did.

Was I a good wife? I would have liked to be. I never wanted to break up our family. If I had relationships outside marriage, it was because I felt there was nowhere else to go. The attention of others was good for my self-esteem, the sex a mood uplifter. Ideally, I would not have been with any other man after marrying Nakul. But I have no regrets. I would have missed out on invaluable and insightful exposure and lessons had I stayed homebound.

Of course, Nakul tried to buy any wishes his wife and children may have had. He let his money do the loving. I wanted Kabir's first birthday to be as memorable as Vani's had been forgettable. Nakul came good on the occasion. He spared no effort in throwing a bash where those invited—and even those not—would talk for years. It was no less than a grand wedding. A lavish banquet, creation of a mini Disney-themed park, a band, return gifts for all children who attended—every other birthday party in town would pale in comparison to what Kabir's was. Guests came from far and wide, and included relations, friends and professional acquaintances. Those from outside town were put up in a five-star hotel, with their taxis, flights and trains paid for by Nakul. I was pleased with the effort he put in, but I wish he would pamper us with his attention the way he did with his money.

Nakul was deeply affected by the loss of his father, and then of his mother, within a space of a few months. I offered my bosom for him to rest his grieving soul on, but he pulled away further. I wanted to hold him close, but he turned more aloof than before. He hurt me when I could have consoled him, healed him.

Angad was the only one at hand who I could turn to for company. I had to make peace with the devil himself. And give myself to him.

I just slipped into a relationship with Angad.

I was in a state of emotional despair as Nakul moved further away. I could have fallen in love with a pole. I compromised. I settled for whoever was at hand. For the time being. I took Angad at surface value, knowing he was only muck deep down. I gave up seeking utopian love. At least till the kids were older and I was financially secure.

Not that Angad was entirely detestable. I did share good moments with him. Times when he would pamper me, make me feel like a queen, go out of his way to do things for me. We often travelled for work together, and he would make it seem like a holiday. He was at his best when he had my undivided attention, knowing there was no one else around I could be with. His possessive self needed that assurance.

He was at his worst when I had my mood swings, wanted to be on my own, do my own thing. He just needed to know where I was so he could go looking for me if he wanted to, or hear from me if he called. He would lose his head when I questioned him at work, disagreed with him or asked for more money for myself. He would always apologize later, and I would give in for the sake of congeniality between us and in the interest of the business.

I could never predict when he would put me on a pedestal, or when he would try to squash me under his heel. But I had built a resilience in my dealings with him. I checked any impulses to abuse him or even get violent with him, but nothing would stop him from testing my patience. When the dark side of you becomes your dominant trait, I will no longer give any credit to your good side, I warned him more than once. My tolerance levels would then have been crossed and everything will be over between us. I will not care for my personal reputation or business loss at that time; I will come after you and make your life miserable. Because I will have nothing to lose by then.

Angad was not one to be cowed by such threats. He would laugh in my face as if those words were the rant of a child. I was bearing up with him for my own reasons, fully aware it would not always be the case. I knew I was in the wrong by being with him, and I knew he was getting away with wronging me. I had been forced to pawn my self-esteem, health, mental peace and family in my dealings with Angad.

I never forgave him.

I figured out why I was not making the money I should have been. Angad had been playing dirty all along. He got away with it because I went against my hunch and let him handle the accounts, unquestioned.

He had been taking money out of the till at our shops; we had set up three of our own. He had been making cash withdrawals from the bank without supporting justification, he had been marking up expenses and taking kickbacks from vendors, and had been issuing cheques to individuals and companies as expenses that never were. All this and more came to light when I was served notices by the authorities for not depositing taxes as due. I was liable as one of the directors of the company.

When I confronted him, he tried to brush the issues under the carpet, asking me to leave it to him to handle. I demanded we meet the auditors, but they too sang the tune he was singing. I wanted a neutral, independent agency to look into all finances but he kept putting it off under one pretext or the other. When I got one on my own, he refused to cooperate in providing necessary documents and information.

I finally lost it and called him a cheat who had abused me both personally and professionally. I refused to continue working with him, and told him to fork up my stolen share of past profits. Of course, that was too much to expect of him. But I had to try.

I expected him to be apologetic and ashamed of himself—after all, we were also in a relationship, even if illicit. But he went on the offensive instead. He accused me of mismanaging operations and blaming him for it. He went around town badmouthing me—to our landlords, the retail partners, staff, vendors and the industry in general. He painted himself as the victim, and how the business was his idea to start with but I had appropriated all credit—and made his investment worthless.

This approach did not have the desired effect though; it actually backfired. Most people did not believe him; they had been interacting with me directly and were well aware of my contribution and role in building the brand. But an uncertainty spread about the sustainability of the business. Vendors called in their outstandings and refused to supply anything further on credit. Our retail partners did not pay what was due to us; their aisles would be empty should our business pack up. They too would suffer losses in turn. Some key staff picked up alternate jobs rather than be laid off with nothing in hand. Sales fell because we could not produce enough stocks to keep the distribution pipelines flowing.

My worst fears were coming true as I saw the business I built crumble around me. I was tired. I no longer wanted to hear run Nikita, run, in my head. I wanted to stay put. At home.

Angad's dark side had become his dominant trait. He had pushed me over the threshold of my tolerance levels. He would know my threats were not the rant of a child. He had been warned.

I want out. Totally. I want to have nothing to do with you. Personal or professional. Give me a fair offer for my shares, and the company is all yours. And don't ever try to meet me after that.

I finally mustered up the will to walk away from my brand and my partner. And told Angad so while returning from a meeting. He was humming an old Dev Anand romantic number while I spoke. Really, he taunted without missing a beat of the song.

Yes, I had warned you. The limits of my tolerance have been breached, I said.

You don't have to overreact. Whatever it is, we will sort it out, he said while continuing with the song. He was a gifted singer, and I had enjoyed him singing on better days. He sounded irritating now.

There is nothing to sort. Just pay me my dues and we will be done, I said.

The company is worthless without you. So the value of your shares is zero. Here, take your money right now, he said while extending an empty palm toward me.

I am sick of your insults. I don't know how I allowed you to even touch me.

Ouch! Now that hurts. But I know you are upset, you will get over it soon. Come on, stop fuming. We had a very productive meeting, let's not fuss over inconsequential stuff.

It might be trivial for you, but it's not a game I am playing to entertain myself. Stop the car and drop me off right here.

Sure. What should I do with the videos? Should I send them with the stuff you remove from your office?

What videos?

The ones we made together, memories of our love.

I don't recall any such videos.

Of course you won't. How could you have noticed being shot? You make love with your eyes closed.

I froze when he uttered those words. Maybe my heart had failed me and rigor mortis was already setting in. How will Angad dispose of my body? Just then, he braked the car with a jerk at a traffic junction and I snapped out. You bastard, you will not get away with blackmail, I told him and got out of the car before he could stop me. I noticed his smirk disappear. I ran across the road to a taxi stand and took one home.

I held on to my tears till I was home. I opened the main door and made a dash for the bedroom. To find Nakul sitting on the bed, smiling in my direction. What are you doing here? I asked. I could not have asked for a more welcome sight in that moment. I didn't know whether to laugh with joy or to cry with the sorrows I was carrying.

It's my home if my memory serves me right. So I can be here, I suppose, he said.

Of course you can be. But I wasn't expecting you back until the end of the month.

Can't a man surprise his wife?

What was happening, I wondered. What games is the universe playing with me? Nakul had not shown such love in years. I don't even remember when he was last so playful and cheerful around me. It's as if I had gone back in time to our courtship days. And why today? Just the day I told Angad I wanted him out of my life. A day when I decided I would no longer allow anything or anyone to hold my life to ransom. A day when I had resolved to do everything on my terms, and all those who have a problem with that be damned. A day I reminded myself I wanted nothing but my home, with my family in it. Nakul wasn't even supposed to be there. Was the universe listening to my thoughts? Was the universe in a generous mood, giving me what I was seeking?

I dropped my bag on the floor and ran towards him. I jumped on to the bed and curled up with him. I buried my face in his chest and started crying. Sobbing actually. He put his hand behind my head to support it, and did not interrupt me. He let the tears flow for as long as I wanted them to. Eventually, I looked up. My eyes were red, my face wet, my hair a mess and my nose runny.

I am sorry, baby, I said.

Sorry about what? he asked.

About everything that happened.

What happened?

I am sure you know.

Maybe I do. But I don't want to assume anything. Is there something you want to tell me?

Yes.

I blurted everything out. About everything that transpired between Angad and me. From the moment he spotted me at TGI Fridays and till our early evening drive back that day. Including his video blackmail.

Is that it? he asked.

More or less, I said.

I had an inkling but could not be sure.

And?

Give me your phone.

I did. He dialled Angad's number. Even before he had completed his hello, Nakul started off. Listen, you bastard, I know what you have been doing to my wife. She has told me everything about the two of you. So you cannot blackmail her on that count. In fact, you should worry about your home should your wife get to know anything. Her politician father will feed your balls to his dogs and they won't even burp when they are finished with you. Think before you harass Nikita on any front from now on. She's not alone. Not now. Not ever. Now fuck you and fuck off.

Nakul hung up without waiting for a reaction. He had stayed calm while speaking but I am sure Angad got the message and would not even think of coming near me from then on. Except to pay my dues. Nakul got up, took my hand and led me to the terrace. The moon was shining bright.

Now what? I asked.

I fucked up too, baby. We are even now, he said.

I didn't want to know what he had done. It was not important. He was home. With me. For me. I had wanted nothing else. And now I had it. How could any other information be of consequence? We both looked up at the moon and whispered a silent thank you for taking loads off our shoulders and bringing us together.

We are good then, I asked.

Yes, baby. Let's go have dinner now. I am sure you are famished. You must have been fasting all day.

It was Karva Chauth.

# About the Author

**Ajay Jain** identifies himself as a storyteller. He is an author, photographer, traveller and the founder of Kunzum, an independent bookstore in New Delhi, India. He has written several printed and electronic books covering travel, fiction, business and personal development. He is a regular on the speaking circuit, and his motivational talks are much sought after. He holds degrees in mechanical engineering (Delhi College of Engineering), management (FORE) and journalism (Cardiff, UK). In the past, he has worked in technology, sports management and media sectors. You can find him at ajay@ajayjain.com and kunzum.com.